Studies in International Performance

Published in association with the International Federation of Theatre Research

General Editors: **Janelle Reinelt** and **Brian Singleton**

Culture and performance cross borders constantly, and not just the borders that define nations. In this new series, scholars of performance produce interactions between and among nations and cultures as well as genres, identities and imaginations.

Inter-national in the largest sense, the books collected in the *Studies in International Performance* series display a range of historical, theoretical and critical approaches to the panoply of performances that make up the global surround. The series embraces 'Culture' which is institutional as well as improvised, underground or alternate, and treats 'Performance' as either intercultural or transnational as well as intracultural within nations.

Titles include:

Khalid Amine and Marvin Carlson
THE THEATRES OF MOROCCO, ALGERIA AND TUNISIA
Performance Traditions of the Maghreb

AF611701

Patrick Anderson and Jisha Menon (*editors*)
VIOLENCE PERFORMED
Local Roots and Global Routes of Conflict

Elaine Aston and Sue-Ellen Case
STAGING INTERNATIONAL FEMINISMS

Christopher Balme
PACIFIC PERFORMANCES
Theatricality and Cross-Cultural Encounter in the South Seas

Matthew Isaac Cohen
PERFORMING OTHERNESS
Java and Bali on International Stages, 1905–1952

Susan Leigh Foster (*editor*)
WORLDING DANCE

Helen Gilbert and Jacqueline Lo
PERFORMANCE AND COSMOPOLITICS
Cross-Cultural Transactions in Australasia

Helena Grehan
PERFORMANCE, ETHICS AND SPECTATORSHIP IN A GLOBAL AGE

James Harding and Cindy Rosenthal (*editors*)
THE RISE OF PERFORMANCE STUDIES
Rethinking Richard Schechner's Broad Spectrum

Silvija Jestrovic
PERFORMANCE, SPACE, UTOPIA

Silvija Jestrovic and Yana Meerzon (*editors*)
PERFORMANCE, EXILE AND 'AMERICA'

Ola Johansson
COMMUNITY THEATRE AND AIDS

Ketu Katrak
CONTEMPORARY INDIAN DANCE
New Creative Choreography in India and the Diaspora

Sonja Arsham Kuftinec
THEATRE, FACILITATION, AND NATION FORMATION IN THE BALKANS AND MIDDLE EAST

Daphne P. Lei
ALTERNATIVE CHINESE OPERA IN THE AGE OF GLOBALIZATION
Performing Zero

Carol Martin (*editor*)
THE DRAMATURGY OF THE REAL ON THE WORLD STAGE

Carol Martin
THEATRE OF THE REAL

Y. Meerzon
PERFORMING EXILE, PERFORMING SELF
Drama, Theatre, Film

Lara D. Nielson and Patricia Ybarra (*editors*)
NEOLIBERALISM AND GLOBAL THEATRES
Performance Permutations

Alan Read
THEATRE, INTIMACY & ENGAGEMENT
The Last Human Venue

Shannon Steen
RACIAL GEOMETRIES OF THE BLACK ATLANTIC, ASIAN PACIFIC AND AMERICAN THEATRE

Marcus Tan
ACOUSTIC INTERCULTURALISM
Listening to Performance

Maurya Wickstrom
PERFORMANCE IN THE BLOCKADES OF NEOLIBERALISM
Thinking the Political Anew

S. E. Wilmer
NATIONAL THEATRES IN A CHANGING EUROPE

Evan Darwin Winet
INDONESIAN POSTCOLONIAL THEATRE
Spectral Genealogies and Absent Faces

Forthcoming titles:

Adrian Kear
THEATRE AND EVENT

Studies in International Performance
Series Standing Order ISBN 978–1–4039–4456–6 (hardback)
978–1–4039–4457–3 (paperback)
(*outside North America only*)

You can receive future titles in this series as they are published by placing a standing order. Please contact your bookseller or, in case of difficulty, write to us at the address below with your name and address, the title of the series and the ISBN quoted above.

Customer Services Department, Macmillan Distribution Ltd, Houndmills, Basingstoke, Hampshire RG21 6XS, England

---

Performance, Space, Utopia

Cities of War, Cities of Exile

Silvija Jestrovic

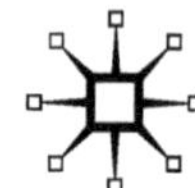

© Silvija Jestrovic 2013

All rights reserved. No reproduction, copy or transmission of this publication may be made without written permission.

No portion of this publication may be reproduced, copied or transmitted save with written permission or in accordance with the provisions of the Copyright, Designs and Patents Act 1988, or under the terms of any licence permitting limited copying issued by the Copyright Licensing Agency, Saffron House, 6–10 Kirby Street, London EC1N 8TS.

Any person who does any unauthorized act in relation to this publication may be liable to criminal prosecution and civil claims for damages.

The author has asserted her right to be identified as the author of this work in accordance with the Copyright, Designs and Patents Act 1988.

First published 2013 by
PALGRAVE MACMILLAN

Palgrave Macmillan in the UK is an imprint of Macmillan Publishers Limited, registered in England, company number 785998, of Houndmills, Basingstoke, Hampshire RG21 6XS.

Palgrave Macmillan in the US is a division of St Martin's Press LLC, 175 Fifth Avenue, New York, NY 10010.

Palgrave Macmillan is the global academic imprint of the above companies and has companies and representatives throughout the world.

Palgrave® and Macmillan® are registered trademarks in the United States, the United Kingdom, Europe and other countries.

ISBN 978-1-349-33242-7 ISBN 978-1-137-29167-7 (eBook)
DOI 10.1057/9781137291677

This book is printed on paper suitable for recycling and made from fully managed and sustained forest sources. Logging, pulping and manufacturing processes are expected to conform to the environmental regulations of the country of origin.

A catalogue record for this book is available from the British Library.

A catalog record for this book is available from the Library of Congress.

10 9 8 7 6 5 4 3 2 1
22 21 20 19 18 17 16 15 14 13

Contents

List of Illustrations

Series Editors' Preface

The 'Studies in International Performance' series was initiated in 2004 on behalf of the International Federation for Theatre Research, by Janelle Reinelt and Brian Singleton, successive Presidents of the Federation. Their aim was, and still is, to call on performance scholars to expand their disciplinary horizons to include the comparative study of performances across national, cultural, social, and political borders. This is necessary not only in order to avoid the homogenizing tendency of national paradigms in performance scholarship, but also in order to engage in creating new performance scholarship that takes account of and embraces the complexities of transnational cultural production, the new media, and the economic and social consequences of increasingly international forms of artistic expression. Comparative studies (especially when conceived across more than two terms) can value both the specifically local and the broadly conceived global forms of performance practices, histories, and social formations. Comparative aesthetics can challenge the limitations of national orthodoxies of art criticism and current artistic knowledges. In formalizing the work of the Federation's members through rigorous and innovative scholarship this series aims to make a significant contribution to an ever-changing project of knowledge creation.

Janelle Reinelt and Brian Singleton

International Federation for Theatre Research
Fédération Internationale pour la Recherche Théâtrale

Acknowledgements

There are many people who encouraged, advised and above all inspired me in the process of writing this book.

First of all I wish to thank Professor Janelle Reinelt and Professor Brian Singleton for including this book in their series 'Studies in International Performance' and for their continuous support, thought-provoking feedback and friendship. They made me feel safe and secure in the challenging personal and intellectual journey of writing this book.

I am also grateful to Paula Kennedy, Benjamin Doyle and the team at Palgrave Macmillan for their great work and patience in putting up with my deadline extensions. My special thanks go to Penny Simmons for her wonderful editorial work and for making the last stages of the process fast and easy.

The generous support of the Arts and Humanities Research Council (AHRC, UK), through their Small Research Grant Award and Research Leave Award, secured both resources and time to write this book. I am also grateful to the Social Sciences and Humanities Research Council of Canada (SSHRC) and Professor Christopher Innes for supporting the early stages of this research. I am thankful to the University of Warwick and my colleagues in the Department of Theatre, Performance and Cultural Policy for their support and collegiality.

The Belgrade chapters of this book would not have been possible without help from artist Nikola Džafo, Borka Pavićević and Ana Miljanić from the Center of Cultural Decontamination, Vesna Mrdja from the *Vreme* magazine archive, *Dah* Theatre, Ksenija Radulović and the Serbian *Theatre Museum*, and Professor Milena Dragićević Šešić. A great conversation with my friends, playwrights Jelena Mijović and Petar Grujčić, one summer evening in Belgrade after Radovan Karadžić had been captured inspired the chapter on Seductive Performatives. The experience and memory of living and protesting in Milošević's Serbia I share with too many people to name here. I am thanking them all for making my life in Serbia in the early 1990s bearable.

Mladen Ovadija and Mair Musafija shared their Sarajevo contacts with me. Safet Plakalo of Sarajevski Ratni Teatar (SARTR), Zlatko Topčić of Kamerni 55, Pozorište Mladih, Nermin Tulić and Željka Buka, Lejla Pašović and MESS, and Vojka Djikić, editor of *Sarajevske sveske*, all generously shared their memories and experiences of life and theatre in the besieged Sarajevo. They provided me with stories, books, images and information without which I would not have been able to write the Sarajevo chapters of the book. I am most grateful to actor/director Admir Glamočak for his insight into the cultural life of Sarajevo during the war and for sharing photos and material from his private archive with me. Milija Gluhović shared his thoughts, inspiring stories and important suggestions for these chapters too. Natasha Davis helped me with Sarajevo photos.

My chapter on Exile is made of many voices and they come from: Željko and Pejka Grubić, Radakovići and Stankovići of the Petkovci group, Jelena Vulović, Dragoslav Tanasković, Dragana Varagić and Dušan Petričić, and the late Professor Dragan Klaić. Joanne MacKay Bennett's friendship made me feel at home in Toronto and I am thankful for her proofreading of this material. Sharing thoughts on performance and critical theory with Professor Veronika Ambros made me write more and procrastinate less. Somewhere in the Cities of Exile are also Erith and Adam, Lisa, Yana, Marjan and Sanja...

I thank Dragan Todorović for being my partner in travelling to cities of war and to cities of exile, and my parents Ljiljana and Miloje Jestrović for looking after my daughter while I had to be away on research trips for this book.

Admir Glamočak wanted the photos he shared with me to be signed 'Courtesy of Friends from Sarajevo'. Following his lead, I dedicate this book to my daughter Ana Isabella Todorović, my inspiration and driving force – a little traveller to so many cities – and to our friends from Belgrade, from Sarajevo, and from all the *exilic non-places* that have become our homes.

Introduction: Cities of War, Cities of Exile

'We will build a prettier and *older* Vukovar.' So responded General Veselin Šljivančanin – one of the key figures of the Yugoslav People's Army during the downfall of Yugoslavia – after a viewer called in to a live TV interview with the General and asked him to explain the senseless destruction of one of the most beautiful baroque towns in Croatia, for which Šljivančanin's army was responsible. Commenting on the siege of Sarajevo, another city that had become a military target, architect and former mayor of Belgrade, Bogdan Bogdanović, wrote: 'Much as I ponder the abnormalities of our current civil war, I cannot comprehend why military strategy should make the destruction of cities a main – if not *the* main – goal' ('The Ritual Murder of the City', 53). The war in the Balkans that took place between 1991 and 1995 forms the context of this book. It has been variously viewed as ethnic strife, religious conflict, or civil war, but seldom has it been described as a war against cities led by people who shared Šljivančanin's alarming mind-set.

Nearly twenty years after the war, this book looks back at its two most iconic cities – Sarajevo and Belgrade. The former was a symbol of suffering and urbicide, the latter was the centre of the war-mongering machinery that orchestrated that urbicide. In both places, the conflict – between urban culture, which was understood as cosmopolitan, hybrid, open – and the logic of national imaginaries of homogeneity, asserted with heavy artillery – played out on a daily basis. Performance and theatricality became modes of being and acting in the city, even strategies of physical and ethical survival. Yet, so often it is exile, both as marginalization *within* and exodus *from* the city, which emerges as the defining consequence of living in Sarajevo or Belgrade in the 1990s.

My choice of Belgrade, Sarajevo, and subsequently, Toronto, as primary examples of the exilic city, has been informed by reasons that are both scholarly and personal.

First, Belgrade and Sarajevo offer a fascinating comparative case study not only because the two cities belong to the same historical narrative of civil war and breakdown of Yugoslavia, but because of the ways in which their various performances both complement and contradict one another. I am particularly interested in how their performance practices positioned communal versus national identity, asserted continuity and discontinuity as political categories, and added new dimensions to the notion of urban space as a site of resistance. Performing the city in the besieged Sarajevo was a personal and political act of asserting continuity in the face of death and destruction. In Belgrade, safely located a few hundred kilometres away from the war zone, urban performance had the opposite function. There, performing the city foregrounded discontinuity as a *sickness of place*, and resisted the official political propaganda that insisted on tradition, normalcy, and national homogeneity.

Performing the city in Belgrade took a different approach than it did in Sarajevo. Hence my use of the terms *city-as-action* – that I relate more to Belgrade and its radical and spectacular political performances – and the *city-as-body,* that I identify with Sarajevo. Despite the destruction of Sarajevo's landmark buildings and the impossible conditions of living under siege, the city continued to exist through performances of civil resilience. At times, the citizens virtually embodied destroyed cultural landmarks through concerts and performances on the ruins. Toronto, viewed here as an exilic city from the perspective of immigrants from the Balkan wars, offers a specific amalgamation of the city-as-action and the city-as-body, not via palimpsests of history and struggles of belonging, but rather through an unmediated experience of both *place* and *placelessness.*

Second, this particular material opens a wider conceptual discussion on space and place, community and resistance, and utopian moments that emerge through various kinds of performances – from those belonging to theatre to those that reside in the spheres of political rituals and performances of everyday life. The settings of the cities of war, on the one side, and the city of exiles, on the other, place the performance and critical theories that I have turned to in new, and often extreme, contexts. Sometimes, I have introduced notions that seem applicable to specifics of my case studies. I use *political memory of place,* for example, to explain the spatial and temporal dimension of the palimpsest of Belgrade's central pedestrian zone. Other times, my framework has required a broader interpretation of concepts that inform performance and critical theories. Thus, I have applied the concept of restorative architecture – *spoila* – to explain the concert performance on Sarajevo ruins as a specific mode of performative reconstruction of the city's mind-map. Similarly, Marc Augé's notion of *non-place* has been reworked in the context of exile and immigration to examine what happens *in the comfort of exilic non-places*. While Jill Dolan's *utopian performatives* emerged in my discussion of all three cities, not necessarily when nor as expected, I have used the term *seductive performatives* to describe those instances when a more sinister side of utopia in performance surfaced. Finally, my analysis of performance in the cities in question allowed me to see the possibilities of theatre and performance in situations of extreme existential or ethical crisis. The case studies of Belgrade, and even more of Sarajevo, provide us with glimpses of performance at its most fundamental level, neither as a commodity nor as an intellectual exercise – but as a bare necessity.

My relationship to all three cities has been both deeply personal and shaped through the political. I lived in Belgrade for 15 years and in Toronto for ten – hence, on my personal map, these two cities have been linked dialectically through experiences of belonging and exile. Although I have never lived in Sarajevo, it has always embodied the notion of Yugoslavia for me. More than any other place in the Balkan bloodbath, I equate Sarajevo's destruction with the loss of Yugoslavia – not the communist state, but its multicultural spaces.

The first part of the book 'Belgrade: the City of Spectacle', which focuses on the theatricality of civic disobedience and political protests, has in the most part been written from the first-hand experience of a witness/participant who was part of a larger, political collective. Here, my relationship to Belgrade is that of an *insider- who-has-left*. The *insider-who-has-left* reads the city between the lines. She knows the city almost too well, yet her knowledge has been cured of nostalgia. *The insider-who-has-left* claims the attitude of intimacy shaped by sharp, critical distance.

The second part, 'Sarajevo: Imaginaries and Embodiments', looks at the city from the position of an *intimate outsider*. The city has been part of the *intimate outsider's* personal landscape. *The intimate outsider* speaks the language of the city, has favourite city haunts, and understands local jokes, yet she has always been a visitor to the city rather than a citizen. *The intimate outsider* examines the relationship between the city – its architecture, its public and private spaces – and moving, performing bodies. She deconstructs imaginaries constructed though the gaze of outsiders, at risk of unwittingly imposing her own.

The third part of the book, 'City of Exile', is situated in Toronto, with some references to other exilic cities. The exilic city is a place constituted through fragmented personal and collective experiences. Hence, the positions are never stable. Sometimes, *the-insider-who-has-left* and the *intimate outsider* trade places. At other times, they amalgamate, or become so fragmented that the main mode of being and engaging with the exilic city is only possible through *improvisation*. The exilic city is both a personal and a collective space, yet for exiles from the Balkan wars a collective identity is difficult. Shared places of the past are contested and memories can be minefields. To speak about the exilic collective, shaped by the experiences of Yugoslavia, the war and the emigration, is ethically possible only through fragments of individual stories and voices. It is never spoken in everybody's name. For that reason, the final section of the book examines place, identity and community in the exilic city through distinct, individual narratives.

Part I
Belgrade: The City of Spectacle

> *THE SPECTACLE IS NOT a collection of images; rather, it is a form of social relationship between people that is mediated by images.*
>
> Guy Debord, *Society of Spectacle*

In my attempt to understand and explain Belgrade as a city of spectacle, I turn to Guy Debord's famous concept. It suggests that the nature of spectacle is all-encompassing and its power seductive. Of course, Belgrade could never have epitomized Debord's metropolis of the highly developed Western world. As a city situated on its geographical and economic edges, the 'wonderments' of Belgrade are not manufactured so much through power and capital, but rather through a permanent state of crisis.

In 1967, when Debord wrote *The Society of Spectacle*, his seminal work that inspired the student uprising in France in 1968, Belgrade was the capital of socialist Yugoslavia under the steady and firm rule of President Tito. Nevertheless, the events in France and the United States had an impact on the students of Belgrade University, who were dissatisfied with the existing social climate and began protesting in June 1968, much in the manner of their fellow students in France. The root of their dissatisfaction was not capitalist society, but the increasing inequality of their socialist state. The students, joined by a number of faculty members, 'occupied' the Faculty of Philosophy over a period of several days. Just when the riot police were about to take over, President Tito, surprisingly, appeared on national television to address the students and to welcome their criticism. Reportedly, Tito then joined the protesters in the traditional dance of kolo symbolically marking the end of the student unrest. As a result, the protests were quickly defused and the status quo was restored. In *The Society of Spectacle*, Debord distinguishes between two kinds of spectacular power – *the concentrated*, which has epitomized regimes prone to totalitarianism; and *the diffuse*, which has represented the Americanization of the world. The spectacular power that shaped Belgrade in the late 1960s in its capacity to absorb and water-down political unrest – as embodied in Tito's sudden alliance with the protesting students – and, under different guises into the late 1980s, epitomized a velvet-gloved version of Debord's concentrated spectacle.

In her book, *How we Survived Communism and even Laughed*, Slavenka Drakulić describes an Eastern European version of the other aspect of Debord's notion – the *diffuse* spectacle:

> In the newspaper and on TV revolutions looked spectacular: cut barbed wire, seas of lighted candles, masses chanting in the streets, convulsive embraces and tears of happiness, people chiselling pieces from the Berlin Wall. A famous Hollywood director once said that movies are the same as life with the boring parts cut out. I found that this was precisely right. The boring parts of the revolution had simply finished up on the floors of television studio cutting rooms all over the world. What the world has seen and heard were only the most dramatic and symbolic images. That was all right, but it was not all. Life, for the most part is trivial.
>
> (p. xiv)

The main trait of the Americanization of the world, which for Debord is the core of the *diffuse spectacle*, has to do with the 'freedom of choice to the vast range of new commodities now on offer' (*Comments on the Society of Spectacle*, p. 8). Filtered through the modern media, the end of communism and the disintegration of the Eastern Block – from the fall of the Berlin Wall to the carnage in the Balkans – might appear as offerings for consumption, but that is not the only aspect which turns these events into *spectacles*. Drakulić highlights the process of 'editing' and the part it plays in the Hollywoodization of the events. In this fictionalization of Eastern Europe however, the loss of the trivial is not so much a loss of the ordinariness of existence, as a loss of its political complexity. Spectacular society of any kind thrives on simplifications. The freedom of choice that the diffuse spectacle brings presupposes a cancellation of ambiguities that provides a Hollywood ending for the fall of the Berlin Wall, or a consumer-friendly, good guys versus bed guys scenario of the bloodshed in the Balkans. The question is: how do the perception and the memory of the real, from the perspective of both onlookers and participants, impact the relationships and actions in a society? What is the actual guiding force – is it a complex reality both extraordinary and banal, riveting and boring? Or is it a somewhat less ambiguous but more entertaining version?

From the late 1980s to the present day, Belgrade has become a city that reinvents itself through various forms of spectacle. Elements of both – the concentrated and the diffuse spectacle – have shaped Belgrade as a city of competing and contesting spectacles and counter-spectacles. In 1989 – the year of the fall of the Berlin Wall, the peaceful collapse of communist regimes across Europe, and of the Chernobyl catastrophe – Debord published *Comments on the Society of the Spectacle* only to diagnose that the spectacular society had entered a new and even more powerful phase. Debord recognized that the two types of spectacular power – the condensed and the diffuse – have amalgamated into an *integrated spectacle* that now permeates all of reality. For Debord, the synthesis of defused and condensed spectacle has been shaping a global system of domination marked by features such as generalized secrecy, increased technological renewal, and the integration of state and economy. Yet in the integrated spectacle of liberal democracy, he recognizes roots and traits of both capitalist and totalitarian regimes:

> Whereas Russia and Germany were largely responsible for the formation of the concentrated spectacle, and the United States for the diffuse form, the integrated spectacle has been pioneered by France and Italy. The emergence of this new form is attributable to a number of shared historical features, namely, the important role of the Stalinist party and unions in political and intellectual life, a weak democratic tradition, the long monopoly of power enjoyed by a single party of government, and a need to eliminate an unexpected upsurge in revolutionary activity.
>
> (*Comments on the Society of Spectacle*, pp. 8–9)

In the late 1980s, from a cultural and political climate that shares most of the aforementioned attributes of the integrated spectacle, albeit in different proportions and different ideological frameworks largely dominated by a combination of communism and nationalism, Belgrade emerged as a spectacular city.

The same year that Debord's *Comments* were published, Slobodan Milošević reached the peak of his popularity and became President of Serbia, further fuelling the nationalistic frenzy across the country. Although his regime thrived on Tito's legacy of concentrated spectacle, a society of integrated spectacle started to emerge in tandem with nationalism, offering itself as a new ideological possibility and even a new lifestyle, not only in Serbia but across Yugoslavia. It appeared on different levels from the awakening of individual religious zeal to the introduction of pluralism into the political system giving rise to numerous political parties, most of them with nationalist orientations. At the time of Debord's suicide in 1994, the spectacle of bloodshed in the Balkans, filtered and packaged for consumption through mass media, emerged as yet another form of integrated spectacle. This integrated spectacle acquired new layers, hovering between images of mass graves on one side, and the wonderments of the capitalist market on the other.

Aska and the Wolf: counter-spectacles

Against this backdrop, Belgrade has embodied a spectacle of both radical integration and resistance, where the binaries of the concentrated and the diffused spectacle have given way to an even deeper ethical ambiguity. Belgrade became a Janus-faced city: the centre of Milošević's war-mongering machine and the focal point of its most stubborn resistance in Serbia – with numerous intertwined and problematic layers in between. For over a decade, downtown Belgrade was turned into a stage of political struggle where performance and daily life, politics and spectacle, state power and its opposition, constantly competed. Belgrade became a site where dramaturgies of political protest were exercised. These activities fell in line, by and large, with the global protests that, as Baz Kershaw argues, have 'developed a new range of performative strategies. Through these strategies, protest has gained new kinds of synecdochic relevance to its socio-political contexts, and this suggests that it has drawn on new sources for radicalism in performance.' (*The Radical in Performance* 109–10).

The events of political protests against the regime (from 1991 to 2000) emerge as counter-spectacles since they try to resist an imposed illusory unity. Debord claims that the 'spectacle appears at once as society itself, as a part of society and as a means of unification.' (*Comments to the Society of Spectacle*, p. 12) However, the counter-spectacle, even when it tries to invent its own means and its own vocabulary, does not seek an alternative to the spectacular, but its contrary. For the political protests of the Serbian opposition, spectacle was a necessary strategy of both maintaining the momentum of the resistance and of capturing the attention of the world media.

It was late Saturday morning on 9 March 1991, three months before the civil war, when the first big riot of the opposition against the regime of Serbian president Slobodan Milošević took place. Tens of thousands of protesters gathered in the heart of Belgrade – then the capital of Yugoslavia. Protesters filled the main city square around the monument of Knez Mihailo in front of the National Theatre and were spreading out into the main pedestrian zone of Knez Mihailova street. They demanded free media, open access to information and called for an end to Milošević's presidency. When the police tried to prevent the leaders of the democratic opposition from addressing the crowd, Vida Ognjenović, the artistic director of the National Theatre, opened the door of the building and allowed the protest to continue in the theatre balcony.[1] To stop the riot, the regime deployed the army, sending tanks into the streets of Belgrade. The protest became violent, the police fired water cannons and tear gas at the protesters, stones were thrown at shop windows, cars turned upside down. Walking home from the protest through back alleys, eyes still itchy and watery from the tear gas, I remember passing people with bruised faces and broken noses, and yet the only thing I could think of was Patti Smith's song 'People Have the Power'.[2] In a way, that particular slice of real life was so extraordinary and dramatic to experience, that in that given moment, it could only be comprehended through metaphors and vocabularies not so much of politics, but rather of performance. Hence the Patti Smith song emerged in the midst of chaos.

A few hours later, the official tally of the protest was announced: two people were killed – a young protester and a policeman – a number of protesters suffered serious injuries, and together with over a hundred of his fellow citizens, one of the leaders of the Serbian opposition, Vuk Drašković, was arrested. Late that night, disturbing, uncanny sounds could be heard in the city centre – regular traffic had disappeared as long convoys of tanks advanced down the city boulevards. They almost sealed off the zone around the National Theatre and the Knez Mihailo monument. The next morning, I walked to the protest site. Parts of the pavement were still covered in broken glass. The square and the surrounding streets were unusually quiet and deserted. The military presence and their tanks made the familiar city veneer seem strange. The scenery was dominated by grey sky and olive green metal.

In the afternoon, word was out that a peaceful vigil would take place near Terazijska Česma – a drinking fountain built in the nineteenth century in memory of one of Serbia's rulers. The fountain was located on Terazije square, another city centre landmark, within walking distance from the National Theatre and Knez Mihailova Street. That day, the military closed off the area from traffic and, as night fell, the square and the Terazije strip filled with people, most of them university students. They demanded liberation for the arrested citizens and the resignations of the leading figures of the regime, whom they held responsible for the violent outcome of the protest on 9 March. The evening was cold and the atmosphere solemn. It felt as if the city was dissolving under the weight of tanks that stared blankly at us like gigantic caterpillars. Every once in a while there was a rumour that the authorities had decided to put an end to the protest and that they were sending in more tanks and soldiers, this time not just to throw tear gas. Soon after we gathered on Terazije, an improvised stage was erected in front of the fountain. One of the leading young actors at the time, Branislav Lečić,[3] took the stage asking the assembled crowd to stay put until the army was recalled and the streets of Belgrade were returned to civilians. Almost without interruption, he remained on that stage for several days and nights serving as a kind of MC. Other local artists joined him, keeping the spirits of the protesters high and the constant threat of Milošević's police and army at bay.

There is a story by Yugoslavian Nobel Prize laureate Ivo Andrić, titled 'Aska and the Wolf'. Aska is a beautiful sheep that loves to dance. One day, while she is playing in the woods, the Wolf comes to catch her. Full of fear, almost involuntarily, Aska's little body begins to move, morphing into a beautiful dance. She performs wonderfully, better than ever before. The Wolf watches, surprised, puzzled, bewildered, and Aska dances away into freedom. On those cold March nights in Belgrade, all the performing, singing, dancing, chanting, both on the improvised stage and among the crowd, was an intuitive survival strategy – an act of 'bewildering the Wolf'.

Less then a couple of months later, the first victims fell to the ongoing sporadic military conflicts in Croatia; in the summer, after a short war, the Republic of Slovenia separated from Yugoslavia; and by the fall of that year, the conflict in Croatia had escalated. The city of Vukovar was destroyed and the coastal towns of Zadar and Dubrovnik were shelled, while thousands of refugees were fleeing Croatia towards Serbian and Bosnian borders. After March 1991, street protests against Milošević took place in regular intervals from anti-war processions and vigils in the early 1990s and the student demonstration in 1992, to a three-month-long street protest in 1996–97 and numerous public subversions by the political organization *Otpor* (*Resistance*),[4] non-governmental groups such as Women in Black, and, last but by no means least, artists

Illustration 1 *Kunstlager*, 'Photographing' [Slikanje], photo courtesy of Nikola Džafo

and alternative performance troupes including Dah Theater, Centre for Cultural Decontamination, Plavo pozoriste (Blue Theatre), Škart and others. Well-known scenarios of political demonstrations were replayed, often altered and rejuvenated by innovative concepts and through their use of wit and humour. In general, anti-regime protests responded to the various events that ensued in the dramatic political life of the region in a multitude of ways (Illustration 1).

The regime often chose to answer the demonstrations with a form of counter-demonstration that turned out to be less imaginative and theatrical. The ruling party transported their supporters from various parts of Serbia to Belgrade in buses – since there were not enough of them in the capital to make a critical mass – and staged a rally for the President. Cultural theorist Milena Dragićević-Šešić contrasts these spectacles to their anti-regime counterparts in the following way:

> The free laughter of the months-long carnival demonstrations, the moveable feast, confronted the officially organized, deadly serious ceremonies which marked the Milošević anti-bureaucratic revolution in the 1980s, and their later rallies, right up to December 1996, when Milošević tried to gather his supporters from all over Serbia

> to confront the protest demonstrators in Belgrade. Iconographic stereotypes – same slogans, same photos, same typestyles, same colours, with even the frames of banners stressing the seriousness of the participants, who came to Belgrade convinced that the survival of their state and leaders depended on them. This rally – or rather counter-rally – had no room for improvisation. There was a platform onto which participants climbed according to protocol and procedure. There was no dancing, no wit, and no laughter. There were weapons.
>
> ('The Street as Political Space', p. 86)

These two kinds of political demonstrations clearly illustrate the divide within the country. They correspond to Jurgen Habermas's distinction between Strategic and Communicative action:

> Whereas in strategic action one actor seeks to *influence* the behavior of another by means of the threat of sanctions or the prospect of gratification in order to *cause* the interaction to continue as the first actor desires, in communicative action one actor seeks *rationally* to motivate *another* by relying on the illocutionary binding/bonding effect of the offer contained in his speech act.
>
> (*Moral Consciousness and Communicative Action*, p. 58)

The regime-orchestrated demonstrations and the anti-regime protests not only reveal the different ethics and politics of Habermas's categories of action, but also show how Strategic and Communicative actions operate through different rhetorics and through different kinds of theatricality.

The oppositional protest activities culminated on 5 October 2000 when mass street demonstrations to overthrow Milošević took place for the last time. At first, the police fired tear gas into the crowed, but the protesters managed to take over the Parliament building and to penetrate the headquarters of Radio Television Serbia – Milošević's key propaganda machine responsible for arousing jingoistic passions and fabricating information to justify its war-mongering politics. Later in the day, the police and military crossed over to 'the other side', joining the protesters in a seemingly spontaneous gesture of communal solidarity, which in retrospect turned out to be the fruit of complex and risky negotiations led by one of the key figures of the Serbian Opposition, Zoran Djindjić.[5] After 13 years of rule, after wars in Croatia and Bosnia, after the NATO bombing of Serbia (1999) and the Kosovo disaster, after years of economic decline, and after the most massive brain drain in the history of the region, Slobodan Milošević had been overthrown.

During this entire decade of various forms of counter-spectacles, the strategy of 'bewildering the Wolf' not only became a device of political resistance and a way of channelling potentially violent riots, but had at least two additional functions – to grab the attention of the world media and to provide a means of self-fashioning both individual and collective identity. Moreover, these counter-spectacles were not only a means of 'bewildering the wolves' of both local and global powers, but also a way to tame the inner 'wolves' of inertia, fear and self-censorship.

Histories

On 5 October 2000, the day Milošević was overthrown, I was watching television at my home in Toronto and saw an image from Belgrade that has stuck in my memory to this day. It is dusk, the protesters are leaving the streets to celebrate the big victory elsewhere, the vandalized Parliament building is in the background, while in the middle of the road, a man is sitting comfortably in an antique armchair taken from one of the parliamentary chambers. Traffic passes him by, he makes a victory sign to the drivers, they wave back at him, he stares blankly towards the near-by square of Marx and Engels (as its name makes obvious, a name that dates back to the communist era, and which has since been renamed), then waves again. I find this image iconic as it summarizes in a suspended moment the complex dynamics between individual and collective, between the spectacle of power and the city as a site of subversion. The fancy armchair, one that generations of politicians have enjoyed, is in the street and an ordinary man rests in it. This surreal object/image functions as a synecdoche summarizing the *danse macabre* between civil disobedience and alienated political power in Serbia. However, it is also an act of reclaiming the streets (albeit for a suspended moment) and subverting the dynamics between inside and outside and the power hierarchy. This anonymous man had unintentionally created a piece of live art that vividly commented not only on the immediate event, but created a gestic image, which contained both a backward glance into the political palimpsest of the city and a blank stare into a complicated and uncertain future.

The integrated spectacle of Milošević's era and the one that has emerged after his downfall differ in many ways, yet the relationship to history is key to understanding both of them. Debord writes: 'Spectacular domination's first priority was to eradicate historical knowledge in general; beginning with just about all rational information and commentary on the most recent past' (*Comments*, p. 14). Milošević's regime managed to do that through what I call the *hyperinflation of history* – excessive and strategic usage of history to win political arguments and influence the public. The tactic is to place diverse historical facts and remote historical events on the same plane. As in a *danse macabre*, Serbian victims from the medieval Battle of Kosovo are placed side by side with the dead from the Croatian concentration camps of the Second World War, and with the still fresh corpses of Serbs killed in Croatia, Bosnia, or Kosovo and broadcast on state-run television. *Hyperinflation of history* is the means of the spectacular government by which it becomes the 'absolute master of memories' (*Comments*, p. 10) that enables 'contemporary events to retreat into a remote and fabulous realm of unverifiable stories, uncheckable statistics, unlikely explanations and untenable reasoning.' (*Comments*, p. 16).

The *integrated spectacle* of post-Milošević Serbia employs quite the opposite attitude towards history. It displays various elaborate tactics of willing suspension of disbelief as if ignoring, for instance, the mass graves of Srebrenica long enough would make them disappear from history. Unpleasant and potentially painful issues of Serbia's involvement, responsibility and guilt in the recent history of the Balkans has been most often addressed in two extremely opposing ways, but with an equally self-righteous zeal – by those who only see Serbs as victims and assert this position as a form of resistance to the imperatives of Western powers and by those who, in admitting that Serbs were the sole perpetrators of the war, see the path towards reckoning and reconciliation that will open the door of Fortress Europe. The former are strong in numbers, the latter are fewer, while the majority of the population has chosen escapism as a strategy. This does not necessarily come out of the ruthless denial of war atrocities, but more out of a lack of tools, vocabulary and effective strategies to face recent history and deal with it – not so much insensitivity and irresponsibility, but mere confusion. Yet escapism is never innocent. It is a choice and thereby ideologically shaped against the backdrop of that which it refuses to face. Debord writes: 'The precise advantage which the spectacle has acquired through *outlawing* of history, from having driven the recent past into hiding, and from having made everyone forget the spirit of history within the society, is above all the ability to cover its own tracks' (*Comments*, pp. 15–16). The integrated spectacle of the post-Milošević era offers escapism and selective remembering presenting itself as a healthy alternative to the spectacle of the *hyperinflated history* of its predecessors.

Appropriations and counter-appropriations

Debord pointed out that there is no escape from spectacle as the individual follows 'the language of the spectacle, for it is the only one he is familiar with; the one in which he learnt to speak. No doubt he would like to be regarded as an enemy of its rhetoric; but he will use its syntax' (*Comments on the Society of Spectacle*, p. 31).

Even if the critique of the spectacular society is only possible in a language that has already been formulated by that society, and even with the danger of becoming co-opted, even corrupted, the distinction between spectacle and counter-spectacle is important. This distinction is in the first place ethical, because without it there would be no difference between protests against the regime of Slobodan Milošević and organized public gatherings in his support. In a way, Belgrade's counter-spectacles were born on the ruins of the spectacles of Milošević's regime. The protest events emerged as counter-spectacles in as much as they tried to resist a form of spectacular power of the *concentrated spectacle* defined by Debord as favouring 'the ideology condensed around a dictatorial personality' (*Comments on the Society of the Spectacle*, p. 8) and the lure of the integrated spectacle disguised as a true alternative to communism. Even if a counter-spectacle could only come into being through a borrowed, albeit subverted, language of a spectacular power, and even if at the end of the day, the counter-spectacle gets sucked into the powerful, seductive and irresistible integrated spectacle, its importance is crucial as it still provides critique, ethical parameters and the possibility of intervention. However, these counter-spectacles remained at best on the margins and in the footnotes of the historical narratives, whether shaped and written by the local war-mongering regime or by international powers working to stop such a regime. Still, the notion of counter-spectacle is a reminder that even within a world of integrated spectacle, resistance is not only possible, but necessary.

In what follows I will explore two interconnected aspects of performing Belgrade as a city of spectacle – its theatricality and its various performatives. In Chapter 1, 'City-as-Action', I will focus on the dramaturgy of political resistance and the role of theatricality and performativity in activating the city and negotiating the boundaries of both public spaces and public discourses. In Chapter 2, 'At the Confluence of Utopia and Seduction', I will address the city as spatial practice through ideological and ethical implications of its *utopian performatives* (Dolan, *Utopia in Performance*).

1
City-as-Action

In the mid-1990s, it was difficult to find the usual postcards of the city with images of monuments, squares and parks. There were almost no tourists in Belgrade. Foreign visitors were reduced to journalists, negotiators and envoys with no interest in tourist memorabilia. The only kind of postcards that one could still easily buy from Belgrade street-vendors featured iconic images of various political protests. Some of them were reprints of documentary photographs from the protests, while others depicted the protest's main symbols: a whistle and a broken egg. The whistle was one of the protesters' most used props, alongside eggs which they threw at the Serbian Television building, singling it out as an instrument of a regime that operated through censorship and propaganda. The postcards often looked like propagandist posters of the Russian avant-garde with the conventional inscription, 'Greetings from Belgrade', adding an extra twist. In the year 2000, preceding the end of the Milošović regime, postcards with insignias of the democratic opposition resurfaced, most featuring a raised fist – the symbol of the political organization *Otpor*. Some of the postcards had their inscriptions written in English, but most of these 'Greetings from Belgrade' were written in Serbian Cyrillic.

The postcards were clearly part of the resistance but they were also a means of shaping a new urban identity. They depicted Belgrade as a city of protest, deliberately subverting the habitual postcard iconography that located a place through its national institutions and symbols. By refusing to depict images of official buildings and monuments, these postcards asserted an alternative and hitherto marginalized identity of the city. In the years surrounding the overthrow of Milošević, the production of protest memorabilia iconic of Belgrade's new identity became more prominent. Images that adorned postcards and T-shirts featured a black and white drawing of a raised fist and the anti-Milošević slogan, 'Gotov je!' (He's finished!) – all symbols of OTPOR. After NATO bombed Serbia in 1999, a new series of postcards appeared: images of destroyed buildings, of air raids and explosions that were captioned 'Belgrade by Night' and 'Greetings from Belgrade'. Yet these postcards were more ambiguous in revealing a political position. In other words, they could be from either side of Serbia's internal political conflict. Items such as these were not only telling the recent history of the city but also attested to its shaky, fluctuating identity and its desperate need for refashioning.

During the mass protests in winter of 1996/7, I was already an immigrant in Toronto and could only follow these events at a distance, mostly through letters and messages sent from my friends in Belgrade, and, to a very limited extent, through North American and Serbian media. Among the letters I got from Belgrade in those days was a protest postcard. It looked like pop art featuring pink, green and yellow whistles. On the back of it my friend wrote: 'We are practically living on the streets. It's amazing. Miss you.' Later that year, when my mother came for a visit, she brought a selection of protest postcards and gave me her whistle (which came in handy when we joined other members of the Serbian Diaspora to demonstrate in front of the Serbian consulate in Toronto to express our support). In giving me the protest postcards, both my friend and my mother were asserting the strongest bond that I had to the public life of a city that I had left in anger and hopelessness a couple of years earlier. The protests, in their carnivalesque theatricality and sardonic performativity (Illustration 2), made living in Belgrade somehow still worth it, at least during those few months of the winter of 1996/7. For me those postcards again echoed the Patty Smith song, although in retrospect, I am no longer sure that the notion 'people have the power', expressed so passionately through her music and lyrics, was fully realized as a political force. Perhaps it was only a lullaby.

In any event, if postcards are meant to represent the most appealing features of a place, it was the protest activities that emerged as an integral part of Belgrade and made its citizens feel very proud. In this changing face of Belgrade, nationalist kitsch, strategies of escapism and selective memory competed with the iconography and performance of political resistance. The other side of Belgrade that perceived itself as European and cosmopolitan had been on the verge of losing its subjectivity, hence spectacles of political protest became much more than a pragmatic political strategy. They became a means of reasserting the city's cultural identity and, eventually, a new form of communal

Illustration 2 Protests 1996–97, photo courtesy of the *Vreme* archive

expression. These postcards suggest a heterotopic dimension of Belgrade that has emerged through political protests, revealing the city as a counter-site for staging resistance to its own mainstream politics.

Lastly, the protest postcards depict the theatricality and performativity of Belgrade that the counter-spectacles had created. Featuring documentary images or stylized props of the protest, the postcards suggest the idea of the *city-as-action* – a dynamic and at times conflicting relationship between people-in-motion – a body politic *in mot* – and unshakable architecture, between continuity and rupture, between symbols of power and images of resistance, between spectacle and counter-spectacle. The notion of the *city-as-action* is more than a theatrical metaphor that describes the city as a stage where performances of political power and political resistance are enacted. *City-as-action* implies not only the political struggles but also its dramaturgy and its *mise-en-scène*. It includes the process of making and unmaking the city through action – that is, through a dynamic self-fashioning – and asserts the idea of place as a palimpsest that reveals the city's synchronic and diachronic relations. Theatricality and performativity are key elements of foregrounding the *city-as-action*.

The theatricality of protests is the strategic, conceptual, premeditated aspect of the counter-spectacle. It formulates the language of the protest activities and carries performance codes to confront the regime in power and attract the attention of the world media. As Diana Taylor points out:

> Theatricality makes the scenario alive and compelling. In other words, scenarios exit as culturally specific imaginaries – activated with more or less theatricality. [...] Theatricality strives for efficiency, not authenticity. It connotes a conscious, controlled and, thus, always political dimension that performance need not imply. It differs from spectacle in that theatricality highlights the *mechanics* of spectacle.
>
> (*The Archive and the Repertoire*, p. 13)

Theatricality determined the dramaturgy of the protests and also linked Belgrade's counter-spectacle to other scenarios of political urban resistance. In other words, theatricality forms intertextual and/or interperformative links to other radical performances in history from as far back as the French Revolution[1] to the events of 1968, and, finally, places Belgrade's counter-spectacles in line with the street demonstrations of the late 1980s and early 1990s that marked the end of communist regimes in Eastern Europe and the fall of the Berlin Wall. Conversely, performativity emerges as an element of counter-spectacle that can never be fully premeditated, 'rehearsed' and repeated. It forges its own intertextual or, rather, interperformative links, not so much through the dramaturgy of radical political performances, but through the social, historical, and cultural specificity of the site where it takes place. These connections are both intertextual and intra-cultural as they situate the counter-spectacles of the 1990s within the palimpsest of the city. Hence performativity is the context-specific dimension of the protests, allowing unique and unrepeatable aspects of Belgrade's counter-spectacles to emerge.

Theatricality and performativity became central to the political protests in Serbia, most notably, with the student demonstrations against the regime that broke out at the University of Belgrade in 1992. The theatricality of the counter-spectacle culminated in later years during the months of protest activities in 1996–97 and, to some extent, it also marked the street demonstrations in the year 2000 when Milošević's rule ended. In the following sections of this chapter, I will explore how theatricality and performativity of *the city-as-action* unfold both through theatrical political protests and through politicized artistic performances. How does the interplay between the city's theatricality and performativity activate intertextual and intra-cultural links and what are their political, ethical and spatial resonances? How do the counter-spectacles of Belgrade replay the notion of the carnivalesque in political performance? And how does the theatricality and performativity of these events give rise to new political metaphors, such as the notion of *political decontamination*, and to new interventionist strategies? Finally, I will examine the phenomenon of *political catharsis* as a common element that takes place, to various degrees, in the theatricality of Belgrade through the strategies of *decontamination* and *carnivalization*, as well as within the city's interperformativity.

Theatricality ethics and the fear factor

> *For the first time in my life I'm not unhappy, I'm not afraid – there are two hundred million people in this country, comrades, and each one is afraid of someone. Two hundred million fears, but I'm not afraid of anyone!*
>
> Nikolai Erdman, *Suicide*

When the student protest started with a gathering in front of the building of the University Rectorate in the heart of Belgrade on 15 June 1992, Sarajevo had been under siege for over two months. The student protest was preceded by several anti-war interventions such as the event organized by the Centre for Antiwar Action that took place on 31 May when tens of thousands of people walked through central Belgrade carrying a black ribbon that was more than one kilometre long. This street procession was staged as an expression of condolence to all the people to date who had died in the war in Bosnia. A day before the student protest started, Serbian Oppositional leaders gathered thousands of people in the streets of Belgrade to take part in an intervention called 'Poslednje zvono' ('The Last Bell') meant to signal to Milošević and his regime that their time was up. Yet cultural theorist Milena Dragićević-Šešić argues that the strongest influence on the aesthetics of the student protest might have come from the interventions organized by B92, the local radio station that became famous for its independent and openly anti-regime broadcasting, as well as from some actions of the independent Antiwar Movement. Some of the actions organized by B92, such as 'All the President's Babies' – a gathering of mothers proposing to give their babies to the President since they could not afford to feed them – foreshadowed the theatricality and wit that would emerge in full during the student protests. Likewise, conceptual actions of the civic peace movements, such as *The Yellow Band* – a protest against ethnic cleansing where all the participants wore a yellow band with a sign on it: 'I am a Croat', 'I am a Muslim', 'I am a Jew' and so on – were echoed in the aesthetics of student protests.

However, as Dragićević-Šešić points out, the student protest found its own dramaturgy and language of resistance distinct from any other forms present on the political stage of Serbia at the time, one that was embedded in the architecture and life of the city:

> The most important forms of student protest against the Balkan War in 1992 were linked with the open spaces of the city of Belgrade, creating a new culture of street manifestations which neither the rallies called by the ruling party (since Milošević's so-called anti-bureaucratic revolution) nor the gatherings called by the opposition had previously achieved [...]
>
> ('The Street as Political Space', p. 75)

In the early summer of 1992, students took over the University buildings demanding the independence of the University, Milošević's resignation and new parliamentary elections. The students, who had full control over what happened inside the buildings, organized events, discussions and speakers, and published their own newspaper. Student IDs were checked at the University entrance in order to prevent the infiltration of regime supporters.[2] I, along with a number of my colleagues, took part in the event contributing to a magazine called *Dosta!* (*No More!*) which was conceived at the site a few days after the protest started. As a theatre student, I was fascinated by the shift from the standard means of political struggle towards the highly performative acts that I witnessed during the course of the protest. Students not only theatricalized the protest, they also reclaimed the space – from university buildings to streets – giving a new dimension to the city. My short article for *Dosta!* described some of the events from the point of view of theatricality.

At first, the protest consisted of students gathering in front of or inside the buildings of Belgrade University, making speeches and inviting supporters to do the same. In the second week of the protest, visual arts students organized a happening in the University lobby by making sculptures out of Styrofoam and paper. The sculptures represented a group of desensitized, brainwashed people in front of a television set, an apparent allusion to the media manipulation that the regime exercised on its citizens. A few days later, a long protest procession, entitled 'Prisoners of Shortsightedness', took over downtown

Belgrade's quotidian life. Students walked in a row like prison inmates, with numbers attached to their shirts. The procession ended when students left a list of their demands in front of the closed doors of the National Assembly. The procession was meant to signify the status of young people in contemporary Serbian society (Illustration 3).

Arguably the best known student procession, 'Coffee with the President', involved students walking some ten kilometres from downtown Belgrade to Dedinje, the posh area of the city, where the President lived. Since the President had ignored the student protest entirely, the students decided to pay him a personal visit, to have coffee with him and to discuss their demands. The procession was stopped a few hundred metres away from the residence by heavily armed police squads. The symbolic attempt to have coffee with the President on the one hand, and the police protecting the impenetrable doors of the President's villa on the other was telling in respect of the city's power demographics. In the symbolic realm, the students walking to the President's doorsteps and the blunt and forceful denying of access by the police, showed all too clearly the alienation of Milošević and his apparatus from a significant part of the public. Dubravka Knežević, playwright, dramaturge and lecturer at the Faculty of Arts, and one of the founding members

Illustration 3 Student protests, photo courtesy of the *Vreme* archive

of the magazine *Dosta!*, described a spin-off event to 'Coffee with the President':

> A few days later they performed a theatrical replica of the same procession, called 'Five O'Clock Coffee'. For this event, fine arts students made two-metre-tall rag puppets of the President and his wife, architecture students designed a stage representing their house, and the whole procession, with flowers and the list of demands in the fore, was repeated. What could not happen in reality happened in this *Grand Guignol* – 'the president' received the students' appeal and was left to make his decision overnight.
>
> ('Marked in Red Ink', p. 413)

While installations like the Styrofoam sculptures reclaimed the regime's institutions and commented on their politics, walks and street processions became a means of mapping and reclaiming the city. These walks and processions also revealed ways in which the power structure reconfigured the city as the students marked and performed in the areas that were off limits for ordinary citizens – the building of the National Assembly, for instance, and the street where the President lived. They charted out a not-so-obvious *Forbidden City* within the city.

By the end of the protest, after many more events of a similar kind had taken place, I witnessed a transformation of a pragmatic political realm into a semiotic and symbolic one. As I have noted elsewhere, semiotization is the first instance of the theatricalization of a political protest, which lies at the very root of counter-spectacle.[3] This includes not only codes and messages brought into the protest from political reality, but also a process of re-coding. The course of political action develops signs and codes that replace everyday political vocabulary with images, metaphors, allusions and symbols. This process is somewhat similar to the Situationist technique of *détournement*, or rerouting, embezzlement, misappropriation. *Détournement*, as counter-spectacle, uses the pre-existing language of the spectacle, but searches for ways to turn it on its head and subvert it. To some extent, the *détournement* strategies of the student protest – the semiotization and theatricalization of their actions to reclaim the city and its institutions – paved the way for the numerous counter-spectacles that followed.

Strategies and dramaturgies exercised during the student process influenced many events of political street theatre, both planned and impromptu, as well as the interventions of OTPOR, a political organization that consisted mostly of university students and came to prominence in the late 1990s. In August 1999, for instance, over two thousand people attended OTPOR's mock celebration of President Milošević's birthday. This was a resounding success since OTPOR protests usually occurred without a permit and were not widely announced in order to decrease the risk of police intervention. The idea of celebrating Milošević's birthday had strong intertextual/intertheatrical references to the lavish celebrations of Tito's birthday, also dubbed Youth Day, where thousands of young people entertained the President in a large stadium performing precisely choreographed exercises accompanied by speeches and projected images. The satire inherent in this reference is evident in its allusion to the similarities between the somewhat dictatorial rule of Tito and his enjoyment of the cult of personality and Milošević's personal style as a ruler (Illustration 4). The celebration of the President's birthday involved a scenario of improvisational activities, acting, props and a degree of fictionalization of the streetscape where the event took place. One of the participants played the role of the President dressed in a dark suit, sitting in a comfortable chair and smoking Havana cigars. Other participants were invited to write birthday cards on a board behind the President or bring him presents that included handcuffs, a one-way

Illustration 4 Protest 1996–97, photo courtesy of the *Vreme* archive

ticket to the Hague, and a strait jacket – a counter-spectacle that preconfigured Milošević's end in the prison cell in Scheveningen.

The student community was central in carrying out the counter-spectacles of the 1990s, openly expressing their resistance to the regime in various instances of reclaiming streets and official institutions. Nevertheless, the same could not be said for the University governing bodies and faculty members, whose political views, alliances and action differed widely. In the fall of 1991, Mirjana Miočinović, one of the most prominent theatre scholars of former Yugoslavia, voluntarily resigned her position as Professor of Yugoslavian Drama and Theatre at the University of Belgrade's Faculty of Dramatic Arts. Her resignation was a gesture of political protest and a refusal to participate in the public and institutional life of a country that, in the name of its citizens, promoted deadly, war-raging, jingoism. Her gesture was largely ignored by the media and by most of her colleagues. In an interview more than ten years later for Serbian theatre magazine, *Teatron*, Miočinović was asked to comment on her resignation and the public reaction to it:

> In 1991 Milošević's politics were widely supported and therefore didn't need to be openly repressive. My own case confirms this: it was enough to just ignore my gesture. But things would have been different if, particularly that year, the University used its power and showed that it did not accept a politics that was committing crimes and had been openly criminal already. If that was the case, Milošević's regime would have either been overthrown then, or it would have become openly repressive to us (I mean Serbs in Serbia) and it would not be able to recruit its supporters so easily. It's their own business that to this day my colleagues ease their conscience by claiming that they were helping their students through 'dark times', while they only prolonged the 'dark times', which ethically, psychologically, and professionally destroyed their students. For me this was the downfall of our profession.
>
> (quoted in Medenica and Radulović, 'Nemam tu šta da tražim', p. 40)

The student protest was a way of performing the role that institutions of higher education should have played in the society – to serve as places of dialogue and critique and to stand up to the regime. Instead, the students were left mostly to their own devices, which limited the efficiency of their interventions. Still, the theatricality of their protests played out as a social and ethical force.

As Miočinović pointed out, the regime in those years had no need to be openly repressive because fear was already in the air. Time and again friends and colleagues shared their anti-regime views in private but kept silent in public. Some openly admitted that they feared for their jobs, their safety, even for their lives, pleading for one's right to be afraid in 'dark times'.[4] In any case, even if it did not immediately bring down the regime, the theatricality of the student protest went a long way towards counteracting the fear factor. The student protest of 1992 was longer and subsequently gathered more participants than the protest on 9 March 1991 and the mainly student-led demonstrations that took place on Terazijska Česma. It was not so much that Milošević created a new critical mass of opponents in one year, but that those who disagreed with his politics in private became a little less afraid to express their views publicly. In other words, the theatricality of the student demonstrations made the city safe enough as a site of political protest thus enabling many more people to overcome their fears.

In that light, the theatricality of the protests not only offered new urban iconography and renewed dramaturgies of political intervention, but openly expressed an ethical standpoint. To join or not to join the protest, to be or not to be against Milošević's regime, was more than a political gesture – it was a moral choice. In 'dark times', perhaps more than ever, such choices irrevocably determine and alter individual and collective identities. Therefore, theatricality and performativity became a means of foregrounding the ethical dimension of Belgrade's self-fashioning through political protests.

Angels in the City: rituals of political decontamination

In 1998, Belgrade's theatre company *DAH* (*Breath*)[5] created a site-specific performance entitled *Angels in the City* at the Roman Fortress Kalemegdan – a beautiful park in the heart of the city overlooking the river Danube. In *Angels in the City*, actors/angels guide the audience through Kalemegdan's most scenic lookouts and vistas only to reveal its violent history of dungeons, torture chambers and execution sites. The aim of this 'tour' was political: to cleanse the place of its historical baggage.

By the time *DAH* theatre's 'angels' arrived to decontaminate Belgrade's major historical landmark, the wars in Croatia and Bosnia were over and the last chapter of Milošević's regime had started to unfold in Serbia. Still, *Angels in the City* sent an important message. The performance was about the need to exhume the remains and confront the past, but also about letting the scars of history heal. It was conceptualized as a guided tour, where homeless angels appeared disguised as tramps and warriors armed with broomsticks, newspapers and a bucket. The tour guide revealed the performance site as haunted by competing and contesting histories: on the left, the river with an isle in the middle of it called War Island; on the right, the Museum of the Yugoslav Army, below, a former Austrian prison and above, a Turkish citadel. He further pointed to five unmarked execution sites from different periods of the city's turbulent history. The angels measured the space with their bodies to mark the spots that needed to be cleansed from history. Then they grabbed their broomsticks and the cleansing ritual began. By theatricalizing violent history, the performers tamed its inflammatory potential and made it manageable, even tragi-comic at times. The concept worked against the nationalistic rhetoric that believed in a future built from the ruins of the past. *Angels in the City* cleansed by rendering historical obsessions absurd. Dijana Milošević, the co-founder of *DAH* and the director of this performance explains: 'In the performance we were cleansing ourselves from history but we were cleansing history itself as well. [...] we can say that we performed a healing process' (DAH website). *Angels in the City* was, however, only one amongst many works by local artists who saw the political dimensions of their work as acts of cleansing and healing in both a satirical and a shamanic sense.

As the country was falling apart, antagonistic histories were strategically unleashed to awaken national pride and pathos and to remind people that the Other – more often than not perceived as the enemy – was about to strike again. History became the fuel for nationalistic passions and a means of legitimizing killing. When Slobodan Milošević came to power in the late 1980s, he emerged as the protector of Kosovo Serbs who felt endangered by the growing ethnic Albanian population. His central argument on the Kosovo issue, as well as the territorial claim, evolved around a heroic battle that Serbs fought there against the Turks in the Middle Ages. When Croatia declared independence in 1991, Serbian media bombarded the citizens with the Second World War history of Croatia – a dark period when Croatia had become a fascist puppet state, housing one of the most notorious concentration camps where hundreds of thousands of Serbs, Jews and Gypsies had been murdered. The idea was to suggest how the new Croatia could not be anything else but a revival of the fascist one, where Serbs were going to be tortured and killed all over again. This was meant, of course, to prompt the citizens of Serbia to take up arms to protect their 'brothers and sisters' in Croatia. During the war in Bosnia, the medieval card was played again as the media and the patriotic mainstream culture worked overtime to remind the public of the five hundred years of slavery under the Ottoman Empire (from the fourteenth to the nineteenth century), maliciously suggesting that Bosnian Muslims were a shameful reminder of that occupation. History was used again to reinforce the idea that to fight in Bosnia meant not only to protect the 'ever-endangered' Serbs, but also to save Christianity from Muslim fundamentalism. Hence, in times when new wars are waged in the name of lost battles dating from the Middle Ages, the idea of cleansing history emerges not only as a witty riposte, but also as a necessary and timely one.

In such a context, it is no surprise that medicinal metaphors of cleansing and healing dominated the narrative of civil disobedience and political protest in Serbia during Slobodan Milošević's regime and simultaneously poured into various performance practices. The counterculture frequently explored symbolic acts of decontamination, healing and hibernation to estrange the reality marked by growing nationalism, xenophobia, war, poverty and fear. Medicinal metaphors as an artistic means of confronting everyday life in Serbia started with the projects of Led Art (Ice Art) – a group of artists from diverse fields active from 1993 and through the Centre for Cultural Decontamination which opened in 1995. Avoiding cultural institutions, Led Art and the Centre for Cultural Decontamination often used the city as stage, turning its streets into sacred places of collective political cleansing. The word decontamination was most frequently used as descriptive of their site-specific interventions. It is essentially an estrangement strategy. Isolation of a person, object or space from its surroundings is the first step in the decontamination procedure. Likewise, artistic devices of estrangement counteract the automatization of perception by isolating a subject from its habitual context, forcing the audience to see the familiar in a new and often surprising light.

Led Art, founded by visual artist Nikola Džafo, identified freezing and hibernation as central metaphors in Serbian political and cultural life, hence ice is both part of its name and was used in numerous sculptures, installations and performances that the members of the group created. In one of their manifestos, Led Art declared:

> Refusing to take part in destruction, murder and robbery, we are uprooting ourselves from traditional institutions. [...] We are finding a new path. [...] In other words, Led Art creates its projects in urban environments, outside official artistic venues, using unexpected places to stage its exhibits and performances (trucks, skating rinks, garages, streets).[6]
>
> ('Načela', Led Art 1999, p. 18)

Illustration 5 The Led Art truck, photo courtesy of Nikola Džafo

In May 1993, the group made a spectacular entrance onto the countercultural scene parking a refrigerated truck in the centre of Belgrade (Illustration 5). The inside of the truck was turned into an exhibition venue for a project called 'Ice Art'. Loudspeakers installed on the roof of the truck played Radio B92's live broadcast of the event.[7] The radio commentary suggested that the citizens of Serbia lived in 'a time out of joint', where things freeze in the middle of spring. The metaphor could be further stretched to suggest that seemingly normal everyday life in Belgrade was absurd in the light of the war raging only a few hundred kilometres away in Bosnia. Each visitor was given an army coat before entering the exhibit to keep warm. Inside the truck was a display of objects captured in ice blocks. The installations ranged from overtly political and ironic, to personal, abstract and nostalgic. One installation displayed a kitschy Venetian gondola figurine[8] stuck in the frozen water of a sewer pipe (Illustration 6); in another, entitled 'Summer Time Blues', a pair of old running shoes stood arrested in a block of ice.[9] An untitled ice sculpture captured a clock and a bullet from the latest war in Croatia,[10] while in the corner of the truck, an old Yugoslavian flag was stuck in a barrel of lard, refusing to freeze (Illustration 7). The author, Raša Todosijević, named this one 'Gott liebt die Serben' alluding to the fascist dimensions of Serbian nationalism.

Illustration 6 'Gondola' by Nikola Džafo, photo courtesy of Nikola Džafo

The symbolism of the ice sculptures is twofold. On the one hand, freezing is a way of preserving something from decay. Led Art is a hibernation tactic – a strategy of lowering the temperature in order to survive the cultural, political and ethical ice age into which the former Yugoslavia had fallen. On the other hand, installations made of statutory flags and frozen bullets also assert an unambiguous critique of war and the existing political situation. By offering army coats to protect visitors from the cold inside the truck, the artists suggested that everyone, no matter how uninvolved, was in a way part of the war and implicated in the unfolding Yugoslavian catastrophe. Hence the hibernation metaphor turns full circle from having a positive connotation as a preservation strategy, to standing for passivity and political cowardice that makes innocent bystanders complicit in the crime.

The medicinal metaphors of Led Art have a shamanic quality. By freezing the 'evil' objects (i.e., the bullet from the war in Croatia), the artists symbolically disable them from their usual power. The context shifts from political to metaphysical: an object frozen in reality is also frozen in time and prompts spectators to isolate it and to contemplate it. Freezing things from kitschy figurines to bullets is a way of arresting them and subsequently decontaminating the cultural space. In a series of performances entitled 'Crime Reconstruction' (Illutrations 8

Illustration 7 Inside the Led Art truck, photo courtesy of Nikola Džafo

Illustration 8 'Crime Reconstruction', photo courtesy of Nikola Džafo

and 9), Led Art further explored this idea. The project was advertised as a 'free healing' offering to measure the fevered temperature that the political situation in the Balkans had raised in various communities. The artists conducted a random survey asking the following questions: 'Do you have enemies? Have you ever had subversive thoughts? Did you read Kafka's *Process?*' (*Led Art*, p. 103). Since most of the answers were positive, Led Art diagnosed that most of the population was in danger of dying due to a high political temperature and prescribed a remedy called 'The Balkan Chalk Circle' – an obviously ironic toying with the title of Brecht's famous play. 'The Balkan Chalk Circle' was based on a method used in criminal investigations to mark the spot where a violent crime has taken place. The contours of the victim's body are outlined in white chalk to fix the position in which the victim has been found at the crime scene (Illustrations 8 and 9). Led Art performed numerous variations of this technique in a number of places – from street pavements to skating rinks – and in various occasions – from the student protest in Belgrade in 1994 and 1997 to New Year's celebrations in the city of Novi Sad in the year 2000. The political subversion of the project was overt, suggesting that the entire population of Serbia was held hostage by Milošević's regime. 'Balkan Chalk Circle' was a means of reclaiming and embodying public spaces at a time when voices of political opposition were silenced

Illustration 9 'Crime Reconstruction', photo courtesy of Nikola Džafo

and the counter-culture was made invisible. On another level, the idea was a shamanic one – everything harmful and evil remains captured within the contours of the white chalk. In its leaflet for the 'Crime Reconstruction' project, Led Art states: 'We draw contours of the body in white chalk, so evil becomes arrested in the drawing. Art is placed in the service of protection' (*Led Art*, p. 103). The drawing becomes an effigy and a death mask which does not harm but protects its owner by scaring evil spirits away.

How successful, then, was Led Art in healing and protecting through its installations and performances? For example, Led Art used the 'Balkan Chalk Circle' method on the streets of Belgrade during the student protest in February of 1997. A number of protestors volunteered for the performance, lying on the pavement while artists from Led Art outlined the contours of their bodies in white chalk. This happening was a reaction to the police violence that had taken place a few nights before when protestors had been brutally beaten. The 'Balkan Chalk Circle' became a means of mapping the streets of Belgrade as sites of violent political crimes and a playful whistle-blowing strategy to keep the police at bay.

The faith of 'Ice Art' was different. Although the state-run agricultural company that donated the refrigerated truck had agreed to permanently house the exhibit, the night after the opening, the truck's cooling mechanism mysteriously broke down. The owners of the truck claimed that the damage was beyond repair and nothing could be done. Artefacts were taken out onto the street pavement and left to melt.

Evidence that the evil captured in the ice had escaped as the blocks melted resurfaced years later, when in 2001 a refrigerated truck full of dead bodies from Kosovo was found in a Serbian lake (Illustration 10). It was an obvious attempt of Milošević's regime to obliterate traces of the atrocities committed in that province during the conflict in 1999. Oscar Wilde wrote, 'Life imitates art and not the other way round' ('The Decay of Lying', p. 789). In this horrific parallel between art and reality, Wilde's thought was somewhat reworked – life no longer imitated art, death did. Thus, death became the final political metaphor of the 'Frozen Art' prefigured in the sculpture 'Summer Time Blues' – a pair of running shoes captured in a block of ice with nobody to wear them, could only stand for loss and void.

Medicinal metaphors of the Serbian counter-culture and the political opposition finally became institutionalized when on 1 January 1995, veteran dramaturge and activist Borka Pavićević, members of Led Art, young theatre director Ana Miljanić and playwright Dubravka Knežević

Illustration 10 Life Imitates Art, photo courtesy of Nikola Džafo

opened the Centre for Cultural Decontamination in a restored building called Pavilion Veljković. Their aims were playfully outlined in the following maxims: the Centre 'starts with the premise that the overwhelming contamination makes the demarcation line between the sick and the healthy impossible', therefore it 'investigates, diagnoses and heals various forms of reality' using 'action as a therapeutic methodology', while members of the Centre are not 'health workers, but researchers in healing methods' (*Led Art*, p. 116). The centre is housed in a haunted space (Carlson, *The Haunted Stage*) of fragmented history, where the private and the political have often collided, changing the function and identity of the building. Before the Second World War, the Pavilion was a gallery of modern art owned by the wealthy Veljković family. After the war it was appropriated by the State and turned into a storage facility.

The new life of the building started with an event advertised as *The First Decontamination*. It began in the courtyard of the Pavilion with sounds of air-raid sirens – a chilling reminder of life in the war zone, a premonition of the NATO bombing of Serbia that would take place some four years later, and a signal to the visitors to enter the dilapidated building. Inside the huge bare space surrounded by cracked walls, the music of Schumann and Mozart replaced the air-raid sirens, while members of Led Art offered heart-shaped ice popsicles to the guests. On the walls was a display of photos and drawings found on the site that attested to the Pavilion's turbulent history. The opening ceremony was both a way of uncovering the building's past and a cleansing ritual of a haunted site. On its opening day, the Centre for Cultural Decontamination gave the old Pavilion a new identity – offering it to the public as a cultural and moral shelter. A few months after its inauguration, in May 1995, the Centre put on an exhibit called *Living in Sarajevo* (*Živjeti u Sarajevu*) about life in a city that was still under siege. Later that summer, the Centre also organized a workshop entitled 'What can we do to stop the war in Bosnia?', a gesture of protest against ethnic cleansing in Srebrenica and Žepa. From its opening to the present day, the Centre has produced and hosted numerous events – performances, happenings and exhibits as well as political discussions that have been more or less absent from mainstream debate – Serbia's responsibility for the Srebrenica massacre, for example, and other similar topics.

Projects of Led Art and the Centre for Cultural Decontamination have not only been a means of reclaiming cultural space and estranging its dominant politics, but have also revealed a deep, organic connection between rituals of political cleansing and the city. Their medicinal metaphors and acts of decontamination have uncovered geopathological

(Chaudhuri. *Staging Place*) relationships between the citizens and their city – where political and ethical issues become manifest in a sickness of place and sickness with place. The geopathological condition emerged from the gap between two cultures that became very distinct during the Milošević years – and which the end of his era has still not fully bridged – a cosmopolitan, pacifist, rock and roll culture on the one side, and a nationalistic, warmongering, 'turbo-folk' culture[11] on the other. In Belgrade's street vernacular, this social and political gap has been identified as a rift between 'rural' and 'urban' culture, reflecting the two major political streams in Serbia that often collided in numerous street protests and were the subject of various site-specific performances: one that still wanted to fight medieval battles and the other that wanted to be decontaminated from history.

Finally, how strong was the remedy that various performances of political cleansing provided? In other words, how wide-reaching was the work of Led Art and the Centre for Cultural Decontamination? Performances of decontaminations and medicinal metaphors had a paradoxical dimension: they were a means of political empowerment on the one hand, and desperate shamanic acts after all the official political remedies had been exhausted on the other. In 1996, the Centre for Cultural Decontamination and Led Art went their separate ways. The parting from the Centre was highly performative and entitled *Escape from the Centre*. When Led Art issued a statement and sent it to all the local dailies, only *Beorama* magazine – a city-guide publication with limited readership – published it. Playfully, using metaphors of cleansing and hibernation, Led Art explained its departure:

> After a year and a half of activities, Led Art is forced to freeze its activities in the Centre for Cultural Decontamination. This self-imposed exile is a result of the Aest-Ethic cleansing as Led Art refuses to be just a decorative feature of the Centre. The final decision was made on May 17th 1996, on the date of the third anniversary of Led Art, [...] with the announcement of the action *Escape from the Centre*.
>
> Led Art takes over the concept of decontamination with the view not to stop on the edges of the city [...]. The project *Escape from the Centre* starts with a tour 'Aj SAD –Kragujevac' [Kragujevac is another major Serbian city. SJ].
>
> (*Led Art*, p. 129)

The activities of the Centre remained mostly in Belgrade and in its determination to remain uncompromised and uncontaminated, it almost embraced self-marginalization. Led Art searched for more immediate ways to engage with the public and constantly struggled against marginalization to escape the trap of preaching to the converted, which often emerges as a result of strategic self-marginalization. The title of their project, *Escape from the Centre,* thus alluded both to the Centre for Cultural Decontamination and to the rift between the centre and the margin in a geographical and cultural sense. *Escape from the Centre* was asserted as a critique of the Centre for Cultural Decontamination for its elitism – its Belgrade-centredness. To become more visible and widen the impact of its work, Led Art was ready to go beyond Belgrade and beyond big cultural centres and began its tour entitled *Journey into the Heart of Serbia* – a clear allusion to the title of Konrad's novella *In the Heart of Darkness.*

Despite their different strategies, performances of cultural and political decontamination were not only gestures of anti-regime protests but also constant reminders to the citizenry that civil disobedience was a moral responsibility and an obligation. The opening of Led Art's gallery (the Art Clinic) in the city of Novi Sad in November 2002, two years after Milošević's regime fell, suggests that the process of decontamination is not over. Also in 2002, the Centre for Cultural Decontamination produced a performance titled *Warriors' Bordello* in the 'Museum of 25 May'. In communist times, the museum – named after President Tito's birthday – used to be dedicated to his achievements. *Warriors' Bordello* aimed to decontaminate the place from its history and unmask the macho war culture deeply embedded in both communist and nationalist mythology. In March 2006, after Slobodan Milošević had died in his prison cell in the Hague, his body was brought back to Belgrade and displayed in the 'Museum of 25 May' so his supporters could pay their last respects. The events around Milošević's funeral looked like a grotesque re-enactment of the glory days of his Socialist Party. Soon after, in the Summer of 2006, I met with Borka Pavićević, who still ran the Centre for Cultural Decontamination. She commented: 'Now we must decontaminate the Museum again!'

Interperformativity of place

In his book the *Haunted Stage,* Marvin Carlson suggests that, through its capacity for doubling and 'ghosting', performance establishes relations not only to other texts and performances, but also to actual past and present sites that it recreates or renegotiates. The links and relationships between theatrical/ theatricalized and 'real' spaces can be both diachronic and synchronic – performance can refer or even spring out of actual contemporary sites whose history is still in the making. As much as it counts on tradition and cultural memory, theatrical references to other spaces might rely on short-term memory of the community. A space used, recreated, or alluded to in a theatre production might not be quite 'haunted' (Carlson, *The Haunted Stage*) yet, or at least not entirely – it might be an integral part of the audience's contemporary cultural and social experience. The real space might be still in the process of being shaped, as its theatricalized doubling unfolds. In that sense, an effigy of the actual space is never a mere reproduction, it is always a renegotiation as the link between theatrical and 'real' space becomes dynamic and interactive. The reality and the unstable position of a historical space in the making influences and alters the meaning of its theatrical and performative renderings. In return, the theatricalization of an actual space reshapes its future meaning in cultural memory.

I will call this complex phenomenon *interperformativity of place* – identified, in the broadest sense, as a theatrical/performative allusion of a visual, aural or verbal nature to a cultural space outside designated theatrical and cultural institutions. In other words, *interperformativity of place* allows for sounds and sites of an actual locale to iconically or symbolically penetrate the fabric of the performance. The phenomenon is closely connected to the political and cultural life of a city as a performance space. *Interperformativity of place* counts on a collective knowledge and memory of shared urban spaces – their history, meaning and function in the life of a community.

Interperformativity of place is fully realized in the reception/participation process as the participating audience makes the final link between the performance and the spatial reality within which it unfolds. In some cases, the audience is able to establish spatial interperformative references even when the creators and performers have not consciously intended to do so. This form of the audience's concretization most often occurs when spectators/participants have a richer experience of the place than the performers. In such a case, spatial interperformative references are established almost solely through the audience's memory and they become the performative equivalent to dramatic irony. To elucidate this point in the context of Belgrade, I will consider a performance I witnessed, which at first glance, had nothing much to do with Belgrade's counter-spectacles of resistance. The event in question was a street performance of the French troupe Générik Vapeur at the Belgrade International Theatre Festival (BITEF) in the fall of 1994.

The performance, entitled *Bivouac* and translated in the Festival's programme as *Emotional Journey*, started in the heart of the city by the monument of Knez Mihailo across the street from the National Theatre. The performers were dressed in blue body suits with blue make-up on their faces. As a moderate crowd of theatregoers gathered, the performers started to roll huge empty barrels followed by punk music blaring from the loudspeakers. They took the assembled spectatorship to the city's main pedestrian zone, leading to Kalemegdan fortress. As the procession progressed, the music became louder, the performers as street clowns and acrobats climbed the fountains and streetlamps, curious passers-by joined the procession, the audience multiplied, walking turned into a slow run and then into a stampede. The theatrical procession overtook this part of the city, making any other street activity impossible and creating a truly carnivalesque atmosphere. The procession quickly erased any demarcation line between the audience and the performers, temporarily freeing the street from its daily routine and order. It ended on the top of the Roman fortress, Kalemegdan, overlooking the river, where the performers stacked the barrels into a pyramid and set them on fire, followed by applause and cheering from the audience. As the procession was nearing its end and the energy level of everyone involved was about to reach its peak, a feeling of liberation overcame the spectator/participants as if they had just undergone a ritual of political decontamination.

The Marseille-based troupe is committed to street performance that makes the everyday sights and sounds of a city strange. Générik Vapeur turns ordinary street life into a liberating chaos inviting the audience to experience a familiar urban landscape in a new way. Their performances are based on flexible scenarios allowing the city not only to become the theatrical stage, but also to provide the final shape of the performance. *Bivouac* was created in 1988 and since then it has toured numerous European cities. It was also performed in Japan and China.[12] Each performance of *Bivouac* is different, since the show's *mise-en-scène* depends to some degree on the street architecture where it is performed – its fountains, statues, trees, and lamps that the performers use as set and props. The performance is further shaped by the street's culture and history through the energy and the shared urban experience of its inhabitants.

As its subtitle in the Festival's catalogue suggested, *Bivouac* aimed to take everyone involved on an 'emotional journey' arousing energy, creating the atmosphere of a rock concert and a sense of bonding amongst the participants. In some other city, this street procession would have probably been a highly entertaining carnivalesque event, perhaps prompting critics and theatre scholars to write about the possibilities of attaining an Artaudian, theatrical experience. In Belgrade of 1994, the performance unintentionally acquired striking political dimensions. The part of the city where the procession took place had been – since 1991 – a place of political protests and riots against the warmongering regime of Slobodan Milošević.

Searching for the most suitable spot for their street theatre to unfold, the performers accidentally chose the itinerary of the political protest that took place on 9 March 1991 in Belgrade – the first riot of the Serbian opposition against the ruling regime. As did the performers and the audience of *Bivouac,* the protesters – three years earlier – had also gathered around the monument of Knez Mihailo facing the National Theatre to demand that Slobodan Milošević and his regime step down. When, in order to stop the protest, the police used tear gas and water canons, the protesters ran down Knez Mihailova Street smashing windows and streetlights in anger and despair. In retrospect, the stampede of the political protest seemed like a violent and chaotic version of Générik Vapeur's street theatre.

When the street theatre of Générik Vapeur came to Belgrade, the events of March 1991 were still vivid in the memory of the citizens regardless of their political orientation. It was the first anti-regime mass protest whose violent *mise-en-scène* and tragic outcome confirmed that the struggle for political change in Serbia would be both long and difficult. For the democratic opposition and its supporters, the event left the bitter taste of defeat. Finally, the pathway and drama of this riot was to be relived through many political protests to come, including the student protest of 1992. Many of us who ran enthusiastically after the Générik Vapeur performers, overcome with the illusion that the street was ours again, had run down that same street many times before, chased away with tear gas, water-canons and police batons.

In this once-favoured city strip, even on quiet days citizens could easily feel like strangers as traces of urban civic culture had been rapidly erased. Knez Mihailova Street, with its old nineteenth-century facades and modern galleries, bookstores and cafés was one of the places where both the city's mainstream and its counter-culture were created and shaped. At one end of the street is the Serbian Academy of Arts and Sciences – the keeper of cultural tradition, which in the late 1980s started to degenerate through nationalism. At the other end is the nightclub, *Akademia,* which in the 1980s became the cradle of the city's alternative rock and roll culture. In the 1990s, as the search for national identity got out of control, street musicians played jingoistic songs under the balcony of the Serbian Academy of Arts and Science and 'turbo-folk' – the preferred music of the new crowd of young war profiteers – silenced rock and roll in the *Akademia*; both the traditionalists and the proponents of the counter-culture were in a sense exiled from the street.

On regular days, the pavement of Knez Mihailova Street was packed with street vendors selling nationalistic insignia and war uniforms. From their improvised counters and even from some of the nearby cafés, 'patriotic' songs were played calling for hatred and killing. In contrast to these sights and sounds of the street, in front of the Knez Mihailo monument everyday around noon, a group named Women in Black would gather in silent protest against the war and the regime, steadfastly enduring insults from 'patriotically' inclined passers-by. Inasmuch as this daily performance was an act of civic resistance and disobedience, the marginalization of this group, overpowered by the blustering iconography of the street, was also a mark of helplessness and the fruitlessness of all attempts to change society.

An exhibit entitled *Art and War*, by author Dragan Todorović, opened in the spring of 1994 in the gallery of the Belgrade Cultural Centre, also located on Knez Mihailova Street. This project attested to the devastating effects of this new kind of street culture as well as to profound socio-political polarization. Todorović gathered and exhibited a variety of ready-made objects that could be bought on the street, including Disney figurines dressed in the uniforms of Serbian para-militaries, liquor bottles in the shape of Serbian monasteries, and war uniforms for two-year-olds. This bizarre installation was juxtaposed with photos from the war in Bosnia and Croatia to point out how seemingly comical and innocent objects had become deadly weapons of jingoistic hatred and propaganda. Art critics and regular gallery visitors loved the exhibit, but the proponents of the new street culture of Knez Mihailova did not, and some even threatened to blow up the gallery.

This micro demographic of Knez Mihailova Street pointed once again to the unbridgeable gap between the two city cultures – the cosmopolitan, pacifist, rock and roll culture on one side, and the nationalistic, warmongering, turbo-folk culture on the other, reflected the two major political streams in Serbia that often collided in numerous street protests. The performance of Générik Vapeur temporarily cleansed the street of the vendors and singers who had been trying to capitalize on the nationalistic frenzy and enabled the illusion that the urban culture of the city had finally prevailed. Moreover, it tapped right into the mythology of Belgrade's 'urban' culture, mixing the two strongest ingredients of the collective 'emotional journey' that Belgrade's 'urban guerrilla' had undergone in the past few years – the energy of a rock concert with the atmosphere and rebelliousness of a political protest. Theatre critic Aleksandar Milosavljević described the effect the French performers had on the spectator-participants as a performance of cultural decontamination:

> Indirectly, energetic street performers of the Génértik Vapeur troupe spoke about us and our reality as if they knew that in the past few years (from 1990 to 1994) the heart of Belgrade had become *ruralized* – provincial mentality took hold of the city systematically destroying its urban culture and consciousness. The French performers ran through the centre of Belgrade emitting powerful rock and roll energy, which reminded us that this city used to belong to its citizens before it was taken over by the buyers and sellers of nationalistic insignia, who now dance on the Kelemegdan fortress to turbo-folk tunes.
>
> (Milosavljević, 'BITEF je gotov – sezona je pocela', p. 186)

When Génértik Vapeur came to the Belgrade International Theatre Festival the troupe found itself in a 'haunted' performance site. Unexpectedly, their street procession invoked in the audience a strong sense of symbolic political cleansing from oppression and the illusion of reclaiming Belgrade's favourite street, very much in line with the Led Art project and activities of the Centre for Cultural Decontamination. This performance, which instantly erased the barrier between audience and participants and created the atmosphere of a carnival, was not necessarily intended to be politically relevant. The audience, who had lived through a highly politically charged reality at the given performance site, read into the show an inter-performative reference that the actors might not even have been fully aware of.

The recent past of the city and the everyday political reality of its central street asserted itself into the body of the Génértik Vapeur performance as a palimpsest. The French troupe inscribed its performance codes onto the fabric of the city – onto a pre-existing text of political struggle, violence and despair, strongly imprinted into the cityscape of the time. For the audience-participants, the actual performance became a tool to reach and confront the underling text in which their own history was being written through a profound *political catharsis*.

Carnivalization

When the mass protest started in 1996–97, the voices of Serbian opposition were doubly marginalized by Milošević's regime, on the one side, and by the international community, on the other. Political, economic and cultural sanctions, imposed because of Serbia's involvement in the Bosnian war, completely isolated internal oppositional voices. The situation became even more paradoxical in 1995 when Slobodan Milošević signed the Dayton Peace Treaty which ended the war in Bosnia, dramatically shifting his international public image, albeit for a short period, from Balkan dictator to one of the key players of the peace agreement. When Dubravka Knežević published her article, 'Marked with Red Ink', in *Theatre Journal* almost a year after Slobodan Milošević signed the Dayton peace agreement and on the eve of the 1996–97 protests, she precisely described the marginalized position of Serbian oppositional voices:

> [...] lack of information about what was happening on Belgrade's streets, lack of support even from colleagues abroad, and disregard not only by the Serbian government but also by the international community keep telling us that there is less and less sense in what we are doing. Halting the spirit of freedom, freezing it, driving it into hibernation, even erasing it – everything that could not be accomplished by the Serbian regime despite all its efforts during these five war years was accomplished by the International authorities, by the measures they keep taking to stop or thwart the regime itself. Three years of UN sanctions did not destroy the Serbian ruling party, but they did diminish an already fragile opposition. The sanctions have not in any way endangered the popularity of the Serbian president; on the contrary, they have strengthened and even expanded his power.
>
> (p. 417)

Soon after Knežević's article was published in the winter of 1996/7, a series of everyday protests started taking place in Serbia's major cities that yet again mobilized Serbian opposition. The protests, started after the electoral commission refused to accept the obvious victory of the democratic Opposition in the municipal elections, turned into months of street spectacle. Overcoming the political lethargy that had engulfed the Serbian anti-regime voice, the counter-spectacle was ready to strike back. On a symbolic level these were acts of reclaiming a political voice hitherto ignored both by the regime and by the international community. The regime, however, continued with its tactic of treating the opposition as almost non-existent. Since the majority of the media in Serbia was state-run or controlled, any information on events that challenged the ruling regime was either manipulated or ignored. The media painted an idealized picture of a proud but demonized Serbia, standing harmoniously behind its President and his ruling party, while the political Opposition and its supporters were but a handful of misguided souls.

In the winter of 1996/7, however, the protesters made a spectacle of noise, light and buffoonery to assert their presence and their voice. The noise-making, using everything from pots and pans to loud music, was another cardinal feature of the protests – an answer to the local media policy of boycotting the event and a symbolic act of silencing the dominant political voice. To make their presence visible, protesters lit up their street processions with all sorts of devices from candles to fire works symbolizing the act of breaking through the oppressive system of 'darkness' created by the ruling political party. The protest activities were at least two-fold – targeting a particular political issue on the one side, and trying to communicate to the international community, on the other.

Illustration 11 Street performance of *Magbeth*, Protest 1996–97, photo courtesy of the *Vreme* archive

In their brief reports, the state media often referred to the protesting public as 'the forces of chaos and mindlessness'. Protesters foregrounded the absurdity of such a label by wearing buttons with the inscription 'I'm the force of chaos and mindlessness'. This somewhat anecdotal detail illustrates the tendency to identify 'the sources of radicalism in the performance of political protest [...] with the irrational, the uncontrollable, the dark side of the human' (Kershaw, *The Radical in Performance*, p. 120). Although seemingly innocent, this characterization has real ideological ramifications – for how could something anti-structural, something lacking in any kind of arrangement, give rise to alternative political arrangements? Kershaw points to the importance of the dramaturgical analysis of protest performances in order to counteract this notion of political performance as chaos. In other words, the semiotization and theatricalization of protests as processes of structuring and meaning-making determine not only the strategies of the protests, but also their ideological effects and their political efficiency.

The protest challenged the political power structure and its institutions and, at least temporarily, reclaimed the streets of Belgrade and other major Serbian cities. Out of the 'chaos' of noise and light, the community of protesters created an alternative cityscape, subverting and shifting the function and meaning of its main landmarks and disrupting the habitual dynamic of street life. They were not only upsetting the prevailing political order, but, in an almost Brechtian sense, they were making it strange. Its various public interventions involved different types of theatrical semiotization in the form of pageants, processions, farces and morality plays (Illustration 11). The elaborate scenarios of Belgrade's counter-spectacles were not only usurping the city, the meaning and authority of its institutions, and the structure of its everyday life, but they were also creating an alternative structure of everyday life. This structure was evolving around the most urgent matter concerning both public and private life in the city – resisting an oppressive political regime.

Humour and satire are proven sharp, political weapons. The genre of farce, which has never been co-opted by law and order and is closely linked to buffoonery, often finds its way into the dramaturgy of street protests. During the Serbian demonstrations in 1996–97, some very elaborate 'protest farces' were staged, such as the one called 'Broken Cars' (Illustration 12). According to the official media, the role of a few thousand policemen, surrounding the location where the everyday protests took place, was just to regulate the traffic. As a reaction to that, protesters decided to drive to the site. The protest scenario suggested that all the cars should break at the same time so that the police would really have their hands full. Some of the participants were dressed up as mechanics or physicians, carrying various tools for fixing cars. Near one of the cars, a group of 'mechanics' and 'experts' examined a small scratch with a lens and a stethoscope, and asked a nearby policeman to help them diagnose the problem. Another driver played with a couple of wires to 'fix' his car, claimed to be into 'alternative healing' and asked a policeman to touch the wires and donate some of his bio-energy. Another participant warned the driver to be careful because a 'car can explode from too much negative energy'. Other drivers honked their horns in rhythm, or simulated road rage with mocking allusions to the ruling regime. In the course of this event each car became a mini-stage where a variety of protest farces were enacted.

Street demonstrations always contain a didactic dimension that establishes, in the most general terms, the polarity between right and wrong, justice and injustice, good and bad. In the urgency of political protests there is a morality lesson for the authorities, and to some degree for the world community as well. The notion of the morality play underlines the theatricalization of political protest, not necessarily on the

Illustration 12 'Broken Cars', photo courtesy of the *Vreme* archive

dramaturgical level, but on the metaphoric one. During the 1996/97 series of demonstrations in Serbia, protesters overtly used elements of the morality play genre. They worked out a strategy of giving subtle political lessons to the police on site by offering to 'Have a Photo With Your Guardian Policemen' or by having 'Reading Sessions' in which protesters read poetry and books about modern democracy to the police. This kind of interaction shifts the protagonist-antagonist polarity in its attempt to agitate and convert the side that represents the instrument of power (Illustration 13).

Observing some of the events described above, an Italian journalist wrote: 'This will be the first regime overthrown by buffoonery!'[13] Indeed, in most forms of street demonstrations there are common elements of comedy, satire and improvisation as they depart from traditional, one-dimensional scenarios of street demonstrations. On the one hand, the dramaturgies of these events belong to new kinds of semiosis of political protest unfolding globally that, as Kershaw argues, 'tend towards greater polyphony and heteroglossia, [where] multiple referenced images were added to monologic slogans, and the slogans themselves became more aphoristic and punning. Satire and caricature

Illustration 13 Protest 1996–97, photo courtesy of the *Vreme* archive

were welded to images suggesting desired ideals and Utopias' (*The Radical in Performance*, p. 122). On the other hand, these 'weapons' of political struggle have their roots in the tradition of political and satirical theatre, in the practice of comedians, clowns and rogues, rather than in the arsenal of professional politics.

In his study of the theatricality of street demonstrations, Richard Schechner in *Environmental Theatre* asserts that political protests, as well as various forms of environmental theatre, are by definition always outside established cultural and theatrical institutions. Although street demonstrations as theatrical activity are indeed anti-institutional, their relationship to the cultural establishment can be more complex than Schechner suggests. The relationship between theatre and theatricalized political activities varies depending on how political the institutional theatres are in a given social and cultural context. This relationship is a dynamic one with a constant possibility for renegotiation. During the era of communist regimes, East European theatrical institutions, although often funded by the State, were venues for political issues and subversions. Thus, anti-institutional elements could come to life *within* cultural institutions, not only outside of them. In common with political street protests, they often use humour and improvisation to express political content. Furthermore, theatre histories in this part of the world include stories of forbidden performances and artists, the arrest of theatre practitioners for staging topical political allusions too boldly and, of course, of audiences ready to recognize and applaud this kind of subversion. The protests scenarios reveal links to local cultural and artistic practices in Diana Taylor's sense of the archive and repertoire dichotomy:

> The repertoire, on the one hand, enacts embodied memory: performances, gestures, orality, movements, dance, singing – in short, all those acts usually thought as ephemeral, non-reproducible knowledge. [...] The repertoire requires presence: people participate in production and reproduction of knowledge by 'being there', being a part of the transmission. As opposed to the supposedly stable objects in the archive, the actions that are in the repertoire do not remain the same. The repertoire both keeps and transforms choreographies of meaning.
>
> (*The Archive and the Repertoire*, p. 20)

The process of semiotization merges political and theatrical, while the notion of carnivalization connects street demonstrations to the realm of embodied practices, allowing for alternative perspectives – whether it be from the cultural fringes or hidden within the institutions – on the unfolding historical current to emerge.

The theatricality of political protests consists of overlapping categories of efficiency with those of play and pleasure. One of the strongest impressions of the Serbian 1996–97 protest is the image of people of all ages and social strata taking over the streets and dancing together. The Bakhtinian notion of the carnivalesque describes this sense of a collective, communal body that undermines the distinction between observers and participants and, as Schechner points out in 'The Street is the Stage', captures the transgressive tendency in the theatricality of political protests. Bakhtin writes that: 'Carnival celebrates temporary liberation from the prevailing truth of the established order: it marks the suspension of hierarchical rank, privileges, norms and prohibitions' (*Rabelais and his World*, p. 10). Political protest is, to some extent, marked by the suspension of the prevailing order, unmasking, by means of carnival and theatricality, its dominant truths and norms. Milena Dragićević-Šešić links carnivalization directly to the theatricality of the city:

> It seems that the carnivalization of the city during these protests, although spread over just a few months, managed to put life itself on stage. Walking as a form defined these protests and symbolized their spirit. The efforts made to win freedom of movement through the city were physicalized. Noise, too, became fashionable (envisaged as a static action, generic noise during TV news), and so movement and noise grew into new forms of protest which linked and opened up the city in new ways.
>
> ('The Street as Political Space', p. 75)

Carnivalization asserted the notion of the *city-as-action*, playing out and subverting its conventional static and dynamic. Unlike carnival, political protest aims to provoke an actual rearrangement of the power structure. Manifestations of subversion of the prevailing order and hierarchy emerge as symbolic acts through which protest activities strive to alter the political reality. The notion of carnival suggests an ambiguity, almost a paradox, inherent in the theatricality of political protest. Carnivalesque points to the dualities or synergies between efficacy and entertainment (Schechner), real and imaginary (Kershaw), but also to the paradoxical ambiguities between the cathartic that finds fulfilment in ritual purgation, and the radically political that partakes in the process of historical change.

Political catharsis

Whether as a conscious conceptual choice of the performers or a by-phenomena that occurred in a guest performance of the foreign street theatre troupe, the notion of political purgation asserts itself as a dominant metaphor of performing the counter-spectacles of Belgrade. Through their various decontamination metaphors and strategies – Led Art, the Centre for Cultural Decontamination and Dah Theatre on the one hand, with carnivalesque political protests and the reception of Générik Vapeur's guest performance in Belgrade on the other – all shared a desire for a *cathartic experience*. Let's call this experience *political catharsis*, it springs from the sense of oneness with the performance event and the larger historical picture within which the performance becomes inscribed. This cathartic experience requires a shift in focus from the spectacle to the experience of the participating public.

Political catharsis is most strongly experienced in events that express the highest degree of carnivalization. Although in a Led Art exhibition or happening, the audience experiences a profound sense of oneness and political understanding exemplary of Jill Dolan's utopian performatives, it is unlikely that the audience-participants would be aroused to the kind of celebratory frenzy and release of energy and emotions as experienced during the protests of 1996–97 and in the Générik Vapeur street procession. In the case of the former, the discursive political element maintains a central place in the activation of the audience-participants, allowing intellectual distance to keep the aspects of emotional involvement and enjoyment in the spectacle under control. In the latter, the spectacle takes over, allowing the enjoyment and the emotional energy to play the main role in governing the dramaturgy of the event. Although the discursive political element is still inscribed into the spectacle, distance, in the Brechtian sense, is blurred.

Since the music and movement of a collective body mobilizes the public even more than the political cause in question, the dramaturgy and *mise-en-scène* of the carnivalesque in radical political protest play the key roles in enabling the experience of *political catharsis* to take place. For instance, the overpowering sounds coming from the loudspeakers and the energetic performers of Générik Vapeur made the public run after them recreating the physical movement of the protesters that had taken place in the same space a couple of years earlier. The street procession of Générik Vapeur in Belgrade caused the audience to relive a dramatic political experience that marked their recent past and still resonated in their present realities. Through intentional and, in the case of Générik Vapeur, unintentional spatial inter-performative references, these performance evoked not only a kind of emotional 'cleansing' from political trauma, but also a sense, or rather the illusion, of political empowerment. The performance endowed the audience with a sense of reclaiming their cultural and political space as the French troupe temporarily 'decontaminated' the heart of the city from oppressive politics. Hence the Belgrade audience, who recognized the emotional *spiritus movens* of their own political struggle in the physicality and raw energy of Générik Vapeur's performance, had a cathartic experience – a truly utopian moment, embodied not only in the sense of oneness with the performance event, but also in the illusion of an unquestionable political victory.

It also somewhat prefigured the carnivalization of the city during the protests of 1996–97 where music also played a crucial role in mobilizing the public body. Some of the most memorable, empowering and glorious moments of these protests are connected to the procession of drummers, led by the locally famous Dragoljub Djuričić, and the citizens who walked everyday through the heart of Belgrade in tune with the rhythm of the drums. A Roma song, accompanied by powerfully sounding brass bands, became the protest anthem. Its beautiful lyrics stood as a political metaphor for the absurdity of everyday life in Serbia. The lyrics are about a 'time out of joint' where the 'darkness of war' has covered everything. Yet there is a mysterious and uncanny sign appearing in the sky – the sun and the moon are shining at the same time ('Nema sunca ni meseca/ prekrial nas ratna tama/ Mesečina, mesečina, joj, joj/ sunce sija, sunce sija/joj joj [...]'). The song was played every day during the protests of 1996–97 and also in subsequent protests and other gatherings. People always sang and danced along. This dance, like the song itself, was a paradoxical mixture of opposites oscillating between empowerment and liberation on the one hand, and political despair on the other. Music poeticized the political protest of 1996–97, while the performance of Générik Vapeur invoked politics when it was least expected. Nevertheless, in both cases political life was experienced and comprehended through metaphors of civil disobedience unfolding in an excess of symbolic gestures and carnivalizations. In both cases, political sentiments were experienced through catharsis.

Baz Kershaw cautions about overusing the carnival link in relation to radical political performances, especially in ways in which it clouds both the efficacy and cultural specificity of particular protest activities. He points out that the notion of political protest as carnivalesque emphasizes a cathartic and almost self-sufficient aspect of the protest, a kind of holiday from everyday life, and backgrounds the role of such events in the process of global historical change. Kershaw writes:

> An approach which mainly stresses the aesthetics of the protest, especially through an analogy to the carnival, offers a useful model, but its concentration on *formal similarities* tends to detract from the protest's contribution to the major ideological shifts of specific periods.
>
> (*The Radical in Performance*, p. 108)

Nevertheless, the radical in political performance oscillates between catharsis and estrangement – between the utopian realm of community, freedom, equality and abundance established in the process of carnivalization, and political pragmatics, strategies and negotiations. Arguably, the radical requires carnivalization as a means of expression of its political urgency and as a scenario to fulfil its quest for change. Yet, while it serves the radical in performance, the carnivalesque also offers a playground for release of political tensions – the experience of protest as a holiday from everyday life as Kershaw suggests. In other words, carnival appears as a strategy of radically political performance and a means of empowerment, but it also, paradoxically, makes it easier for the regime to restore the status quo. Carnival is the utopian performative (Dolan) of the protest. It reveals a need for the cathartic amidst the radically political. This mixture of the emotional and the political cannot, despite the best of efforts, be fully set apart – it has emerged as both a vital and dangerous element regardless of the ideological and aesthetic orientation of the performance. Often, however, the cause can get somewhat lost in the pleasure of participation in the spectacle.

In this light, the carnivalesque dynamics of the political performances in Belgrade could be described *as one step forward towards political efficacy, two steps backwards towards the carnival.* The elaborate theatricality of the protests in Belgrade and other cities not only attempted to usurp the regime but also to mobilize the public and to send a message to the world that there was a critical mass of Serbian citizens who were actively against Milošević, and who felt strongly that he and his regime were not their legally elected representatives. These four months of ongoing street spectacle granted the Serbian Opposition a couple of minutes on CNN and eventually, the regime's acceptance of the electoral victory.

As a memento of these protests, a friend in Belgrade keeps a photo on the wall of her 'guardian policeman' taken during one of the political performances in the winter of 1996/7. In it, she is standing in the crowd with a triumphant smile, holding flowers and hugging a young man in a police uniform. He tries to hide from the camera but smiles a little. I wonder what this photo represents now, after these spectacular days of protests are almost a forgotten event? A memory of a small and already-faded political victory, or something else? Street protest is a peculiar celebration of political freedom in spite of its obstacles and regardless of its danger. Whether successful or compromised, tragic or triumphant, no political outcome can stand up to that moment of utopian reconciliation between all the good sides and bad sides, all justices and injustices – to the moment of *political catharsis*, when the photo of my friend and her smiling policeman was taken. This photo is a memory of what no political reality can achieve: the pleasure of counter-spectacle.

2
At the Confluence of Utopia and Seduction

> *Utopian performatives describe small but profound moments in which performance calls the attention of the audience in a way that lifts everyone slightly above the present, into a hopeful feeling of what the world might be like if every moment of our lives were as emotionally voluminous, generous, aesthetically striking, and intersubjectively intense. [...] The performatives under consideration here allow fleeting contact with a utopia not stabilized by its own finished perfection, not coercive in its contained, self-reliant, self-determined system, not messianic in its zeal for a particular social arrangement, but a utopia always in process, always only partially grasped, as it disappears before us around the corners of narrative and social experience.*
>
> Dolan, *Utopia in Performance*

Some of the radical performances that took place in Belgrade – both on the streets and in performance venues – during the 1990s, embodied Dolan's notion of utopian performatives offering the sense of 'magical' empowerment and gestured towards a transformed society. In a way, this whole book is about various utopian performatives stretching from Belgrade and Sarajevo to exilic Toronto, from theatres to street happenings, to political protests and into everyday life. Some of the utopian performatives experienced through the theatrical, political, and ultimately dramatic life of these cities worked even more proactively than the way Dolan has described, operating as interventionist strategies, not just as wishful thinking. Nevertheless, the spectacles and counter-spectacles of Belgrade that set the climate for Milošević's climb to power and the events that followed for over a decade, usually under the sign of political protest, equally embodied and problematized Dolan's concept.

Dolan counts on a kind of ethical and political common sense behind the experience of utopia in performance, when she writes:

> rather than resting on an old humanist legacy of universality and transcendence, utopian performances let the audience experience a processual, momentary feeling of affinity, in which spectators experience themselves as part of a congenial public constituted by the performance's address.
>
> (*Utopia in Performance*, p. 14)

Put simply, the notion of utopian performatives presupposes that the 'hearts' (and one might add, minds) of the participants involved in the theatrical event are 'in the right place'. I would ague that these ethical dimensions are not always guaranteed. As is well known, one person's utopian dream could be another person's worst nightmare.

Dolan seems aware of this paradox, though, as she tries to offset it by charting ideological and practical boundaries for her concept. She places her utopian performatives within the ideological framework of transnational humanism, although it is often very hard to resist the gravity of the local and, at times, the lure of the national as a bonding principle. Yet there is a somewhat binding aspect that emerges through the experience of utopia in performance that Dolan acknowledges through her Austinian example of the performative utterance as action. Utopian performatives reverberate or carry actual consequences into reality, sometimes even long after the performance is over. I would argue that utopian performatives often have a seductive element because they rely on an alchemy of the emotional and the intellectual which is both necessary, to make the humanistic dimension of the experience palpable, and dangerous, since the ideological and ethical dimension, even if clearly charted out, could never be entirely fixed or guaranteed.

I will be examining the multifaceted experience of utopia in performing Belgrade from the early expressions of nationalistic frenzy in the late 1980s to the political performances and protests in the 1990s, and, finally, to the integrated spectacle of post-Milošević's Belgrade. My interest is in three different categories of utopian or pseudo-utopian elements in performance. The first category concerns events that epitomize various aspects of Dolan's utopian performatives as spatial practices that marked different historical moments of performing Belgrade. Although it does not diverge from Dolan's conceptual outline, the second category points to utopian performatives as ideologically and politically unstable; while the third category, that I have named *seductive performatives,* often appears similar to Dolan's concept, but in fact represents a different set of phenomena integral to the integrated spectacle of the post-Milošević era.

Congenial publics

I will briefly examine two performances, both produced by Yugoslavian Drama Theatre in Belgrade, that actively related to two crucial, interconnected moments in socio-political destiny, not only of the city, but also within the wider context of Milošević's reign and the downfall of Yugoslavia. The two performances in question are *The Battle of Kolubara* (*Kolubarska Bitka*) that premiered in 1983, and *Power Keg* (*Bure baruta*) that opened in 1995. Both theatrical events have in common the key elements of Dolan's notion of utopia in performance, enabling the audience to share a 'momentary feeling of affinity' and 'experience themselves as part of a congenial public'. They also epitomize Kershaw's definition of performance efficacy – 'the potential that theatre may have to make the immediate effects of performance influence, however minutely, the general historical evolution of wider social and political realities' (*The Radical in Performance,* 1).

During the protests in the mid- and late 1990s, *Powder Keg* epitomized some of the finest utopian performative moments that reinforce Dolan's definition of this notion and become acts of political resistance. Like *Powder Keg, The Battle of Kolubara* created an alchemy of the ideological and the emotional and activated the audience, but in a very different direction and through a very different political ethos. These two performances embody competing and conflicting politics behind utopian moments in performance. In *Battle of Kolubara,* utopian performatives were made palpable and powerful through nationalistic sentiments. In *Powder Keg,* the possibility of a better future lay in deconstructing the violence and absurdity fertilized through nationalist utopias. While in this study my interests and main focus are predominately with utopian performatives that are closer to the ethics inherent in Dolan's sense of the term, it is impossible to study them without considering their other versions – their ethical counterparts as it were.

Back to the future: *The Battle of Kolubara*

During the 1980s, a wave of plays and performances focusing on the history of the Serbian nation appeared. This theatre repertoire[1] emerged while Tito's Yugoslavia still seemed relatively stable and followed the country to its downfall. The ideological set up of Tito's Yugoslavia required a multicultural approach, epitomized in the ethos of 'brotherhood and unity', while local patriotism and nationalism were strongly suppressed. Thus, when only three years after Tito's death the *Battle of Kolubara* was staged with the attitude of foregrounding national consciousness, for the majority of theatregoers and critics it did not appear as dated and reactionary as the later criticism of this work pointed out – rather the performance had the allure of political subversion. It was understood as an assertion of a hitherto deliberately marginalized historical narrative.

The script for *The Battle of Kolubara* was a dramatization of the epic novel *The Time of Death* (*Vreme Smrti*) by Dobrica Ćosić – a dissident in Tito's time and allegedly the greatest bard of Milošević's time. When his popularity was at its peak, Ćosić was considered the 'father of the nation' – a spiritual voice of Serbian national identity. The novel, *The Time of Death,* is often viewed from two conflicting positions – either as a Bible for Serbian nationalists or as sentimental and dangerous third-rate literature for those holding more cosmopolitan views. The dramatization by Borislav Mihajlović Mihiz focused on the part of Ćosić's grand epic that takes place on the battlefields of the First World War, reinforcing the notion of Serbs as historically heroic warriors. In her critical analysis of the nationalist aspects in Serbian theatre during the 1980s, scholar and critic Ksenija Radulović looks into this novel beyond its ideological interpretations in order to understand its nationalist sentiment and appeal. She finds, both in the novel and its dramatization, a view on the issues of Serbian history that is less univocal than it had been assumed, with expressions of patriotic passion mixed with passages about diplomacy and tolerance. Nevertheless, Radulović finds that these 'two aspects are not properly balanced – neither in the novel nor in its stage adaptation' ('Nacionalni resentiman na sceni', p. 10) with enough complexity to aid the historical issues. The novel left room for interpretations that glorified Serbian patriotism and sacrifice in the First World War, implicitly asserting that Serbs had fought against foreign oppressors far more than the other nationals of the Yugoslavian federation. This view, considered to be a kind of parallel historical narrative, did not go well with the tendency of the Yugoslavian 'brotherhood and unity' model to neutralize historical differences among the nations participating in the Federation. Thus, the staging[2] of this dramatization also corresponded to a rapidly spreading sentiment of suppressed Serbian national history and identity within the boundaries of Tito's Yugoslavia.[3]

All these factors – textual and contextual – might have played into the unprecedented success of the performance. The line-ups for tickets were unusually long, the show was sold out months in advance, and a lot of people went more than once to see this quite conventionally and statically staged show. When the actors sang the traditional Serbian war song from the First World War (*Marš na Drinu*), the audience rose to their feet and sang along. When the main protagonist, who played the role of a real historical figure, General Mišić, greeted his solders with the phrase 'God help you, brave soldiers!' (*'Pomoz Bog, junaci'*), the audience responded in unison with 'God help you!' (*'Bog ti pomogao'*). In response to every scene that reported the successes of brave Serbian solders on the battleground, the audience cheered and applauded. This collective improvisational performance of nationalistic sentiments has a striking resemblance to religious rituals such as the traditional salutation and blessing used in the Roman Catholic Mass as well as in liturgies.[4] Dalibor Foretić, a Croatian theatre critic, described the experience of seeing *The Battle of Kolubara* in February of 1984, a few months after the show opened in Belgrade:

> Of course, the auditorium was packed. There were many people who were standing during the two and a half hours long performance. I remembered that I had already read in newspapers about standing ovations at the opening night of this show. Actual survivors of the battle for Kolubara were present in the auditorium applauding the actors, while the actors applauded back at them. This show, that has currently overshadowed all the others in Belgrade, is indeed a very special phenomenon. [...]
>
> According to everything I saw and read, *The Battle of Kolubara* seems to be above all a phenomenon of spectatorship. When I asked at the Yugoslav Drama Theatre who was to be credited for the enormous popularity of this show, I was told: history and Ćosić...
>
> (quoted from Vučetić, *Teatron*, p. 13

The phenomenon of this performance, its 'spontaneous community' (Turner, *From Ritual to Theatre*; Dolan, *Utopia in Performance*) of spectator/participants, as well as the novel *Time of Death*, and finally the authorial figure himself – Ćosić, perceived as the spiritual father of a nation oppressed under communism – all belong to the cultural production that partakes in the making of the national imaginary. In *Imagined Communities*, Benedict Anderson points out that what is important for the national imagination is not so much history, but biography, not scientific facts, but collective myths. What characterizes his notion of imagined communities and gives rise to nationalism is a search for a sacred or private language proper to that community. He writes that 'nationalism has to be understood, by aligning it not with self-consciously held political ideologies, but with larger cultural systems that preceded it, out of which – as well as against – it came into being' (Anderson, *Imagined Communities*, p. 19). Nationalism, thus appears as a result of cultural production, a myth-making phenomenon, a construct woven with the help of fiction rather than history, and finally, we might add, strengthened through communal utopian performatives.

Although the utopian in performance that the audience experiences in *The Battle of Kolubara* is quite obviously situated within the realm of the national imaginary, rather than in the ethos of transnationalism where Dolan prefers to place them, the concept of utopian performatives still works. Utopian performatives of *The Battle of Kolubara* have most of the characteristics that Dolan points out in her elaboration of the concept, as the audience experiences the 'sense of hope, possibility and desire' (Dolan, *Utopia in Performance*) to freely express a communal identity, albeit nationalistic, that was hitherto felt to be suppressed. 'Spectators might draw a utopian performative from even the most dystopian theatrical universe' (*Utopia in Performance*, pp. 5–6) which in this case is the carnage of the First World War. Utopian performatives of this production quite obviously 'exceed(ed) the content of the play' (*Utopia in Performance*) as they became a means of self-fashioning a national identity. As Radulović observes: 'Going to see *The Battle of Kolubara* was more than a theatre outing, it almost became an obligatory part of a national ritual' ('Nacionalni resentiman na sceni', p. 10).

I would argue that this phenomenon is not a mere appropriation of the concept within a nationalist, and thus ethically dubious, framework, but that what was happening during the performances of *The Battle for Kolubara* were proper utopian performatives. The people who were participating as artists and audiences in the utopian performatives of this production, as well as others involved in various creations of the national imaginary, were not just a gathering of extremists. Reviews of the production were mixed and ranged from praising the production for its powerful handling of an important historical issue, to finding its nationalism in poor taste.[5] Yet the show attracted a wide variety of audiences from First World War veterans and leading religious figures, to prominent intellectuals and theatre critics – some of whom regretted their patriotic passions a few years later and became Milošević's most vocal opponents. In the early to mid-1980s, the rediscovery of a national history, identity and religion was a subversive political activity against the backdrop of an allegedly, artificial, collective Yugoslav identity imposed by the communist regime. National imaginaries gave the illusion of a progressive alternative to flawed communist rule. The community that sang the patriotic songs in *The Battle of Kolubara* perceived itself to be part of a genuine historical counter-narrative.

The experience of utopian performatives is perhaps fleeting, but their socio-cultural impact reverberates far beyond the ephemeral performance event. In this production, as in any other, utopian performatives take place in brief and somewhat unrepeatable moments, yet the audience keeps returning to the theatre to replay these particular moments. In the concluding remarks to his review, Foretić also hinted at ominous dimensions of this performance: 'I am terribly afraid of times where the theatricality of life becomes stronger than the liveness of theatre. Yet I feel that the performance around *The Battle for Kolubara* surpasses the theatrical meaning of the show itself' (in Vučetić, 'Invitation to the Battle', p. 12). Utopian performatives contributed to the creation of an imagined community that, while sentimentally looking backwards at the past, moved towards the future. The efficacy impact of 'laughter, tears, applause and other active audience responses' (Kershaw, *The Radical in Performance*) of this performance is evident. Although situated in the context of the historic past and although somewhat old-fashioned in its aesthetics, *The Battle of Kolubara* was a performance about the future – awakening sentiments and constructing an ideology that would have a very real political and existential impact in the years to come. These utopian performatives, and others that were similar, indeed haunted the Balkans of the 1990s.

Two concretizations of *Powder Keg*

Powder Keg could not be more different from the *Battle for Kolubra* – in its dramaturgy, in its aesthetics and in its political metaphors. Written by young Macedonian playwright Dejan Dukovski and directed by Slobodan Unkovski – a bard of Macedonian theatre – the play also premiered on the stage of the Yugoslav Drama Theatre over a decade later, in 1995. Reworking the pattern of concentrated circles à la Schnitzler in *La Ronde*, Dukovski creates the effect of an accelerating and self-perpetuating violence as the culprit in one scenic circle becomes the victim in another, and so on. Scenes start with ordinary, even innocent, dialogue that gradually becomes volatile and culminates in violence and often murder. The play opens with an ironically named character, Angele, who sits down beside an old man with crutches at a neighbourhood bar and inquires about his brutal injuries. The old man describes a crowbar attack that left him with broken bones, spinal injuries, three missing toes, and a leg shortened by two inches. The dialogue continues in the following way:

ANGELE: Do you know who beat you?
DIMITRIE: Who?
ANGELE: I did.

(Dukovski, *Powder Keg*, p. 2)

Dukovski's play has no plot, narrative or characters that could be extrapolated to stand on their own outside the structural circles in which they unfold. Yet *Powder Keg*, written during the downfall of the former Yugoslavia, contains a strong political resonance without making overt political references and claims. The play's structure of circles within which violence perpetuates and accelerates echoes the culture of guilt and revenge that had begun to emerge in the region. Hence, *Powder Keg* was quickly taken as a metaphor of Yugoslavia's downfall and as the dramatic political reality continued to unravel, the performance acquired new levels of interpretation and new forms of audience response.

Theorists such as Felix Vodička, Roman Ingarden and Patrice Pavis have used the term *concretization* to signal that the meaning of an artistic work is completed only through the process of its reception. The notion of *concretization* maintains that text/performance is not a fixed entity that can be understood in a particular way once and for all. It exists only upon completion of a 'reading'/reception process, which is always situated in history. In the following passages, I will describe two performances of *Powder Keg* that overtly foreground this point and where the process of *concretization* is highlighted as a two-way street – not only 'a reading' from the audience into the 'performance-text', but also a parallel re-reading reinforced by the actors' improvisation and the audience's participation. As in the *Battle of Kolubara* for that matter, *the re-reading* and *the reading into* – the concretization of the text – goes beyond the text and the staging and dives into the current historical moment.

The first *concretization* took place during the protests of 1996–97 when walking in the city as a performative political gesture became one of the most recognizable protest codes. The walks, present in various forms in the urban struggle against Milošević's regime, such as the processions against the war in Bosnia and radical performances during the student protests of 1992, came to prominence particularly in periods when the authorities forbade protest gatherings, as was the case during the 1996–97 demonstrations. Everyday, thousands of citizens went to the city centre for a walk keeping the protest both alive and spectacular under the auspices of a quotidian activity.

A couple of years before the start of the radical street performances and walks in Belgrade and other Serbian cities, when Slobodan Unkovski was rehearsing *Powder Keg,* he enhanced the ending by adding a circular procession of all the characters (most of them dead) – a farewell walk. Forming a funeral procession, each character was going to both his/her own funeral and the funeral of the others, they all walked in circles. This *mise-en-scène* solution corresponded with the dramatic structure of the play and with its theme of violence and passion.

One evening, during the 1996–97 protests, the procession of *Powder Keg*'s dead personages lasted longer than usual – the actors used the farewell walk of their characters to pay tribute to the street protests that were taking place near the theatre. The audience was quick to recognize the allusion. Some of them joined the actors on stage and reinforced the political gesture by turning the end of the play into a mini-protest walk. Both the audience and the actors co-operated in transforming the funeral procession of a theatrical performance into the *mise-en-scène* of a real-life political protest. This intervention enriched both the theatrical and the political metaphors that overlapped during this utopian performative moment. In other words, the procession at the end of the production acquired new meaning – it was clearly a gesture of political protest, a means of empowering both the actors and the audience not only as contributors to a theatrical event, but also as citizens. The extended, improvised procession ambiguously resembled a prisoner's routine daily walk – a metaphor for the position of Serbian citizens dating back to the 1992 student protests. After all, the procession was a farewell, a funeral, which made the idea of the political efficacy of the protests somewhat ambiguous. In retrospect, the funeral procession/protest walk could be further interpreted as a prefiguring of the mass funeral procession through central Belgrade that would take place five years later – the farewell walk, to which I will return later, for assassinated Premier Zoran Djindjić.

This link between performance and political reality was obviously not intended from the beginning, since the show had been mounted a couple of years before the protests. Interpretation – both on the side of the actors and the audience – preceded the process of semiotization. In other words, interpretation initially enabled the language of performance and the semiotic system of the political protest to become mutually translatable. There is a distinct performativity established in the immediacy of the experience of the given theatrical structure in the moment when it transforms itself into a *mise-en-scène* of political protest. The subversive act of the audience joining the actors at the end of *Powder Keg*, the merging of the theatrical and the political, the mutual exchange of energy, the spontaneous camaraderie between performers and audience, and the unintended tragi-comic link between a political procession and a funeral procession could never be fully semiotized. It makes for a profound moment of utopia in performance. Yet the interplay between the semiotic and the phenomenological moments of the performance event, between its theatricality and its performativity, between rehearsed and spontaneous gestures on stage and in the auditorium, brought about a similar experience of energy, camaraderie and utopia in *The Battle of Kolubara* – a work, aesthetically and ideologically, very far removed from *Powder Keg*.

The second concretization of *Powder Keg* occurred in 1999 during a guest performance at the National Theatre in Belgrade, when the mainly student-run organization OTPOR (Resistance) became one of the key actors in Serbia's radical political performance, introducing the symbol of a raised fist as a new protest icon. At the end of one of the performances of *Powder Keg*, actor Voja Brajović was supposed to utter the final words of the play: 'I'd like to tell you something…' and then to collapse. Instead, he stood up, opened his hospital gown – his costume – and revealed a black T-shirt with the inscription 'OTPOR – DO POBEDE' ('RESISTANCE – TO VICTORY') written in large, white letters with the image of a raised fist underneath. The rest of the ensemble followed suit, raising their fists – a gesture the audience greeted with a 15-minute-long standing ovation. With these and other acts of political subversion, theatre 'proper' incorporates the sense of unpredictability and the urgency of street protests. Stepping through the proscenium arch and merging with the audience, either physically or symbolically through political gestures and allusions, the performers left the safe zone of stage illusion, and took one step closer to the radical counter-spectacles of the street.

The actor, Brajović, was awarded the title of 'The Most Resistant Serbian Actor' through an unofficial street ballot organized by OTPOR.[6] The protagonists of the performance later described this event as the most exciting moment they had ever experienced in theatre. The extent of the political subversion the actor's gesture was further enhanced by the fact that the performance was not taking place in the Yugoslavian Drama Theatre, demolished in a fire two years earlier and in the process of being rebuilt, but on the stage of the National Theatre that was temporarily housing some of the Yugoslavian Drama Theatre repertoire. During Milošević's era, the National Theatre was the stronghold of the regime's cultural ideology. Its management and core artistic team were mostly populated by Milošević's apparatchiks, a fact which was reflected in the theatre's aesthetic and repertoire, as well as in the resignations of several of the most prominent members of the National Theatre ensemble. The political subversion during the performance of *Powder Keg* further reinforced the image of the National Theatre as the regime's institution, which comments from the management of the National only confirmed. The artistic director of the theatre and a prominent member of Milošević's party described the incident as a 'striptease on the stage', while the deputy director of the National's Drama Programme asserted the following:

> With this gesture the actors exiled themselves from our stage. After their building burned down, we offered the Yugoslavian Drama Theatre to play on our stage on Mondays when we don't have performances. It was a gesture of goodwill which the ensemble of *Powder Keg* exploited by reciprocating with an undignified gesture inappropriate for this institution. Theatre is not a place for political exhibitionism. For that they have the public square, they can take off their clothes there, if they wish.
>
> (quoted in Ćirić, 'Majca i pesnica [T-Shirt and a Fist'])

In addition, the management of the National described the audience's lengthy applause as an 'uncivilized' and 'anti-theatrical' gesture. In his ironic commentary to the reactions from the National, theatre critic Aleksandar Milosavljević emphasized the absurdity of such a reaction: 'Now we can expect a radical but efficient move [from the regime's side S.J.] – getting rid of the audience that applauds in theatre' (Milosavljević, 'Htedoh nesto da vam kaze...' ['I'd like to tell you something...'], *Vreme*, no. 468, 25 December 1999: http://www.vreme.com/arhiva_html/468/14.html). Needless to say, after this incident – which prompted a lot of support for Brajović and the other actors in the show, including congratulations from the director Unkovski – the National Theatre revoked its hospitality and the management of the demolished Yugoslavian Drama Theatre had to look for a new space to perform Powder Keg.

Uneasy convergence

Although there is a gap of over ten years between *The Battle of Kolubara* and *Powder Keg*, this gap is not an empty one, but is rather a chronotope of desires, conflicts and political tensions that these two productions, in all their aesthetic and political differences, epitomize. Their differences are crucial in order to understand Belgrade's counter-spectacles of the 1990s and the cultural and ethical claims they stand for. In order to illuminate the mechanism of Belgrade's utopian performatives, of which both *Powder Keg* and *Battle of Kolubara* were a part, it is worthwhile to look at points of juncture of their uneasy convergence.

Firstly, both events played into the production of cultural imaginaries, albeit from opposite, even conflicting, ends. In other words, a comparative view of these two performances reveals the axes along which the conflict between the two cultures run – one epitomized in the political spectacle that the Milošević regime represented, the other best embodied in counter-spectacles of radical political performance. The collision of the two cultural imaginaries is expressed in dichotomies such as cosmopolitanism vs. nationalism, urban vs. rural, modernity vs. tradition, liberal vs. conservative, rock n' roll vs. folk, and so on. The latter – shaped and mythologized through the culture and ethos that *Battle of Kolubara* and its audience represented – displayed all the key features of Anderson's notion of nationalism as an imagined community. The former presents a much-needed counterpart to the nationalist imaginaries, establishing, nevertheless, alternative imaginaries that require their own stories, mythologies, anecdotes and other ingredients to maintain the production of counter-culture.

Secondly, the dramaturgy of performative gestures in *Powder Keg* and *Battle of Kolubara* unfolds through a similar mechanism – they are both based on an improvised breaking of the fourth wall where audience and actors meet each other half-way and in both cases the bonding ritual is prompted through political sentiment. Finally, both events foreground the audience and reinforce the bond between the actors and the audience best described through Turner's notion of spontaneous community:

> Is there any of us who has not known this moment when compatible people – friends, congeners – obtain a flash of lucid mutual understanding on the existential level, when they feel all the problems, not just their problems, could be resolved, whether emotional or cognitive, if only the group which is felt (in the first person) as 'essentially us' could sustain its intersubjective illumination?
>
> (*From Ritual to Theatre*, pp. 47–8)

From the point of view of the audience, who sang patriotic Serbian songs and gave standing ovations to the actors playing First World War

Serbian solders, the experience of going to see *The Battle of Kolubara* was nothing short of feeling like they were part of a group of 'compatible people' – of people who were 'essentially us'. Likewise, it was an 'essentially us' moment when the actors and the audience members came together on stage to transform the end of a performance into a protest walk, and it was a moment of 'lucid mutual understanding' when an actor revealed the word RESISTANCE printed on the T-shirt underneath his costume and when the raised fists on stage were greeted with exaltation and long applause from the audience. Hence, both performances, albeit through different aesthetic and ideological premises, epitomize Viktor Turner's notion of spontaneous community – a concept that for Dolan is a 'springboard' to utopia in performance.

Last, but not least, there is a symbolism to performance spaces in relation to these two productions – *The Battle for Kolubara* and *Powder Keg* – too neat to overlook. Both shows – one evoking nationalist passions, the other dealing with a circle of violence as a tragic outcome of such passions – were produced by a theatre called the Yugoslavian Drama Theatre (whose prominence was established through decades of collaborations from artists across Yugoslavia). In October 1997, due to an accident, a fire broke out in the theatre, leaving the building almost completely destroyed. There is no political background to this incident, except, perhaps, as a symbolic echo – the theatre went down in flames, like the country it had been named after. The country, however, perished in the flames of war. As for the theatre, even though its flames were no more than the consequence of poor wiring, it was hardly innocent. Until its reopening in 2003, the repertoire of the Yugoslavian Drama Theatre was performed on the stages of other theatres, such as the National Theatre in Belgrade (until the *Powder Keg* incident). While *The Battle of Kolubra* fit perfectly into the ethos, politics, and ideology of the National Theatre during the Milošević regime, *Powder Keg* was truly out of place on its stage and within its boundaries. *Powder Keg* brings forward utopian performatives of another generation – the generation victimized through the national imaginaries of *The Battle of Kolubara* and other imaginaries of a similar nature – which has to do with place as much as with time. This relationship to place, in fact, is perhaps where the most important distinction between the utopian performatives of these two shows lies. The former seeks to enhance the bonds of place, history and tradition, reinforcing a *Blut und Boden* ethos, the latter is ill at ease with place – be it the stage of the National Theatre or the violent territories of a crumbling Yugoslavia.

Three walks through Belgrade: from utopia to geopathology and back

In her articulation of the concept of utopia in performance, Dolan foregrounds time rather than space as the key to its unfolding:

> While many commentators typically conceive of utopia as a space [...], performance allows us to see utopia as a process of spending time. Performance's temporality excites audiences with a slight disorientation; its spatiality often anchors it to an imagined place, a 'what if' of matter and expression. But performance always exceeds its space and its image, since it lives only in its doing, which is imagining, in the good no-place that is theatre.
>
> (*Utopia in Performance*, p. 13)

Although, utopia in performance often reverberates beyond the immediate theatrical event, it is a communal experience that happens within the present tense of the performance. Dolan stresses the temporal dimensions of utopia in performance, which does not offer social imaginaries of a better place or escapist strategies, but in some ways a sense of possibility of an improved present for the spontaneous community that experiences the utopian moment together.

Nevertheless, I would like to briefly revisit the issues of place in relation to utopia in performance. The spatial component is important not only as it determines utopian performatives through its material aspects, but also as it shapes the experience of utopia through its conceptual and ideological dimensions. I would argue that in addition to the temporal component and the notion of the utopian performative as process, the foregrounding of space and place is a key to understanding utopian moments in both performance as well as in a wider context. My usage of the terms *space* and *place* is based on Michel de Certeau's distinction whereby he defines place *(lieu)* as 'the order (of whatever kind) in accord with which elements are distributed in relationships of co-existence. [...] A place is thus an instantaneous configuration of positions. It implies an indication of stability' (*The Practice of Everyday Life*, p. 117). In contrast to the stability of place, 'space is composed of intersections of mobile elements. It is in a sense actuated by the elements of movement deployed within it. [...] In short, *space is a practical place*' (p. 117). In accordance with Dolan, by place and space I do not mean the *non-place* of an ideal future, but flawed heterotopias of the *here and now* of the performance event.

A brief turn to the etymological root of the word *utopia* shows that its links to the notion of place are both unavoidable and somewhat paradoxical. The word *utopia* is derived from Greek *u* meaning *no* and *topos* meaning *place*. Literally, utopia means 'no (not) place' – negation of place. Conversely, by being insistently *Other* than the place within which it has been imagined, utopia remains forever linked to it. Louis Marin, writing on the city as a utopic figure, describes the 'no place' not as a topos, but as a point of view:

> The viewpoint is fixed at a totalizing point of view. One can see all. But the eye placed at this point occupies a place that is an 'other' point of view: it is in fact impossible to occupy this space. It is a point of space where no man can see: a no-place not outside space but nowhere, utopic.
>
> (*Utopics*, p. 207)

Marin suggests that the utopic point of view is a panoramic perspective from above. The perspective within which utopian performatives take place is quite the opposite; it is the view from below – a perspective of someone who is both onlooker and participant in the utopic moment.

Utopia, in the context of Belgrade's protest culture at least, emerges less as placelessness, but rather as a yearning for place, not necessarily *Other* in physical and geographical sense, but *Other* in an ethical sense. The strengthening of Milošević's regime, for example, brought not only wars and economic breakdown in its wake but a cultural shift that rendered cosmopolitanism, urban culture and any form of critique of the regime, suspect. The iconography and ethos of nationalism pushed urban culture underground, changing the face of the city. Leading cultural institutions and even some alternative venues were taken over by Milošević's apparatchiks and war profiteers. The struggle for political and social justice embodied in political protests and other performances during the 1990s was also a fight for a cultural space – for the city that was becoming increasingly alien to its citizens. The 'spontaneous community' that came to being, at various public and private sites in Belgrade, embodied a lost civic space. Belgrade's utopian performatives sprang from yearning and loss, while their dramaturgy was being shaped by a desire to reclaim the city as a site of political and cultural resistance.

Dolan's utopian performative is heterotopic in nature – not perfect, but realizable – and it comes with an expiration date which could be only moments away. Utopian performatives are realized through dynamic relationships to place; through acts that challenge, negotiate and shape real spaces. They go beyond their emotional effect, even beyond their political resonances, turning into spatial practices and becoming interventionist strategies.

In return, spatial concepts and practices that share strong political dimensions all have utopian aspects. Foucault defines *heterotopia* against the concept of utopia, which represents arrangements that have no real space:

> There also exist, and this is probably true for all cultures and all civilizations, real and effective spaces which are outlined in the very institution of society, but which constitute a sort of counter-arrangement, all the other real arrangements that can be found within society, are at one and the same time, challenged and overturned: a sort of place that lies outside all places and yet is actually localizable.
>
> ('Of Other Space', p. 352)

Ambiguity is inherent in Foucault's definition of heterotopic spaces described as those spaces 'endowed with the curious property of being in relation with all the others, but in such a way as to suspend, neutralize or invert the set of relationships designed, reflected or mirrored by themselves' (p. 352). Theatre is one of the examples that Foucault uses to illustrate his concept, since, along with other heterotopic spaces, theatre 'has the power of juxtaposing in a single real place different spaces that are incompatible with each other' (p. 354). *Heterotopia,* like utopia, suggests an inherent dimension of 'otherness' in both real and imagined spaces, even if we have initially recognized them as familiar.

Taking his cue from both Foucault and Lefebvre, Edward Soja points out that heterotopic space is indeed made/produced through action – whether the acting is physical, conceptual or symbolic. He works against the binaries of *Perceived Space* (the directly experienced world) and *Conceived Space* (subjective, 'imagined' space), and draws from Lefebvre's concept of *Lived Space* – that operates between the dualities of subjective and objective – to introduce his version of the concept, which he calls *Thirdspace.* Soja defines it as a 'strategic meeting place for fostering collective political action against all forms of human oppression' ('Thirdspace', p. 22), and also as a 'distinctive way of looking at, interpreting, and acting to change the spatiality of human life' (p. 21). The concept points to the inseparability of the historical, the social and the spatial, and promotes a 'third possibility' dialectics that does not culminate in synthesis but seeks instead 'to disorder, deconstruct and tentatively reconstruct the entire dialectical sequence and its logic' (p. 21). Soja's *Thirdspace* is an open and inclusive space of action and intervention. It is the where and how of radical performance activity. Utopian dimensions of Soja's *Thirdspace* are inherent in the concept of space as a meeting place that fosters intervention and challenges existing structures of authority.

Inspired by Foucault and Soja, Una Chaudhuri coins the neologism *geopatholgy* in the context of theatre and drama to theorize the notion of place as a problem which 'unfolds as an incessant dialogue between belonging and exile, home and homelessness' (*Staging Place*, p. 15). Foucault's concept is realized as a relationship among different and often incompatible spaces; Soja's *Thirdspace* is established through action – through becoming, rather than being, to echo Hegelian categories; while Chaudhuri's notion emphasizes the relationship between person and place. Even the concept of *geopathology* involves utopia, as Chaudhuri sees 'heterotopic relations' as a means of overcoming the 'sickness' of place.

In the following section I will look at the intrinsic relationship between utopia in performance and the politics of space as they unfolded through political performance practices of walking in Belgrade during the 1990s. I will investigate how Dolan's utopian performances are realized through different kinds of *walks* – from protests to funeral processions. More specifically, I will examine three different city walks that epitomized both the political and the communicational aspects of walking: (1) the protest walks that marked the aforementioned 1996–97 protest activities; (2) a processional performance, *Worried September* (1997), that unfolded in different parts of the city – from its centre to the suburbs; and finally (3) the several kilometres-long funeral procession of Serbian democratic Premier Zoran Djindjić, assassinated in March of 2003.

'Miki, come for a walk'

In his famous study *The Practice of Everyday Life*, Michel de Certeau describes the act of walking in the following way:

> The ordinary practitioners of the city live 'down below', below the thresholds at which visibility begins. They walk – an elementary form of this experience of the city; they are walkers, *Wandersmänner*, whose bodies follow the thicks and thins of an urban 'text' they write without being able to read it. These practitioners make use of spaces that cannot be seen; their knowledge of them is as blind as

> that of lovers in each other's arms. The paths that correspond in this intertwining, unrecognized poems in which each body is an element signed by many others, allude legibility. [...] the networks of these moving, intersecting writings compose a manifold story that has neither author nor spectator, shaped out of fragments or trajectories and alterations of spaces: in relation to representations, it remains daily and indefinitely other.
>
> (p. 93)

Walking was central to performing Belgrade during Milošević's era and even in marking crucial events in the years after his downfall. The relationship between the walkers and the city was perhaps passionate, but in their knowledge of spaces they were not 'blind as lovers in each others arms' – they were rather self-conscious in asserting their visibility. Yet the manifold, fragmented narrative composed through protest walks did not obscure the roles of authors and spectators. Even if individual anonymity was at times unavoidable, the collective identity of the walkers was self-evident and further reinforced though the walks. The walks had their target addressee and whether one took the role of author/participant or the role of spectator, it was not only impacting the communication circuit the walks had charted out, but more often than not the delineation between author/participant and spectator implied an ethical and/or political choice. Walking, as a practice of everyday life was foregrounded, but not so much as a poetic gesture or as a metaphor, rather it became an aesthetic device and above all a political statement. The 'ordinary practitioners of the city' made the everyday practice of walking through Belgrade extraordinary.

Even though Belgrade's highly politicized walks in most cases strip the practice of its poetic metaphors, de Certeau's decoding of walking in the city offers a way into 'reading' the utopian performatives of walking as integral to the palimpsest of Belgrade. Two key aspects of de Certeau's take on walking in the city are particularly relevant to this context – walking as a counterpoint to the language of power and walking as a pedestrian speech act.

During the protest of the Serbian democratic coalition and the student movement in the winter of 1996/7, walking was not only symbolic of the relationship between the city and radical performance practices, but it was also a practical device to subvert various by-laws that the State imposed to prevent mass demonstrations. As the State prohibited public gatherings, walking was a way around the prohibition that turned it into a euphemism of protest activity. In a tongue-in-cheek manner, the leaders of the

Illustration 14 City walks, 'Life Saver', Led Art, photo courtesy of Nikola Džafo

Opposition and of the student movement would invite the citizens not to join the protest, but to take a leisurely walk through central Belgrade every day during the three-month-long protest activities. Every afternoon downtown Belgrade, as well as the centres of other major Serbian cities, filled up with hundreds of thousands of walkers (Illustration 14). A practice of everyday life became a gesture of civil disobedience.

De Certeau writes:

> The language of power is in itself 'urbanizing', but the city is left prey to contradictory movements that counterbalance and combine themselves outside the reach of panoptic power. The city becomes the dominant theme of its political legends, but it is no longer the field of programmed and regulated operations. Beneath the discourses that ideologize the city, the ruses and combinations of powers that have no readable identity proliferate; without points where one can take hold of them, without rational transparency, they are impossible to administer.
>
> (*The Practice of Everyday Life*, p. 95)

Walking emerges as an activity of counterbalancing the mechanisms of control and surveillance that to some extent also determine ways in which the city is ideologized. However, the protest walks subvert power mechanisms in a very different way than the habitual, everyday practice. In this case, walking is not a means of escaping the reach of the panopticon; on the contrary, the walking is taken out of its habitual context of relative invisibility and made deliberately transparent. These walks subvert the authority of an oppressive State by taking it at face value. For instance, one of the most famous student interventions of this kind was called 'Traffic Light' and it was a reaction to one of many prohibitions that ensued during the winter of 1996/7 in order to disable the protest walks. Namely, the protesters were allowed to use only the pavement leaving the roads clear for cars. This was also a way to undermine the protests by ignoring the hundreds of thousands of people who were taking part in them, an attempt to maintain the illusion that all the vital elements of daily city life – such as traffic and public transportation – were functioning as usual without interruption.

The 'Traffic Light' intervention subverted the regime's tendency to yet again neutralize and render the protest activity invisible. The protesters decided to obey the semiotics of traffic regulations fully – they stood on the sidewalk, waiting for the green light; when the traffic light switched to green, they would step on the road to cross the street, then wait on the other side of the street for the next green light to cross to the opposite sidewalk – they walked back and forth all day long. The police could not intervene, since the students were not breaking the law, yet hundreds of people stepping onto the road at the same time, allegedly trying to cross the street, made regular city traffic flow close to impossible. On the one hand, this intervention embodies De Certeau's notion of spatial order that 'organizes an ensemble of possibilities [...] and interdictions' (p. 98), then the walker actualizes, but also alters and often subverts some of these possibilities. As de Certeau points out 'the crossing, drifting away, or improvisation of walking privilege, transform or abandon spatial elements' (p. 98). In the 'Traffic Light' intervention the spatial order is seemingly observed, but the act of crossing the street was altered both in its performance and in its function. It was no longer a mechanical navigation to arrive from one particular point in the urban landscape to the next. There was no immediate practical purpose in the crossing, only a symbolic political one. The constant moving back and forth from one sidewalk to the other subverted the everyday function of walking in the city and thus its spatial order. On the other hand, in its essence, this approach is not dissimilar to the deliberate naivety inherent in the Brechtian look from below. The students were not breaking the law, but they were rendering it absurd through performance – making familiar daily life strange and political.

Walking became a highly self-conscious activity, a practice of everyday life turned into a performative gesture, rather than a daily pedestrian activity that was taken for granted. This kind of self-consciousness was obviously of a political nature. Not only did the protest walks defamiliarize a practice of everyday life, but in a Brechtian sense, they made it gestic – walking was a gesture and the gist of the political performance – to reveal ways in which the city and its citizens were controlled and restricted. As Dragićević-Šešic points out, through the walks 'the efforts to win freedom of movement through the city were physicalized' ('The Street as Political Space', p. 76). This was also a means to reclaim the ownership of the city – to assert that the city does not belong to those who control it, but to those who walk its streets. The everyday practice of walking was framed and turned into a political statement – the walk was the message. In other words, walking became a semantic gesture.

De Certeau has famously compared the practice of walking to the speech act:

> The act of walking is to the urban system what the speech act is to language or to the statements uttered. At the most elementary level, it has a triple 'enunciative' function: it is a process of *appropriation* of the topographical system on the part of the pedestrian (just as the speaker appropriates and takes on language); it is a spatial acting-out of the place (just as the speech act is an acoustic acting-out of language); and it implies *relations* among differentiated positions, that is, among pragmatic 'contracts' in the form of movements (just as verbal enunciation is an 'allocution', 'posits another opposite' the speaker and puts contracts between interlocutors into action). It thus seems possible to give a preliminary definition of walking as a space of enunciation.
>
> (*The Practice of Everyday Life*, pp. 97–8)

In the particular case of the Serbian 1996–97 protests, what kind of discourse and what kind of space were temporarily established through its rhetoric of walking? Walking was to some extent transformed from a practice of everyday life into an act of reclaiming the public space against forces of unification through which that space had been ideologized. In other words, the rhetoric of walking established radical difference in opposition to an enforced homogeneity. This rhetoric of walking affirmed Bakhtin's heteroglossic dialogue, capturing conflicts and contradictions in social relations that worked against the centralizing discourse of monologic forces.

In this performance of space, the dialogic component was further asserted through Belgrade's protest-related graffiti. The graffiti in Belgrade during the 1990s was closely linked, even integral, to walking as a practice of both everyday life and as a protest activity. Some of it was directly about the walking practice and like the walks, their political messages were encrypted rather than agit prop-style transparent, such as 'Miki, come for a walk' and 'Better to walk than to use the fast trains'. Stylistically, they matched the dramaturgies of the protest performances and the rhetoric of its walks in their parodic and satirical manner, often most transparent in graffiti that played on well-known movie titles and popular culture, such as: 'Protesto III', 'Serbia YUL-assic Park' (YUL was the acronym of a satellite political party to Milošević's Socialist Party of Serbia, led by his wife, Mira Marković), and 'Sloba [nickname for Slobodan Milošević] killed Laura Palmer' – an allusion to David Lynch's *Twin Peaks* series, popular in Serbia at the time. The graffiti not only addressed crucial political issues, most notably the rule of Slobodan Milošević ('Last night I dreamt that you were gone'), and the war ('Will swap two-storey house for one with a basement' to hide in), but they also, through intra-cultural allusions, revealed all the nuances and complexity of the place and its socio-political struggles. They often revealed geopathological dimensions of place underneath the empowering strategies of protest performances – through simple statements, such as 'Serbia is killing me'.

Others required a deeper insight into the local culture. For instance, the graffiti that says 'Don't listen to turbo-folk. Die of natural causes' is not only about one's musical preferences, but reveals a deep cultural rift, analogous to the one epitomized in the two stage performances discussed earlier – *The Battle of Kolubara* and *Powder Keg* – the rift between cosmopolitan urban culture and the local patriotic culture of nationalistic kitsch, disinterested in any anti-regime activity and known for its love of the cheap spectacle of the turbo-folk scene. Turbo-folk culture symbolized escapism from any kind of political responsibility and therefore it thrived under Milošević. In short, this graffiti encrypted a deep socio-cultural issue, a conflict, and a geopathological set of relations, which goes far deeper than one's dislike for the music. Where one stands on the turbo-folk debate, often by osmosis, is determined by where one stands in the street – with the police cordon or against it. This was a crucial ethical choice that not only shaped the collective communal identities of the city dwellers, but, arguably, forever altered individual identities. Thus, the inscription that emerged during the student protest of 1992 saying, 'This is the only term for the examination of your conscience' reveals the ethical depth of participation in these events. And even now, some fifteen years later, the question of examining individual and collective conscience is far from closed even if in Serbia it often gets pushed under the carpet.

Other inscriptions depicted the gist of the carnivalesque dimension of the protests, but also the notion of political performance as communal intervention, such as the one that read: 'Granny Olga for Prime Minister'. Granny Olga, too old to go on the long daily walks, protested everyday from her balcony, and became one of the icons of the protest of 1996–97. This kind of graffiti is the testimony of the spontaneous community that had emerged that winter and temporarily at least, took over the streets of Belgrade.

The language of walks embodied through movements and inscriptions, was hybridized, intertextual, often relying on puns, jokes, irony and paradox. This doubling of voice in the rhetoric of the walks – 'which inevitably leads to an awareness of the disassociation between language and intention, language and thought, language and expression' (Bakhtin, *The Dialogic Imagination*, pp. 368–9) – resists the intention to objectify the meaning that has been complicit in a process of sociocultural and political centralization. The rhetoric of walks and of the graffiti asserts the notion of the public square as a contested space that, in its heteroglossia, retains 'a deliberate feeling for the historical and social concreteness for the living discourse, as well as its relativity, a feeling for its participation in historical becoming and in social struggle' (Bakhtin, *The Dialogic Imagination*, p. 311).

A dialogic reading of Belgrade graffiti reveals a minimalist, yet complex narrative of the city inscribed onto the city through movement. Dragićević-Šešić describes graffiti – including both banners and inscriptions on walls – as movable semantic gestures in line with the notion of walking as language:

> Slogans and catchphrases written on the banners could rightly be considered graffiti of the 1990s. A white wall on which a message is written becomes movable as the whole city is on the move. [...] Graffiti displayed on banners constituted a dialogue between the current authorities and the walkers. They appeared in direct reaction to events, as individual attitudes of someone who had been denied other possibilities of media mediation. Such a dialogue now took place on the walls. Graffiti are always a form of open expression, but now this was more directly and frankly exposed to the masses who interpreted it and added to it, confronting it with other, moving

> graffiti. Thus graffiti lost its original location, as its specific spot, obtaining new meanings by passing through different city quarters.
>
> ('The Street as Political Space', p. 82)

Graffiti always take place in a dynamic, movable context – they could only be deciphered in relation and in dialogue with the ever-changing environment that unfolds around them. Belgrade graffiti did not only allude to walking practices, nor, when inscribed on building walls, did they merely alter the environment through which the walkers moved. Graffiti emerged as walks through the walks. Turning into moving inscriptions, they probed and altered the space of their own enunciation. As de Certeau has pointed out, borrowing from Rilke, bodies walking through the city and graphic inscriptions on walls and banners together formed the moving 'trees of gestures', whose 'forests walk through the streets' (*The Practice of Everyday Life*, p. 102). The only permanence of these 'trees of gestures' emerged in the fleeting shapes of the graffiti.

The walks and the graffiti become means of reclaiming one's freedom of speech and asserting the place of counter discourse in the public sphere. In their semantic gestures, these walks affirm the Thirdspace possibility – a practiced space of intervention 'against all forms of oppression' (Soja, 'Thirdspace'). De Certeau talks about categories of *here* and *there* as the walker's 'framework of enunciation' (*The Practice of Everyday Life*, p. 99) invoking again the 'parallelism between linguistic and pedestrian enunciation'(p. 99) The protest walks foregrounded these elements, or 'phatic *topoi*' (p. 99) as de Certeau calls them, that ensure the communicative potential of walking and also ensure the readability of political codes and messages embedded in the semantic gesture. In other words, the foregrounding of this 'phatic *topoi*' shapes these particular walks as Thirdspace practices. *Here* and *there* refers not only to a spatial near and far – the space unfolding between the start and end point of the protest walk through downtown Belgrade, or the road between two sidewalks, constantly filled with hundreds of people the moment the light turns green, who in fact have no intention of moving anywhere further away from these two points – it is also the temporal near and far, the present and the future, within which the utopian performatives of walking take place. In other words, along the spatial axes of the protest walks' *here* and *there*, a Thirdspace unfolds, while along the temporal axes of *here* and *there* are stretched the moments of utopia in performance. The radical rhetoric of protest walks asserts that Thirdspaces and utopian performatives are never too far away.

Geopathologies

Following years of unsuccessful protests and periods of collective lethargy, the 1996–97 protest was not only a great empowerment for the political opposition, but it seemed to provide proof that civil disobedience in the form of radical political performance could work as a real social force. Nevertheless, over the course of just a few months, the utopian performatives that had helped deliver a political victory faded into endless disputes among oppositional politicians. In 1997, only a few months after the spectacular protest walks, director Ana Miljanić staged a site-specific performance in Belgrade called 'Listen up, Common People!' ['Slušaj, mali čoveče!'], produced by the Centre for Cultural Decontamination. This site-specific performance mapped a transformed Belgrade – the capital of a shrunken and troubled country, shaped by a decade of Milošević's rule. The performance was part of a series of events organized by the Centre for Cultural Decontamination under the slogan: 'Worried September! Reich in Belgrade! Longing for Life!' that explored the role of the citizen and everyday life against the backdrop of the socio-political demographics of the city. Yet it was not accidental that 'Listen up, Common People!' took place only a few months after the protests.

'Nobody will ever make me walk the streets again', was a line I heard frequently from my Belgrade friends and family as they were alluding to their participation in the protest walks and to their subsequent disillusionment. They did 'walk again', at least twice – to overthrow Miloševic´ in October of the year 2000 – and again in March of 2003, to bid farewell to Zoran Djindjić, the politician who was instrumental in toppling the government of Milošević. In 1997, however, Milošević's downfall was a long way away and a grim future, one that brought armed conflict to Kosovo and the NATO bombing of Serbia, still lay ahead. Thus, after the winter of collective optimism, evoked through carnivalesque utopian moments that influenced actual political achievements, a renewed sense of dissatisfaction and political helplessness enveloped Serbia for good reason. September of 1997 was indeed an anxious time. 'Listen up, Common People!' paid homage to the protest activities that temporarily reclaimed the city and turned it into a theatrical stage of political protest, but it was also an expression of disappointment in the aftermath of the protests. 'Listen up, Common People!' used the city as stage and aimed to shake the city from its political lethargy by making everyday life strange. The performance uncovered the city as a political palimpsest – a place caught up in the multiple layers of problems and contradictions that had haunted it ever since Yugoslavia fell apart – and pointed out that nothing had been done to remedy the situation.

The project was inspired by Wilhelm Reich's treatise addressed to common people to show that everyone, no matter how seemingly powerless, is complicit in creating a xenophobic and destructive political climate. Reich's piece was written after the Second World War as a means of understanding the communal psychology that allowed Hitler to happen. Director Ana Miljanić created a series of events on various sites that were meeting places of common people – from the Kalemegdan fortress in the heart of the city to the suburbs. The event forced its mostly middle-class audience to engage with a wider population of the city. It called attention to three groups whose journey was particularly telling of the city's changing identity in the years of the Yugoslavian downfall: pensioners, who were the most hurt by the economic crisis under Milošević's regime (and, paradoxically, his most stubborn supporters), a community of refugees that emerged as a result of the war, and war profiteers, who played a key role in the criminalization of Serbian society.

The performance began in the park of the Kalemegdan fortress – a favorite gathering spot of Belgrade pensioners who come to the park to chat and to play chess. Newly retired ballerina, Sonja Vukićević, disrupted their routine and invited them to waltz with her. Although taken by surprise, the pensioners complied and together with the ballerina made their everyday routine strange. The next event was called 'Passport' and took place at city hall among refugees who queued for hours to get the legal papers that would allow them to stay in Belgrade. There, an actor posing as one of the refugees in the queue, started to recite passages from Reich. People in the queue got worried that the actor might upset the person who was issuing the passports. The happening called *De-Striptease* was in a glamorous downtown shopping area that sharply contrasted the reality of impoverished Serbian pensioners in the park and the queues at city hall. This particular shopping strip, full of designer label boutiques, Italian restaurants and money marts, was the venue of Serbia's new elite that emerged after the disintegration of Yugoslavia. The happening began with a nude model who slowly put on piece after piece of designer clothing that could be bought in the surrounding boutiques, turning herself into a trophy girlfriend for one of Serbia's nouveau riche.

The next site was a busy city roundabout crowded with commuters and newcomers, where the audience boarded a bus to the suburbs to visit a community of Croatian refugees. The refugees were actually Serbs from the Dalmatian region forced into exile as part of a Croatian military operation known as 'The Storm'. Yet, when in 1995 the last convoy of Croatian Serbs approached Belgrade, local authorities brought in the police and the army to prevent them from entering the city centre. The refugees eventually found shelter in grey high-rises on the outskirts, in a setting that could not be further from their native Mediterranean landscape. The audience was brought there to watch a traditional Dalmatian bowling game played every afternoon at the near-by parking lot. For the visitors from central Belgrade, the game made the dull suburbs a bit more playful, almost exotic, while for the Dalmatian immigrants it was a survival strategy – a way of picking up the pieces of a broken cultural identity.

The act of walking in this performance was not so much, or at least not only, an act of inscribing, rather a means of seeing more clearly. Each station of the procession was a quotidian site where everyday activities where taking place, but with added interventions – a twist to make the familiar strange. Thus, for the participants walking was not only a specific language and the making of a statement, but a discovery of self amidst the complex and problematic social fabric of the city.

The performance showed different faces of Belgrade often oblivious of one another. It mapped the city in a very particular historical moment, toying with the boundaries of using its public spaces and the rift between its urban centre and the periphery. It explored ways in which certain spaces were marked and claimed socially, ideologically and politically. 'Listen Up, Common People!' was more than a search for a city's missing centre. In bringing together the contrasting fragments of the city, the performance aimed to counteract passivity as a *modus operandi* of everyday life. It was yet again a means of reclaiming public spaces, albeit on a much smaller scale than in the protest performances.

It forced the audience to venture outside its habitual city routes and by doing so, the performance made visible the link between one's daily itinerary and one's social position. It showed the way space was 'produced' socially, ideologically and politically – not only through how it is used, but also through who uses it. The performance did not so much uncover the palimpsest of Belgrade that reached deep into the history of the city as it showed its newly acquired layers – its history in-the-making. On the one hand, the mostly middle-class Belgrade audience got to visit parts of the city that were quite foreign to them – such as the heterotopias of the suburbs newly populated by refugees. On the other hand, familiar and often-frequented parts of central Belgrade were rendered alien, like the scene in *De-striptease* that foregrounded the extent to which the city was 'owned' by businesses that flourished during and from the war. Transporting the audience to a suburbia populated by refugees, or exposing them to the war profiteers' crass culture of glamour, forced the spectators to share the parallel realities of the city and accept their own roles in shaping its many identities.

Walking as a rhetorical device in 'Listen up, Common People!' reinforces, although with a twist, de Certeau's point that to walk is to lack a place:

> The moving about the city multiplies and concentrates, makes the city itself an immense social experience of lacking a place – an experience that is, to be sure, broken up into countless tiny deportations (displacements and walks), compensated for by the relationships and intersections of these exoduses that intertwine and create an urban fabric, and placed under the sign of what ought to be, ultimately, the place but is only a name, the City.
>
> (*The Practice of Everyday Life*, p. 103)

If in these lines of de Certeau there is an underlying critique of place, then Miljanić's performance puts this critique into the spotlight. However, this is not so much a walk through place as a dream, but more a process of making the familiar sites and sounds of the city strange so as to unmask the *geopathologies* of place. Although some of the scenes Miljanić creates to make the familiar life of the city strange have a surreal, dreamlike, quality, it is the harsh socio-political reality of the place that this city walk wants to uncover. Walking in this performance means to lack a place in a political sense. The performance takes the participants on a route to discover their own dislocation and alienation, and to see the contradictions of a place they had considered their own. In short, the performance revealed the palimpsest of Belgrade's geopathologies.

The performance gathered a modest group of onlookers and audience/participants of the like-minded. Given that the Centre for Cultural Decontamination is not a part of Belgrade's theatrical mainstream, neither conceptually nor politically, the performance received virtually no critical or media attention. The strategic ignoring of voices that challenged the politics of the city and of the country that had ceased to work for mass gatherings was still quite effective when it came to events on a smaller scale. Miljanić's performance did bring about utopian moments, however, as well as some of the strategies of spatial practices as interventions. For instance, the somewhat surreal image of the ballerina waltzing with pensioners in the troubled city's park evoked utopia in performance. There was also a sense of political and theatrical kinship between the people walking through the city enabling the performance to take place. Finally, even unmasking the city as a contested, problematic site that was slowly slipping through the fingers of its citizens who had hitherto claimed a sense of belonging, was a form of active engagement with space – a sort of mini-intervention. By its very nature, an event of this kind lacks the critical mass and the political stimulus to evoke utopian performatives of empowerment. The fact that the participants created a temporal community where they could see and diagnose the geopathologies of place together, as opposed to the rest of the population who either turned a blind eye or were soaked in lethargy, was the only hope for a better future that the participants could experience in the utopian moments of this performance. 'Listen up, Common People!' revealed that underneath the utopian performatives of the city lay a palimpsest: clumsily glued together, layer upon layer of history-in-the-making – a set of problems, a pathology that the carnival of mass protests had not been able to remedy.

Walk post-mortem

The era of walking the city as a form of political practice ended in a funeral procession. In March of 2003, three years after Milošević was overthrown and a year after his extradition to The Hague, Premier Zoran Djindjić, the leader of Serbia's Democratic Party, was assassinated. Behind the killing were members of the Serbian Secret Service and Special Military Forces – an elite army unit that Milošević formed during the war in the Balkans. Although Djindjić acquired true cult status after his death, he was always known as one of the key players in the struggle against Milošević and in bringing an end to his regime. The killing of Djindjić shocked the nation and was immediately viewed as an attempt to set Serbia back from the road towards democracy and towards the West. It was also clear proof that the political game was far from over. Problems beset Belgrade once again.

On the day of Djindjić's funeral, several hundred thousand citizens gathered to take part in the procession. The procession started from the St Sava church in the heart of Belgrade and proceeded to cross one of the longest city boulevards (Bulevar Kralja Aleksandra) towards the cemetery (Aleja Velikana). The route from the church to the cemetery was over ten kilometres long, closed to traffic, but open to pedestrians. Citizens walked behind Djindjić's casket in a solemn silence that was interrupted only by the funeral dirge. I call this procession the last walk not only because it was a final farewell to one of the leaders of the Serbian Opposition of the 1990s, but because this procession mapped the city yet again through a gesture of utopian performatives. In both its political and dramaturgical sense, it referred back to the era of protest walks and was the last of its kind.

Despite the tragic occasion that gave rise to this walk, the procession was closer in spirit to the protest walks of the 1990s than to Miljanić's performative city walks revealing the geopathologies of the place. Inevitably, the procession evoked the memory of the protests walks from the 1990s that had often been led by Djindjić himself. This intra-cultural link further reinforced the sense of spontaneous community and the experience of utopian moments in the funeral procession. The protest walks and funeral procession were mass events and although the context and the mood of the two were quite different, in both cases utopian moments and the notion of Soja's Thirdspace emerged in a symbiotic relationship. In both cases, walking was a collective practice and an act of solidarity and resistance. In the former, solidarity and resistance addressed the regime, and in the latter, although a gesture of mourning, once again the walk was the message – this time asserting that the citizens stood behind the democratic reforms.

In both cases, the imagined community sees itself as 'the better Serbia' that stands up to oppression and obstruction on its way towards democracy and into Europe. And in comparison to the Milošević regime and other right-wing options, this indeed was 'a better Serbia', and yet, as with all cultural and political imaginaries, it was bound not to reach its projected self-image. Immediately after the killing of Djindjić, there was a crackdown on organized crime, particularly on the culprits of the assassination, called Operation Sword (Opercija Sablja). The suspects in the killing were arrested. These operations and the subsequent trials are proof of the deep wound left in society and its institutions from the 13 years of Milosević's regime. A new beginning, a clean start, felt and envisioned through utopian moments in the protest walks or in the funeral procession, proved impossible. The future that these walks mapped has been unfolding slowly and with numerous setbacks. It appeared that even 'the better Serbia' could not escape being tainted by the Balkan bloodbath.

Belgrade rocks: seductive performatives

In 2005, the *New York Times* published an article entitled 'Belgrade Rocks'. It opened with the following description:

> Night falls in the capital of former Yugoslavia, and music fills the air. Everywhere. Along the banks of the Danube and Sava Rivers,

> serpentine chains of music-blasting *splavovi* – floating raft clubs – snake into the inky Balkan night. Fortified by huge meat-kebab dinners and Turkish coffee from Belgrade's myriad cafes, crowds of night owls line up to partake variously of Gypsy bands, electronic mixes, rock n' roll and a distinctly Serbian hybrid known as turbo-folk.
> (www.nytimes.com/2005/10/16/travel/16belgrade.html)

The images of Belgrade that accompanied the article featured young people dancing and chatting in lounges that had been opened in private apartments during the 1990s, most of them as a reaction to the public spaces that had been co-opted during Milošević's regime. This contextual background was missing from the article, and was perhaps irrelevant in 2005 to its predominantly American readers. Other photos depicted the streets of Belgrade, one of which featured people carrying colourful balloons. Underneath, the caption read: 'The National Museum in Republic Square, where partying has replaced protests'. The article was widely circulated among Belgrade émigrés in North America and we were feeling proud. On the one hand, Belgrade's new identity – emerging in an urban scene, a communal life and an alternative culture – was vibrant and unique. But on the other, I couldn't help but think that all that music everywhere, all that rocking and rolling, all those colourful balloons on the Republic Square, were Belgrade's way to avoid hearing and seeing the complexities and contradictions of its own reality.

For almost a decade, starting in the late 1980s and stretching into the new millennium, protest performances in the streets and in other public spaces were more than political gestures and strategies. They became political rituals and, at times, practices of everyday life. A decade of constant repetition of political demonstrations and spectacular protest activities of the political opposition – strategically conceptualized to draw media attention and eventually some international support – turned into a *modus vivendi* and created a kind of public addiction. In the years after the fall of Slobodan Milošević (2000), Belgrade went from being a city of protest – of counter-spectacle, so to speak – to a city of *integrated spectacle* (Debord).

Performance, with its ability to evoke 'pathologies of hope' (Kershaw, *The Radical in Performance*) and spark moments of political catharsis, has become a means of both taming, and feeding into, this addiction. Although during the political protests moments of hope and political catharsis were often experienced, sometimes even on a daily basis, they were never fully realized – never carried to full ethical closure, even after the downfall of Milošević. This addiction to spectacle embodies either an urge for a collective catharsis, a form of ethical escapism and/or a mode of self-fashioning of an urban identity. Above all, spectacle has become a mode of avoiding the complexities of post-Milošević Serbia.

After the spectacular political street protests of the 1990s, spectacle remained the only stable category – an empty signifier – in the confusion, if not loss, of political and ethical parameters. At the heart of this *post-mortem* on spectacle is a notion that I call *seductive performatives.* These performatives appropriate only elements of a content and of a context, realizing only partially their relationship to reality. What seductive performatives lack, then, are the ethical connotations and complexities of the original. These performatives are hard to resist and equally hard to fully dismiss. Seductive performatives are highly engaging but they operate within a caveat: they can conceal, and even undermine real political processes and ethical issues. I will look at two types of *seductive performatives* that have been partaking in shaping Belgrade as the city of spectacle in the post-Milošević era: *Performatives of false catharsis* and *Performatives of comic relief.*

False catharsis

In 2002, two years after Milošević's regime was overthrown, Yugoslavia (still the official name of the country) won the World Basketball Championship in Indianapolis. A mass celebration of the victory was staged in the heart of Belgrade in front of the City Hall. Thousands of citizens gathered to greet the basketball players. People were singing, dancing and chanting, prompted by popular rock singer Dejan Cukić, who served as a MC of the celebration and spoke to the assembled public from the City Hall balcony. This street event would not be any different from other celebrations of national sport victories had its site not been 'ghosted' (Carlson, *The Haunted Stage*) and its dancing and singing not peppered with unintentional inter-performative references. During the 1990s, the area in front of the City Hall and the near-by Parliament building, as well as the Square of the Republic (only a few hundred metres away) had been sites of mass political protests – evoked yet again in the energy of the crowd gathered to celebrate the basketball victory.

The celebration resembled the *mise-en-scène* of one of the earliest large-scale protest gatherings of the citizens and the democratic opposition to Milošević's regime that took place on 9 March 1991. That day the leaders of the Democratic Opposition also addressed the crowd from a balcony, albeit not of the City Hall, but of the National Theatre. The celebration of the sports victory and the political protest are somewhat ironically linked through this inversion. In retrospect, political activism and radical political performance, for quite a long time, could not penetrate further than the realm of theatre and of the theatrical, while a celebration of a sports victory became reinforced with additional political significance through its spatial arrangements. The difference between the two events is that the first one, the protest in March 1991, ended in political defeat, leaving two people dead – a protestor and a policeman; in the 2002 sports gathering, victory had been won in advance and there were no causalities.

Music was another link between the protest and the celebration of the basketball victory. Songs that sent the assembled crowd into a celebratory frenzy were often the same tunes that had prompted the protesters against Milošević (most notably during the winter of 1996/97 when protests took place every day for three months) to sing and dance in the streets as a means of asserting their political rights. The celebration of the basketball victory borrowed to some degree the carnivalizations of the political protests that had preceded it.

Like the utopian performatives of the political protests, *seductive performatives of false catharsis* have the capacity to give rise to a 'spontaneous community' (Turner, *From Ritual to Theatre*) or a quasi 'spontaneous community', but their quotidian ethical and ideological affinities could significantly vary. Moreover, sport has the conditions for *seductive performatives* in its capacity to fuel national imaginaries and to give rise to a utopian sense of bonding and belonging to a group identity. The competition with another group, a rival team often emulating nationalistic constructs of 'us and them', while a sports victory becomes identified as a collective triumph of the nation. The amalgamation of the spontaneous community and the official celebration of the Championship victory temporarily created a specific socio/cultural imaginary. For the citizens of a country emerging from a decade of wars, economic sanctions, the NATO bombing and an oppressive jingoistic regime into a complex future of unresolved political, economic and ethical issues, the celebration of the basketball championship offered an illusion of victory and a false catharsis. In his seminal work on nationalism, Benedict Anderson (*Imagined Communities*) reminds us that narratives of the imagined community spring not from history, but from biography, from anecdotes, myths, popular culture. The celebration of the sports victory weaves a narrative of an imagined community, but in such a way that it unwittingly points to the construction of such a community as Anderson's work unmasks. During the celebration, fans and athletes hugged each other chanting: 'Ko je svetski šampion? Yuga, Yuga' ['Who is the World Champion? Yuga, Yuga' – Yuga is short for Yugoslavia]. But what is Yugoslavia in 2002? Originally coined to signify the union of South Slavs, Yugoslavia by 2002 referred to only two entities – Serbia and Montenegro. Only four years later, with Montenegro's proclamation of independence, Yugoslavia would cease to exist altogether. Yugoslavia in 2002 was already a ghost. On the one hand, the name was a reminder of a country that recently fell apart in a bloodbath. On the other, it reflected an identity crisis – a confusion due to a lost link between the sign and its referent. Yuga, in the cathartic chants of the spontaneous community was no longer a place, only a name, an empty signifier, an illusion.

Cheering for basketball player Dejan Bodiroga, who had scored the winning points in the final game of the championship, the crowd chanted 'Mi imamo svoga Boga on se zove Bodiroga' (Bog means God and Bodiroga is obviously the last name of the player and these two words rhyme in Serbian. The chant translates as follows: 'We have our God, his name is Bodiroga'). In the ghosted space between the City Hall and the Parliament building during the late 1980s, crowds had chanted Milošević's name too, and only a few years later shouted his name again, but this time in protest and anger. During the 1990s, names of various oppositional politicians found their way into slogans and chants. In 2002 – as it became clear that even with Milošević gone, political conflicts and economic difficulties were to remain for a long time – the public seemed to have run out of names of potential leaders worth cheering for. Underneath the energy, transferred from the days of political protests onto the celebration of a basketball victory, was uncertainty and disillusionment. The false catharsis of this spontaneous community that was dispersed a few hours later, and where a basketball player had momentarily become a surrogate god, revealed the depth of communal disempowerment.

The term *seductive performative* echoes in its name, and often in its appearance, Jill Dolan's concept of *utopian performatives*. However, unlike *utopian performatives* that often spring from a communal affinity grounded in shared ethics or ideology and imply a certain idea of an improved present/future, *seductive performatives of false catharsis* lack any specific ideology and ethos and are only concerned with the present moment. *Seductive performatives* are often masked as their *utopian* counterparts, but they are not deliberately attached to any specific politics or ethics – they are a spectacle of signifiers that have lost connections to their referents. *Utopian performatives* are inevitably linked to history, while *seductive performatives* attempt to sever those links. *Seductive performatives* have no future and are often oblivious of the past.

Comic relief

When the leader of the Bosnian Serbs, Radovan Karadžić, accused of war crimes and sought by The Hague Tribunal of Justice, was finally captured in the summer of 2008, the entertainment value that unfolded in the story about his false identity, his hideouts and his life in Belgrade, overshadowed all other aspects of the event. The capturing of Karadžić unravelled in a series of seductive performatives that offered the Serbian public an unexpected escape from serious and complex political, ethical and juridical issues related to Serbia's involvement in the Bosnian war. Karadžić's false identity as a healer named Doktor Dragan Dabić who lived freely in Belgrade for years, made public appearances at symposia on alternative medicine, had his own website and travelled abroad, attracted overwhelming public attention. Instead of ethical and political reckonings, the seductive performatives of the Karadžić story offered comic relief.

This event also became a unique performance of the city. Karadžić's supporters, mostly extreme right-wing parties and groups, organized protest gatherings in the Square of the Republic. Yet these protests were both predictable and overshadowed by the theatricality and performativity of Karadžić's transformation and by 'the doctor's' Belgrade itineraries. His daily routines through Belgrade were repeatedly performed through media broadcasts, recreated first by journalists and curious citizens. A tourist agency followed suit and offered a tour of the city entitled 'pop-art Radovan'. Here is the itinerary provided on the agency's website:[7]

- Departure from Belgrade city centre – Nikola Pašić Square.
- Arrival at New Belgrade, last known Radovan Karadžić residence. Block 45 and Jurija Gagarina St.
- We begin with Karadžić's morning routine and go to the bakery shop. For breakfast – home-made potato pie, his favorite morning meal. He liked to eat ascetic food.
- Of course, morning is the time to check the daily news. Across the street from the bakery shop, we say good morning to the local kiosk vendor and buy a newspaper.
- Walking through the park, we visit the grocery shop where Karadžić was a favorite customer. After a short break in the park, reading the newspaper and chatting with his neighbours, maybe a cold beer on the go, we arrive at the bus stop for city bus 73 in front of the building where he used to live. We'll stop to take some souvenir photos.

- The best part of the tour, a visit to local pub Luda kuća is next. In this rustic ambience, relax and enjoy yourselves the way he used to, maybe recounting some old memories of an eventful life with a glass of wine – Medvedja krv (Bear's blood), a few snacks and the sounds of Serbia's national stringed instrument – gusle – in the background.
- Before ending this fabulous tour, we need to sample the famous pancakes in the Pinocchio pancake shop, located in the old town of Zemun. Of course, the specialty that awaits us is the Karadžić pancake.
- On our return to the city centre, a panoramic sightseeing tour of the Special Court. This was Karadžić's residence after he was caught and before he moved to The Hague. It is also our last stop following in his footsteps.

This 'ghosting' of Karadžić through the streets of New Belgrade has offered a performative refocusing from a public/political figure to a private persona and from political responsibility to the pleasure of seductive performatives. In this performative refocusing from political to the private, all the moral parameters were lost. Karadžić/Dabić became neither good nor bad, just entertaining. Belgrade-based theatre director Gorčin Stojanović attempted to bring the case back into a political and ethical framework when he commented on the pop-art Radovan tour: 'A tour named Following Karadžić's Footsteps should actually be organized in Bosnia, and it should include all the places where horrible war crimes were committed, of which Karadžić has been accused' (http://www.humanrights-geneva.info/Karadzic-s-secret-life-draws-the,3375). Nevertheless, these voices were overshadowed by more entertaining headlines about Dr Dabić's lovers and his favourite pancakes. Karadžić/Dabić had pulled off a second disappearing act – an escape from political responsibility into a spectacle of seductive performatives. The theatricality of the case silenced the possibility of meaningful public debate.

There was something almost witty, theatrical, bold, tongue-in-cheek in Karadžić's transformation into Dr Dabić. A young man who had befriended Dr Dabić was interviewed after Dabić's true identity had been revealed. He said: 'I knew Doctor Dragan Dabić and he was nice. I don't know Radovan Karadžić.' In an interview for the Croatian magazine, *Globus*, film director Emir Kusturica made a similar distinction between Radovan Karadžić, the war criminal, and Dr Dabić – a fascinating character worthy of a movie (according to Kusturica).[8] Kusturica and his internationally renowned band, *Non-Smoking Orchestra*, even sing a song about Karadžić in their performances. In the same interview for *Globus*, Kusturica admits that he doesn't know much about the Croatian general Ante Gotovina, who is also on trial in The Hague for war crimes, but he talks about Gotovina sympathetically and promises to put him in a song too. Kusturica's playful, ambivalent and provocative approach is perhaps less about Karadžić and Gotovina than it is about the critique of The Hague tribunal as it reiterates the hegemonic position of the Western world in relation to Eastern Europe and Third World countries (ex-Yugoslavia and Rwanda). In this context, Karadžić's method-acting transformation into Dr Dabić offers itself as an ironic device – a satirical performance act that mocks the tribunal and, as such, is arguably not fully devoid of political and ethical dimensions.

Yet this interpretation, although not entirely apolitical, is solely based on the reception process, on the pleasure of spectators' witnessing the 'unveiling' of Karadžić as Dr Dabić. Like other seductive performatives in this case, it diverts the gaze from Radovan Karadžić/war criminal to Dragan Dabić/fictional persona, from Sarajevo and Srebrenica to The Hague, from dealing with the cause to the ironic deconstruction of the consequence. The transformation of Karadžić from a political figure to a theatrical persona is a highly dangerous interplay of theatricality and performativity. The seductive performatives of this interplay liberate the public from the need to take a political and ethical approach to the case. If Radovan Karadžić performs a disappearing act and reappears as Dr Dabić, a playful figure that Kusturica compares to Charlie Chaplin, what is the status of his war crimes? In other words, if Karadžić has turned into the fictional Dr Dabić, does the shelling of Sarajevo become fictional too?

3
Epilogue: Endemic Geopathologies

> *Outside and inside form a dialectic of division, the obvious geometry of which blinds us as soon as we bring it into play in metaphorical domains. It has the sharpness of the dialectics of yes and no, which decides everything. Unless one is careful, it is made into a basis of images that govern all thoughts of positive and negative.*
>
> Gaston Bachelard, *The Poetics of Space*

The spectacles and counter-spectacles of Belgrade indicate, albeit in different ways, an ever-returning struggle with place – an *endemic geopathology*. During Milošević's time, the antagonistic, geopathological force was embodied in the political apparatus and in a myriad of ways which defined public and private life. In their attempt to confront the regime in power, the counter-spectacles of Belgrade unmasked geopathological dimensions of place. In the post-Milošević era, geopathology reappeared in the gaze of the integrated spectacle which neutralized ethical and political difference and induced a collective loss of political memory. In sharp contradistinction to the confrontation with geopathology that characterized the radical political performance of the 1990s, the post-Milošević era was defined by a marked *absence* of resistance – that is, an inability to stage a counter-spectacle. How were the radical political performances and political gestures able/unable to counteract geopathology? Were Belgrade's counter-spectacles only symbolic acts of civil resistance that began and ended within their own decontamination metaphors?

I would argue that even when their efficacy temporarily gave way to carnivalesque and cathartic pleasures, Belgrade's counter-spectacles were not only important, they were vital. Radical political performance was not a collective choice, it was a necessity. These counter-spectacles shaped an alternative collective identity of the city and of Serbia as a whole. They offered the tools and the vocabulary for civil resistance and established an ethical standpoint which served as the driving force for social change. Even though the political accomplishments of Belgrade's counter-spectacles were not always immediate, they had a cumulative effect and were quantifiable. Nevertheless, the question remains: *was this enough*?

On 5 October 2000 – the day Milošević was stripped of power – I was in Toronto, glued to the news broadcasts from Belgrade and calling friends and family to get a better sense of what was happening on the streets of Belgrade. That evening, a few of us gathered at a friend's house to celebrate the end of the regime that had driven us out of Belgrade.[1] Living away from the city and thus prevented from taking part in, arguably, the last, big political catharsis unfolding on its streets, we thought about the 13 years of Milošević's rule. Viewed from a broader historical perspective, 13 years can feel like a relatively short time. Measured by wars, destruction, civilian casualties, social and economical devastation, as these particular 13 years had been, it felt incredibly long. When change finally did happen, it came too late: the wars in Slovenia, Croatia, Bosnia and Kosovo had taken their deadly toll. All that the events of 5 October 2000 could promise was a slightly better future and the fulfilment of an ethical and political goal desired by the majority of citizens for over a decade. Why did it take so long? Clearly, there is no simple answer. To unravel the labyrinthine network of political, social and economic factors involved on both local and international levels is neither the intent nor the purpose of this book. Instead, my question will focus on the culture of resistance and radical political performance in Serbia. More specifically, it asks whether Belgrade's counter-spectacles of resistance could have accomplished more as strategies of prevention and intervention. Any response I would argue, must take into account two crucial aspects of the culture of resistance and radical political performance in Serbia, namely: (1) the relationship between private and public spheres; (2) the dependence of radical, political performances on urban centres, particularly, on Belgrade.

Private publics

While the spectacular dimensions of Belgrade's radical political performances were often strategically concocted to increase the voice and visibility of the *counter-publics* (Warner[2]) the everyday life of the *urban guerrilla* (Schechner, *Environmental Theatre*) deliberately unfolded in private and semi-private spaces. Belgrade's urban guerrilla was relegated to a ghetto since, both politically and culturally, public outlets and spaces were co-opted and instrumentalized by the regime. This ghettoization was in part a consequence of silencing and forced exclusion of civil society's oppositional voices from the official public arena. Yet it was also a conscious choice on the part of resisters not to mix with the culture that had emerged as a by-product of the regime. Self-marginalization, a kind of self-imposed inner exile (that eventually led to actual emigration) became a strategy of resistance and an ethical choice, carving out an alternative city-within-the-city. Between the acts of political disobedience, radical performances that carnivalized the city, and political decontaminations of public spaces, Belgrade's *counter-publics* grew assertively *private*.

The strategy of going under the radar was not so much about secrecy, and not even about security, but about creating an alternative public arena that unfolds outside the official public spaces and institutions. Private homes became unofficial galleries, performance spaces, literary salons and cafes. It was the strategy of temporarily turning private spaces into alternative public outlets, as they could never be fully controlled by the regime.

The early and mid-1990s witnessed the emergence of various forms of public activity that took place in private and semi-private spaces, from homemade books and exhibits in private houses to clandestine cafés in people's homes. In 1993, for instance, an exhibit called *Private Public* took place in the house of Belgrade artist, Milica Tomić. Although the gallery of the Student Cultural Centre, *Srećna Galerija* (*Happy Gallery*), was instrumental in gathering the group of Serbian cutting-edge artists involved in the show, the choice to hold the show in the house of one of the participants was a political statement. It was a deliberate gesture to avoid all venues that could be co-opted by the official culture and thus put the project at risk. Refusing to take part in the cultural production of Milošević's Serbia, writer Dragan Todorović issued a single copy of his hand-made book, *Sen & San*. He also handpicked its readers. In the years of economic sanctions imposed on Serbia, when travelling abroad was almost impossible, a café named the *World Traveller's Club* (*Klub svetskih putnika*) opened in a private apartment.[3] Entering one of Belgrade's many nondescript residential buildings and discovering an apartment space full of colours, pop-art rendered communist memorabilia, rock-and-roll music and like-minded people on the other side of an unassuming brown door felt like one had been transported to a world behind the looking-glass. Indeed, in the increasingly claustrophobic Serbia of the

1990s, visiting *Klub svetskih putnika* felt like a trip – like a holiday away from everyday reality.

Another of Belgrade's favourite private/public spaces was located in the centre of the city on Trnska street, in the basement of my friend Jovana Krstanović (a film and TV editor working for Radio and Television B92). It had no official name; everyone just called it 'at Jovana's'. In the spring of 1995, on the eve of my emigration to Canada, I invited some of my closest friends to Jovana's to chat, listen to music, drink and play pool. To my mind, it was the perfect place for a farewell gathering since no other place in Belgrade rivalled the basement club for its unique ambience. At one and the same time private and public, personal and political, the space reflected the spirit of my decision to leave Belgrade. Although emigration was a personal choice, in the light of thousands of other exiles from Milošević's Serbia of the 1990s, I (somewhat naively) believed that all our departures were public gestures not entirely without political weight.[4]

In the film *Ghetto – The Secret Life of the City* (*Geto – tajni život grada*), produced in 1995 by the B92 television channel, the protagonist Goran Čavajda –Čavke (a local rock-and-roll icon),[5] guides the viewer through a selection of Belgrade's public and private spaces. The film begins with Čavke standing on the rooftop of his apartment building gazing at the urban panorama. 'This is Belgrade', he says. 'Everything looks the same as decades ago. But nothing is the same any more.' The film is Čavke's reflection on the Belgrade of the 1990s as he walks its grey streets and visits the few remaining outlets of its urban culture. The binary between outside and inside spaces of the city is strikingly obvious. Čavke observes and comments on the grim, unhappy faces of the pedestrians, walks past vendors selling smuggled goods, shivering beside their stalls on King Aleksandar Boulevard (formerly the Boulevard of the Revolution), and yet, as Čavke comments, they remain silent and politically passive. He walks past the Serbian Radio and Television building, one of the darkest and most formidable institutions of Milošević's power apparatus, and comments on the moral standards of the people who work there. He arrives at the building of the Student Cultural Centre (SKC), once the site of the most influential avant-garde projects and rock-and-roll events of ex-Yugoslavia, only to find its doors locked and its landmark garden-café deserted. Like numerous other cultural institutions, SKC was co-opted by the regime and almost overnight became an artistically dull and insignificant venue. It is only when Čavke ventures to the 'underground' spaces of Belgrade that he finds the city he has loved all his life. There, in abandoned underground parking lots, in dilapidated buildings, in private homes, in secret clubs, Čavke's friends play the music of the counter-culture. Only then, as he joins his friends playing the drums and dancing, does Čavke's face visibly brighten.

Towards the end of the movie, Čavke enters a packed concert hall where hundreds of bodies bounce and sway to turbo-folk tunes. Čavke's frozen face reveals the feeling so many of us shared at the time – the sense that our city had been stolen from us. Although Čavke's tone is one of disillusionment and sadness throughout the movie, at times he is angry and ironic. Exemplifying the importance of voicing political views in the public arena, Čavke's voiceovers provide a running commentary for the film until the moment that he enters the crowded turbo-folk concert. The mass indulgence in the repetitive tunes of turbo-folk – the spectacle of political oblivion – leaves the rock legend speechless. Čavke's blank stare into the dancing crowd reads like a painful realization that all the energy and efforts that went into Belgrade's counter-spectacles were futile. In the next scene, Čavke quickly returns to the 'underground' where he listens to the music of his peers, swaying in time, as if trying to shake off the sounds and sights from the turbo-folk concert hall.

On the one hand, the 'underground' spaces counterbalanced the geopathology of Belgrade's public spaces, state institutions, and even everyday street life, by asserting alternative, more heterotopic spatial relations. On the other hand, although the hidden city-within-the-city was real, its heterotopic dimensions had an almost escapist, illusory quality. The wedge drawn between official and the counter-cultures – between everyday public life and private sites of resistance – was too aggressive to allow for the possibility of a more dialogic relationship. In other words, there was a shared sense in the hidden city-within-the-city that members of the official public – from war profiteers to turbo-folk fans – were beyond conversion. Hence, to share the same public domain meant to acknowledge the legitimacy of the ruling regime and its culture. Withdrawals into the city-within-the-city, resignations from posts in governmental institutions and in the state-run media, emigrations to foreign countries – were all gestures of refusal to participate in the public and everyday life of a state that was committing crimes in the name of its citizens. Mirjana Miočinović, who, as mentioned earlier, resigned from her university post as Professor of Yugoslav Theatre and Drama when the war broke out, commented on her decision: 'I don't see what else I could have done, except commit suicide?' (*Teatron*, 39). Not to take part in the life of Milošević's Serbia was the ultimate act of resistance.

Decontamination spectacles that usurped and subverted everyday life in Belgrade's public spaces, and the emerging private spaces of resistance in the city-within-the city, shared (among many other common features) the fear of being co-opted and sucked into the official culture – the fear of contamination. Watching *Ghetto* makes me remember that this indeed was the only possible way of living in Belgrade in the intervals between political protests. In retrospect, though, I wonder whether the crowds of youthful turbo-folk fans could somehow have been persuaded to listen to different musical and political tunes. Had it been possible to concoct a scenario where charismatic Čavke takes young turbo-folk fans on a tour of the hidden city-within-the-city, I can only imagine what the impact on the public sphere of Milošević's Serbia might have been. If revealed to the youth on the other side of its walls, might the utopian performatives of the city-within-the city have turned into interventions?

'All my life I've been waiting for the chance to sing rock-and-roll in Belgrade'

The title of this section ('Cijeli život čekam priliku da u Beogradu pjevam rokenrol') comes from a song from the 1980s by the Croatian rock band, *Time*, which I have often heard used as a metaphor to describe Belgrade as a desirable cultural centre. On the one hand, this line usually re-emerges in a Belgrade-centred, self-flattering context that asserts the division between the metropolitan city and the provincial remainder of Serbia. On the other, it also describes the city as playful and open. Both of these aspects played a role in performing Belgrade as a city of counter-spectacles during the 1990s and were essential in shaping the identity of the radical political performances. Protest activities were centred in several major Serbian cities but by far most prominently in Belgrade. This defined the dramaturgy and the aesthetics of radical political performances as decidedly urban, enabling new urban guerrillas to emerge and to assert a new cultural identity. At the same time, the Belgrade-centredness of the protests and other performances of resistance prevented the possibility of some wider-reaching interventions.

State-run media was one of the main instruments of power of Milošević's regime. While it could not fully prevent alternative media outlets, such as Radio and Television B92, the state had the power to limit their broadcasting range. Consequently, alternative news broadcasts and other programmes situated in Belgrade and other major Serbian cities could not broadcast much farther than their city limits. No matter how loud and carnivalesque the counter-spectacles of Belgrade were, they went unseen and unheard in large parts of Serbia where inflammatory State propaganda dominated the media. No wonder, then, that Belgrade and other urban centres mostly voted against the war(s) and for democracy and change, while the villages and provincial towns bought into Milošević's war-mongering politics. As I mentioned earlier, Led Art, along with others, realized the limitations of the urban guerrilla and ventured outside the big urban centres on a Conradesque *Journey into the Heart of Serbia*, as the title of their project asserted. The public outside urban centres started to turn against Milošević more significantly when the youth resistance organization OTPOR followed suit by journeying into the 'heart of Serbia' and taking a person-to-person approach in its political agitations. However, that was not until after 1998 when OTPOR was formed.

In the early 1990s, while the carnage in the Balkans was still in its incipience, Augusto Boal visited Belgrade to give a workshop to local theatre practitioners on techniques for resisting internal oppression. Observing the workshop, many of us respectfully concluded that Boal's Theatre of the Oppressed strategies could never work in the Serbian context.[6] Given a theatre scene that was not only highly institutional but involved a well-entrenched star system, Serbian theatre artists would have needed complete retraining both in technique and in their professional outlook. More importantly, many of us believed that the inhabitants of Serbian villages and small towns, accustomed as they were to television, folk concerts and other forms of entertainment, were far too savvy to play along with Boal's participatory strategies.

Even if Boal's Theatre of the Oppressed workshop was too naive for the complex realities of Milošević's Serbia, now, more than fifteen years later, it seems to me that we may have missed the point. Arguably, the workshop was not so much about implementing a specific performance technique to mobilize diverse communities in the struggle against the oppressive regime as it was about asserting the need to work much harder, in whatever way appropriate, to reach out to these communities.

I am allowing myself to imagine another scenario that might not have been entirely impossible. Even though the 'heart of Serbia' could not rally enough willing participants for a Theatre of the Oppressed event to take place, popular television stars were much appreciated and trusted. A great many of these stars took an active part in political demonstrations, often leading protest processions or performing in the streets for the protesting crowd. Yet, they seldom ventured out of Belgrade. In my hypothetical scenario (concocted far too late), I am trying to imagine what might have happened if the leading stars, much loved and idolized throughout the former Yugoslavia, had frequented

Serbia's small towns and villages delivering information that the local inhabitants would not have heard in the state-run media. What if urban guerrillas had exported the infectious carnivalesque atmosphere from the street protests in Belgrade to the rest of Serbia? Could the 'It-effect' (Roach)[7] and carnivalization have been used more assertively as interventionist strategies to narrow the communal, political and cultural divide in Serbia on which Milošević's regime thrived? I am fully aware that this would have been far easier said than done. At least in some areas, such interventionist strategies would have carried the risk of open confrontation and put activists in truly dangerous situations. Yet, these are indeed the risks of reaching beyond one's own followers. Jon Erikson makes a distinction between resistance and intervention:

> 'Resistance', if it always remains only that, consists of symbolic hits to the image of the body politic to make oneself and likeminded others gain a sense or feeling of empowerment, most often without seeking actual redress of grievances. To do that it would need to have some rhetorical force that one's opposition or uncommitted third parties would understand. Usually it is not used as a strategy to participate in a larger polity – which always entails a modicum of compromise and an attempt to understand the fears and desires of people not like yourself – but instead as a tactic to serve and impress one's own constituency.
>
> ('Defining Political Performance', p. 172)

The Belgrade of Milošević's era was a city of resistance. The impact and the potential legacy of its culture of resistance is indeed no small matter. It has been vital in shaping a new civic identity and in establishing an ethical standpoint without which the change on 5 October 2000 would not have been possible. Nevertheless, while strategies of resistance kept the urban culture alive and sustained Serbia's counter-publics, acts of intervention remained few and far between.

Building sites and demolitions

Gorana Petrović labels Belgrade a 'city of the moment' ('grad trenutka'), describing this characteristic as one which is deeply rooted in the city's history:

> As opposed to cities where each epoch has left its material traces, where the new has been built on the legacies of the past, Belgrade

> with turns of epoch and changes of socio-political systems that prompted changes in all aspects of society, has usually reinvented itself from scratch. Over centuries, the city was rebuilt in between destructions – from a Turkish *mahala* to a European city – therefore the possibility for a dialogue between different epochs of the city and different architectural styles has mostly been lost. There are very few cities that have been destroyed so often. Outside the Kalemegdan fortress there are no remaining buildings from the seventeenth century and before. Although Belgrade was at different points a Celtic, Roman, Turkish and Austrian city – the traces of the past were almost non-existent.
>
> ('Beograd Festival', p. 164)

Petrović argues that Belgrade is a city of change whose identity and uniqueness is not so much in static elements, such as its architecture, but in the way the city is lived and practiced – its 'energy'. Let me add another characteristic of this 'city of the moment': its loss of memory.

Only days after the events of 5 October 2000, Željko Mitrović, the owner of Pink Television – notorious for shaping the turbo-folk culture of Milošević's Serbia – gave an interview for Radio B92 – one of the key media outlets in the struggle against Milošević. During Milošević's era, a number of artists and other public figures boycotted Pink TV because of its close ties to the regime. While Radio and Television Serbia bombarded the viewers with war propaganda, Pink brainwashed them with turbo-folk. This symbiosis proved highly dangerous, even deadly, in the unfolding of the Yugoslavian catastrophe. Nevertheless, after the change of power on 5 October, Pink's transition into the new regime was remarkably smooth. In the interview for B92, Mitrović – a former prominent member of JUL, a political satellite party to Milošević's SPS and run by Milošević's wife – explained that he had actually fought the regime on the inside. This assertion would have been laughable had the history and role of Pink TV in Milošević's Serbia not been so quickly forgotten. Journalists who had resigned from Television Serbia for political reasons began working for Pink a few years after the downfall of Milošević. Turbo-folk tunes and stars, promoted on Pink, have grown even stronger, penetrating the local cultural fabric more than ever. Three years after 5 October, writer and artist Mileta Prodanović commented:

> 'Pink' announces its new programme that will investigate the responsibility for atrocities on the territory of the former Yugoslavia during

> the 90s. However, these are the same atrocities that were inspired and prompted by the political party whose prominent member and activist was, in his former life, no other than the owner of TV Pink.
>
> (*Older and Prettier Belgrade*, p. 205)

'What did you do during the war?' appears occasionally as a question in polemical essays, yet it is one that has had little impact on Serbian reality. War profiteers have made easy transitions into the new regime, while the urban guerrilla of the 1990s has disintegrated and dispersed in various directions. The city of the moment 'reinvents itself from scratch', yet its capacity for oblivion enables other personal and collective reinventions. Through this process of reinvention, ethics and political responsibility turn into decorative tropes in the narratives of integrated spectacle of post-Milošević Serbia.

In the summer of 2009, commemorations of the Srebrenica massacre were held in Bosnia and throughout the region. Serbian officials have been conspicuously absent from any public acknowledgement of the war crime. Given that at the time Serbia's leading Democratic Party was holding on to its lead against right-wing nationalists by the skin of its teeth, it was not unreasonable to think that the decision to remain silent was motivated by the potential loss of votes. More pointedly, party members were wary of any official acknowledgement and commemoration of the massacre being perceived negatively and swaying even more voters towards the far right. I would argue that this issue is deeply rooted in the inability to establish a true dialogue with the past in the public sphere, beyond univocal historical narratives that have been pulled out by various regimes, whenever it is politically expedient.

Post-Milošević Serbia neither knows how to mourn the victims of its recent wars nor how to celebrate and cherish the legacy of its antiwar activism that helped to overthrow an oppressive regime. Unlike the city-of-action shaped in the 1990s through counter-spectacles that often relied on both synchronic and diachronic interperformative and intra-cultural links, the Belgrade of the new millennium lives in the moment by severing its ties to the past. Radical political performances and other similar performative gestures that once turned Belgrade's streets into sites of counter-spectacle have no place in the new Serbia. Nevertheless, the legacy of these events might hold the keys to how to deal publicly with a variety of ethical issues that the country is facing. Although the dramaturgies of Belgrade's counter-spectacles would need to be somewhat modified to fit the new era, they embody an attitude and culture of how to dialogically and publicly confront difficult political and ethical topics. The legacy of these performative gestures could provide strategies of both reckoning and reconciliation with the traumatic and ethically multifaceted past. More specifically, the strategic use/usurpation of streets and other public spaces, strategies of theatricalization, decontamination and the interperformativity of place, all of which were integral to Belgrade's counter-spectacles of the 1990s, might provide some dramaturgical and aesthetic forms for dealing with issues of both the past and the present. Through these strategies of performance, rather than through the language of official politics, it might be possible to propose a *Let's talk about Srebrenica* project or to ask, by way of radical performance, *What did you do during the war?* in a manner that is open-ended and dialogic – neither implying accusation nor encouraging an alibi.

A true dialogue with the past requires discussion of both macro-historical and micro-historical events. While central historical narratives of the downfall of Yugoslavia have inevitably been shaped, albeit differently in different parts of the region, the micro history of Belgrade as a city of counter-spectacle, resistance and action is in grave danger of being irrevocably lost. I find this loss symbolized by the ways in which the city – both its grand vistas and its tiny side-streets – has recently been reshaped through building projects and demolitions. In the appendix to his book, *Older and Prettier Belgrade* (2003), Mileta Prodanović writes about Avala Tower, one of the city's symbols and a landmark vista until it was destroyed during the NATO bombing in 1999:

> Avala Tower, destroyed in the NATO intervention in 1999, has not been rebuilt, and it probably never will be. [...] Thus, this tower – at one time the pride of Belgrade and the symbol of progress – continues to live only as a clunky model decorating the window of a defunct shop and as a logo of a state company soon to be put out of business. It will not be long before a more lucrative business moves into the deserted shop in the centre of the city and some bigger and more powerful 'label' gobbles up the clunky tower in the shop window. Avala Tower will be put to rest in one of these 'Belgrade in Old Postcards' – coffee-table books.
>
> (p. 203)

Although big brand names are now evident everywhere from Serbian shop windows to billboards, one aspect of Prodanović's prediction has been proven wrong: the Avala Tower *was* rebuilt. As I was driving into Belgrade one summer evening in 2009, there it was, almost finished and already sparkling against the night sky – *as good as old*. Ever since the tower had been destroyed, the clearing on top of the small mountain Avala, on which it used to stand, was a reminder of devastation and loss. Somewhat paradoxically, the resurrected tower feels more like an embodiment of nostalgia than a sign of its rejuvenation – a presence that can only simulate the filling of the void. In any case, the new/old Avala Tower, creating the illusion of something regained, fits into Belgrade's new culture of erasure. This culture of erasure has been marked not only by communal selective memory, but also by a political and ethical relativism, which has been eroding the struggle for democracy of the 1990s.

While the Avala Tower illustrates the relationship of the city symbols to the central historical narratives of Belgrade on a macro scale, the destiny of Jovana's house embodies erasures of the city's micro history. The secret café in the basement of the house on Trnska Street was a counter-site and a shelter during Milošević's era and, for a short while after 5 October 2000, it held the promise of a new urban culture. Jovana's house was a political statement. In the 1990s, it was part of the hidden city-within-the-city – a place shaped through resistance to the public spaces of Milošević's Serbia. In 1999, during the NATO bombings, Jovana, her friends and her house were the protagonists in Janko Baljak's documentary, *Da li i kod vas bombarduju?* (*Are they bombing over at your place?*). The film depicted everyday life in Jovana's house where a number of her friends found shelter from the bombs, as well as from the oppressive culture outside. During the bombing, the regime did what it could to hijack symbols and strategies of resistance – from the symbol of a target (first worn by the citizens of besieged Sarajevo in recognition of the fact that civilians had become military targets), to attempts at performing the city, such as singing and dancing on the bridges (that had also been declared legitimate targets by NATO forces).[8] The film depicts members of Belgrade's counter-culture crammed together (symbolically and literally) in the basement of Jovana's house – watching their strategies of resistance be appropriated by the regime, while democracy, what they had spent a decade fighting for, was being thrown at them in the form of smart bombs. It bore witness to yet another marginalization of Belgrade's urban guerrilla – this time, under the threat of becoming 'collateral damage'.[9] Nevertheless, Jovana's house, both a shelter and a private/public space of resistance, enabled everyday life to unfold somewhere between fear and laughter – just slightly above the ordinary; almost as a utopian performative. It remained the talk of the town for a short while after 5 October 2000. In 2002, musician and activist Manu

Chao visited the house on Trnska Street during his music tour. Soon afterwards, it was about to be abandoned to one day make room for a new apartment complex.

Lately, the side-streets of central Belgrade have turned into construction sites as owners of small houses have been pushed to sell their properties to private investors and building companies. Jovana's house, however, holds a special place in the culture of the city – it is a ghosted space that contains the legacy and spirit of Belgrade's counter-culture. In other words, her house is an important site in the city's micro history. Establishing its public/private existence as a counter-space during the 1990s, surviving both Milošević's regime and NATO bombs, now it has been standing like an empty shell, hidden behind overgrown shrubs and weeds, awaiting the bulldozers of the new entrepreneurial Serbia. This outcome is both deeply ironic and symbolic of Belgrade's culture of erasure. The site, emblematic of the political resistance of the 1990s, does not fit the profile of the new, democratic Serbia – but has been demolished by entrepreneurs, most of whom made their initial fortune during Milošević's time, more often than not in ways that were contingent upon Balkan bloodshed. In the last scene of the film *Ghetto – the Secret Life of the City*, city-guide Čavke stands on the rooftop of his apartment building overlooking Belgrade. Although Belgrade has changed dramatically since the film was made in 1995, Čavke's final remarks remain poignantly relevant: 'This is Belgrade, the city, which like a black hole, swallows everything – people, houses, the past, everything…'.

Part II
Sarajevo: Imaginaries and Embodiments

Bosnia-Herzegovina casts a spell on all who live there or who were privileged in the past to acquaint themselves with the republic. Sentimentalism plays little part in this – it is through the middle of Bosnia that East meets West; Islam meets Christianity; the Catholic eyes the Orthodox across the Neretva, the line of the Great Schism; Bosnia divided the great Empires of Vienna and Constantinople; Bosnia was perhaps the only true reflection of Yugoslavia. It is both the paradigm of peaceful communal life in the Balkans and its darkest antithesis.

Misha Glenny, *The Fall of Yugoslavia*

I first laid eyes on Sarajevo as a child, coming down from the mountain in a narrow-gauge train. It was truly a joy to see. And as naïve as the etymology may be, it added to the experience: Sarajevo suddenly became a caravanserai which I interpreted as, 'Come, little traveller, and rest your bones.'

Bogdan Bogdanović, *Balkan Blues*

Sarajevo, kristalna sećanja
Sarajevo, od blata i snega
(Sarajevo of crystal memories)
Sarajevo of mud and snow)
...
Pusti oči da vide još ovaj put
Pusti uši da čuju još ovaj put...
(Let the eyes see once again

Let the ears hear just one more time)
Sarajevo....
(from the Yugoslavian rock 'n roll band EKV, 1986)

We were singing a popular song at the top of our lungs by one of the most remarkable rock and roll bands of the former Yugoslavia as the bus wound its way along serpentine mountain roads towards the city in the valley. It was 1985 and we were a group of 15-year-olds from Belgrade on a school trip. The city in the valley emerging through a thin layer of fog was Sarajevo. It was my first visit. Like all proper tourists, I went to see the mosque on Baščaršija, the Orthodox Church near by and the Catholic Cathedral. I stood in front of the monument called the Eternal Flame – Vječna vatra – in honour of all the peoples of Yugoslavia who had fought against the Nazis in the Second World War. I ate *ćevapčići*, a famous Bosnian dish, in a modest-looking eatery where they played old-fashioned folk music from the early 1970s. From the wall, a portrait of Marshall Tito, surrounded by posters of local football players, surveilled the customers hugging their plates, washing their kebabs down with homemade yogurt. *Kod Želje*, as it was called, was considered a famous Sarajevo landmark by everybody in the region. On a rainy day, I took a tram ride. As the Sarajevo cityscape rolled by my raindrop-flecked window, I wondered about the meaning of a sentence often used to describe Sarajevo – 'the city where the clocks of different churches displayed different times'. It was cold and windy as I walked towards the city's Synagogue. Later, I felt cosy sitting in a comfy armchair at the Hotel Europe – an Austro-Hungarian building dating from 1882 – eating *tufahije*, a mouth-watering Turkish dessert of baked apples, walnuts and raisins, that had been naturalized through centuries of Ottoman occupation. The wide-eyed teenager from Belgrade had never before encountered a city that contained so many different places within it.

The city of Sarajevo was established in 1440 by Isa bey Ishaković, a minor local governor under the Ottoman Empire. Before the Turks, Bosnia was populated by Slavic tribes who began to enter southeastern Europe during the sixth century. By the end of the twelfth century, Bosnia was established as an independent state. This medieval state was already different from other European states since it hosted three Churches that coexisted peacefully: the Bosnian Church, which was declared heretical in the thirteenth century and broke its ties with Rome; the Orthodox Church; and Roman Catholic monasteries. In 1463, after years of trying to resist the attacks of Turkish troops, Bosnia was fully occupied and remained under Ottoman rule for 400 years. A common practice in the Ottoman Empire system, called *devshirme* (in Serbian *danak u krvi* – blood tax), was to recruit, or rather to abduct, healthy and able Christian boys, convert them to Islam and train them for the highest positions in the imperial institutions. The main protagonist of Ivo Andrić's Nobel prize-winning novel, *Na Drini Ćuprija*, is one such Christian boy, forcefully taken from his mother and converted to Islam. The boy grows up to become the Grand Vizier Mehmed Paša Sokolović. Haunted by the memory of the separation from his family, he builds one of the most beautiful bridges over the river Drina in the Bosnian town of Višegrad. The Grand Vizier's project of building the bridge becomes an attempt to bridge an individual and collective divide between religions and ethnicities.

Over the course of 400 years, there were numerous uprisings against Ottoman Rule. In 1687 Prince Eugene of Savoy and his Habsburg army almost burned Sarajevo to the ground, but did not manage to defeat the Turks. In the mid-nineteenth century, a rebellion that started in Herzegovina, and was supported by Serbia, Macedonia and Russia, finally brought liberation from the Empire. In 1878, the Treaty of Berlin was signed and Romania, Serbia, Montenegro and Bulgaria were recognized as autonomous. Bosnia and Herzegovina, however, was to be annexed and administered by the Austro-Hungarian Monarchy in 1908. The Ottoman Turks built roads and bridges, erected the first mosque in Sarajevo, a Sufi lodge, a covered market (*bezistan*), a bath-house and a piped-water system, a library, a *madrassa* (Islamic school) and a bridge over the River Miljacka. Austro-Hungarians built railroads, factories, businesses and educational institutions, and established the state museum, today's National Museum of Bosnia and Herzegovina. They also built Sarajevo landmarks, such as the magnificent City Hall and the neo-Gothic Catholic cathedral.

Bosnian writer Dževad Karahasan explains what made Sarajevo unique among other multicultural cities that have experienced a similar turbulent history:

> When it was founded, the city was settled by people from three monotheistic religions – Islam, Catholicism, and Eastern Orthodoxy – and the languages spoken in it were Turkish, Arabic, Persian, Bosnian, Croatian, Serbian, Magyar, German, and Italian. And then some fifty years after Sarajevo was founded, the Spanish rulers Ferdinand and Isabella banished the Jews of Spain, some of whom took refuge in Sarajevo. They brought to the city its fourth monotheistic religion

> and a new culture – constituted around that religion and around centuries of wandering – and they brought new languages too.
>
> Sarajevo became a new Babylon and a new Jerusalem – a city of a new linguistic mingling and the city in which temples of all faiths of the Book can be seen in one glance.
>
> This mixture of languages, faiths, cultures, and peoples living together in such a small place produced a cultural system unique to Bosnia and Herzegovina, and especially to Sarajevo. It was clearly their own, original and distinctive. There were, of course, many regions and many cities in the ethnically and religiously mixed Turkish Empire where peoples, languages, and religions were entwined with each other. Yet there surely was no city – not even in that vast domain – where so many languages, religions, and cultures met and mixed with one another in such a small space.
>
> (*Sarajevo, Exodus of a City*, pp. 4–5)

For better or for worse, three moments in modern history have put Sarajevo at the centre of global events: (1) the assassination of the Arch Duke Ferdinand in 1914 that signalled the Bosnian people's desire for liberation from Habsburg rule and triggered the First World War; (2) the 1984 Winter Olympic games that occurred within the last, relatively prosperous decade of the Socialist Federal Republic of Yugoslavia. It was there that Yugoslav Communist politicians sat alongside Elton John watching GDR skating champion Katarina Witt as she twirled across the newly built Olympic ice rink – the 'suits' of Socialism literally rubbing shoulders with Western pop culture on a stage that was slightly the worse for wear. By the time the Olympics were over, Sarajevo had inherited technical equipment and the infrastructure for large-scale media broadcasts as well as a Holiday Inn built expressly for reporters from around the globe. Less than ten years later, this would all come into play again with the third historical moment that put the city in the global spotlight – the war.

In 1991, after the comparatively uneventful secession of Yugoslavia's northern republic of Slovenia and the bloodbath of the secession of Croatia, we began to speculate if Bosnia and Herzegovina would be the next battlefield of the Balkans. I remember numerous conversations where different scenarios were posited. Some worried that if a war in Bosnia were to break out, Sarajevo would be the next Lebanon, or worse. Others were convinced that war would never happen in a place like Sarajevo. It was too mixed, its close-knit and ethnically diverse community, considered the most Yugoslav of all Yugoslavian cities, would never be divided across ethnic lines. Macedonian scholar Naum Panovski vividly describes what Sarajevo meant in the collective consciousness of the former Yugoslavia:

> [...] Sarajevo meant, in fact, many things: It was a place of braided cultures and religions, languages and alphabets, beliefs and ideologies, races and ethnicities; it was a city where different worlds met, a place where the past met the future, and where politics competed with arts. Sarajevo was also an Olympian city with an enormous heart open to everyone, a *'carsija'* place with an inspiring sense of humour, a 'raja' place with a heartbeat felt all over the country, and a music place like no other music place.
>
> ('Goran Stefanovski's Sarajevo', pp. 47–8)

This image of Sarajevo within the mind-map of the former Yugoslavia was confirmed yet again on 28 July 1991, when the Yugoslav National Broadcast News (YUTEL) organized a protest event against the war entitled *YUTEL for Peace* (*YUTEL za mir*) in the Olympic Hall Zetra in Sarajevo. Numerous musicians and other artists came to perform and voice their demand for peace. The event opened with a live news broadcast by well-known and respected journalists, Gordana Suša and Goran Milić. Their reading of the daily news placed the event even more immediately within the context of crisis and jingoistic politics that put the region on the brink of armed conflict. More than 20,000 people gathered for this event with a great sense of urgency. Although it was only possible to watch *YUTEL for Peace* in Bosnia and Macedonia (other places refused to broadcast the protest), the *political catharsis* and the *utopian perfomatives* of the event reverberated far beyond Sarajevo's Olympic Hall. For a short time, the energy of thousands of people gathering to sing and dance while asserting their rightful desire to live in peace felt reassuring.

In his book, *The Fall of Yugoslavia*, journalist Misha Glenny offers a thoughtful analysis of the chain of events that would lead to the Balkan bloodbath. He points out that 'Bosnia could only be saved if a political party which spanned the three communities had emerged as the most powerful after the collapse of the communist party' (p. 148). Instead, what emerged was a poorly constructed pluralist system based on parties divided along nationalist lines. As a result, Glenny affirms, 'Alija Izetbegović and the Moslem leadership also bear a historical responsibility for the breakdown of the consensus between the three Bosnian communities, for they were the first to organize a political party, the SDA, along nationalist lines in May 1990' (*The Fall of Yugoslavia*, p. 149). Sarajevo Professor of Political Science, Asim Mujkić, problematizes Bosnian *religious nationalism* (Friedland) along similar lines when he writes that: 'the electoral victory of the ethno-nationalist parties in Bosnia in 1990 was accomplished with enormous support from religious institutions, which continues to the present' ('We, the Citizens of Ethnopolis', p. 116). Glenny points out that the ethnic divide in the region was not the only factor in the break-down of Yugoslavia and the war in Bosnia. He also foregrounds the role that foreign powers and their ill-conceived political moves and diplomatic missions played in the unravelling of events. With Germany's premature announcement in December 1991 that it would recognize Slovenia and Croatia as independent states, Bosnia's fate was sealed. Clearly, it was too early for such a decision to be made since to avoid pushing Bosnia into war would have required negotiations and an agreement with the Serbian side. The German decision not only 'made a mockery of the consensual foreign policy which the European Community was striving to build on its way towards economic and political integration' (*The Fall of Yugoslavia*, p. 164), but also put Bosnia in an impossible position. Once Croatia and Slovenia had been internationally recognized, Bosnia could 'either remain in a Yugoslavia dominated by Milošević and Belgrade, which would have been simply unacceptable to all Moslems and Croats in BiH, or he [Izetbegović] could accelerate moves towards independence by holding the referendum [...] thus hastening the onset of war' (p. 164). When Izetbegović announced the referendum and Bosnia started its preparations for independence, war became unavoidable.

On 1 March 1992, a Muslim extremist attacked a Serbian wedding party in front of the Old Orthodox Church on Baščaršija, killing the father of the bride. This 'blood wedding' often appears in Serbian narratives about the beginning of the war in Sarajevo and is cited as one of the immediate events that fuelled the conflict. In late March of 1992, on the eve of the referendum, the first fights began in peripheral, but strategically important, areas of Bosnia. On the weekend of 4–5 April the war reached Sarajevo, preceding the international recognition of an independent Bosnia and Herzegovina on the following Monday. On 5 April, as barricades were being erected and heavy artillery was being assembled in the hills surrounding the city, thousands of panic-stricken Sarajevans took to the streets to hold their last big anti-war protest. Documentary footage of the protest is a record of public worry and political confusion. Anti-war slogans and chants revealed a diversity of approaches: some called for an independent, but multicultural

Bosnia, others evoked the notion of the 'brotherhood and unity' of Tito's Yugoslavia, while still others insisted on a multi-ethnic and cosmopolitan Sarajevo. Whatever their understanding of current politics was, one thing remained clear – the citizens of Sarajevo did not want war. As the protesters peacefully approached the Holiday Inn, which at the time also housed the headquarters of the leading party of Bosnian Serbs (SDS – Serbian Democratic Party), shots were fired from the hotel windows into the crowd. These shots marked another symbolic moment that announced the beginning of the war. Glenny summarizes the events that put Sarajevo back on the world map for the next three years and turned it into the iconic city of the Bosnian conflict:

> The battle of Sarajevo was launched by Karadžić doubtless for strategic reasons, but if successful it would also signal a victory for the primitive and irrational over the civilized and the rational. The case of the Serbs has often been misrepresented and their genuine fears and concerns dismissed when they should have not been. But the behaviour of Karadžić, the Arkanovci and other paramilitary groups, and the JNA in Bosnia-Herzegovina, destroyed their reputation abroad. No injustice had been perpetrated against Serbs of Bosnia or of Serbia to justify this rape of Bosnia-Herzegovina.
>
> (*The Fall of Yugoslavia*, p. 171)

A couple of years before Yugoslavia began to drown in its own bloodbath, I had a curious dream that has stayed with me ever since. I found myself standing amidst the rubble of a destroyed city. I was trying to recognize familiar sights in the ruins that surrounded me. I was trying to read street names and signposts but could not make them out. I believed it was my city but I could not find my home. All the routes were strewn with debris which disoriented me even more. I thought my dream was about Belgrade. A few years later, I realized that I was dreaming about Sarajevo. I was never a citizen of Sarajevo but the destruction of this city was a tipping point for me, one that made me acutely aware that I could no longer be a citizen of Yugoslavia.

In the four chapters that form Part II, I will investigate Sarajevo's iconic image during the Balkan conflict. Specifically, I will look at how the city was performed and shaped through *imaginaries* and *embodiments*. By *embodiments* I mean a variety of practices, from cultural events to civic rituals and performances of everyday life, through which citizens not only sustained their dynamic relationship with the city in the face of death, but also preserved its mind-map and performed its architecture even while Sarajevo's landmarks were being destroyed. Here, *imaginaries* do not have entirely negative connotations but rather work as epistemological tools, sometimes as vital phenomena, that shape the identity of the city. Imaginaries involve a fine dialectics between authenticity and experience on the one hand, and preconceived notions and constructs, on the other. In the case of Sarajevo, they are crucial to the city's identity but they are equally instrumental in its misreading. Imaginaries are not separated from the real. Rather, they exercise and embrace a certain aspect of the real, often the one closest to one's preconceived notions, at times overlooking, if not denying, other aspects. Yet the relationship between notion and experience is a two-way street. Dealing with imaginaries is a delicate process where undoing one set of imaginaries often necessitates evoking an alternative set. In the next segment, I will work through a kind of dialectic triad of the city that could be called the *suffering Sarajevo*, the *resilient Sarajevo*, the *heart-of-darkness Sarajevo* – where each new aspect undoes the imaginaries of the previous one.

4
Waiting for Godot: Sarajevo and its Interpretations

After her first visit to war-torn Sarajevo, Susan Sontag was eager to be more than a mere witness to the violence and injustice inflicted upon the city. Her subsequent engagement with the city of Sarajevo could be read as a reaction to a kind of spectatorial voyeurism, enabled through modern media, where one peeks into the unfortunate lives of others from the comfort of one's living room and where information becomes a substitute for compassion. Later, in her book *Regarding the Pain of Others*, she critiques the relationship between spectating and the pain of others:

> Being a spectator of calamities taking place in another country is a quintessential modern experience, the cumulative offering by more than a century and a half's worth of those professional, specialized tourists known as journalists. Wars are now also living room sights and sounds. Information about what is happening elsewhere called 'news', features conflict and violence – 'If it bleeds, it leads' runs the venerable guideline of tabloids and twenty-four-hour headline news shows – to which the response is compassion, or indignation, or titillation, or approval, as each misery heaves into view.
>
> (p. 18)

In her search for a more engaged activism, Sontag pitched the idea to direct a play to Haris Pašović, a well-known local director and producer. When he agreed and asked her what play she would like to direct, she immediately thought of *Waiting for Godot*. In her writings about this project, Sontag has noted: 'Beckett's play, written over forty years ago, seems written for and about, Sarajevo' ('*Waiting for Godot* in Sarajevo',

p. 88). The production took place during some of the severest shelling of the central city since the beginning of the siege and received significant media coverage in the West; her efforts were both commended and criticized. *Waiting for Godot* emerged as one of the most iconic events in Sarajevo during the siege. In the Western media, the visits of Bono from the famous rock band U2, the performance of the Three Tenors on the ruins of the city, and Sontag's *Waiting for Godot* epitomized the suffering and the resilience of Sarajevo. *Godot* not only became a metaphor of the besieged city, but also fed strongly into the imaginaries of Sarajevo as seen through Western eyes. How is the city of Sarajevo performed and textualized through this project and the subsequent writings about it? What kind of city narrative is created in this process and through Sontag's account of her activism? And how does this narrative stand in relation to other performances of and in the city?

Uneasiness with *Godot*

Ever since accounts of *Waiting for Godot* in Sarajevo first appeared in the media and in academic journals, I have had mixed feelings about the way in which these narratives constructed the identity of the city and canonized Sontag's activism. As a citizen of Serbia living in Belgrade in 1993, I resisted my uneasiness at the time, believing that I had no ethical grounds on which to formulate a critique. Yet I have repeatedly felt the need to unpack this uneasiness in order to understand the city or at least to grasp my own imaginaries of Sarajevo. In writing this book on performing Sarajevo and Belgrade during the war, and the breakdown of Yugoslavia, the question of who is speaking – the distinction between insider's and outsider's view – has become crucial to an analysis of my own position within the discourse as well as to an understanding of urban experience and the narratives of others. In order to assess *Waiting for Godot* in Sarajevo as a performance of the city, then, it is necessary to tackle both the relationship between the actual encounter of Sarajevo with Sontag and the perspectives through which the various narratives of this encounter have been filtered.

After Sontag's death in 2004, Haris Pašović proposed that a street or a city square be named after the US writer, director and public intellectual. It was an initiative that was supported by Muhadin Hamamdžić, the mayor of the city at the time, who maintained that Sarajevo and its citizens were grateful to Sontag for her humanitarian efforts and for her contribution to the history of the city. In 2009, a place was finally chosen: the square in front of the National Theatre where Sontag and

Pašović had first made their deal about producing *Godot*. Pašović offers a rationale for this initiative:

> Sontag was one of the biggest intellectuals of the 20th century, and Sarajevo, as well as the rest of the world, should honour her. She was a great friend of the city. She visited Sarajevo nine times during the siege. She directed this famous show during the siege. She wholeheartedly supported Sarajevo urging for the war in Bosnia to end.
> (http://sarajevo.co.ba/trg-u-sarajevu-nosice-ime-susan-sontag)

I have heard this sentiment echoed in my conversations with a number of Sarajevo theatre makers including Admir Glamočak, the actor who played Lucky in Sontag's production of *Godot,* and Leila Pašović, the producer who worked for both the Sarajevo International Theatre Festival (MESS) and the Sarajevo Film Festival. Sarajevans loved Sontag and greatly appreciated her contribution to the city and she loved them back.

In her 1993 article for the *New York Review of Books* about the staging of *Godot* in Sarajevo, as well as in the version of the article published in the *Performing Arts Journal* (*PAJ*) in 1994, Sontag offered valuable insight into the circumstances of mounting a performance in a city under siege:

> we rehearsed in the dark. The bare proscenium stage was lit usually by only three or four candles, supplemented by the four flashlights I'd brought with me. [...] The theatre's façade, lobby, and bar had been wrecked by shelling more than a year ago and the debris still had not been cleared away. [...] The main obstacle, apart from the stage lighting, was the fatigue of the malnourished actors, many of whom, before they arrived for rehearsals at ten, had for several hours been queuing for water and then lugging heavy plastic containers up eight or ten flights of stairs. Some of them had to walk two hours to get to the theatre, and of course, would have to follow the same dangerous route at the end of the day.
> ('*Waiting for Godot* in Sarajevo', pp. 94–5)

In addition, Sontag makes several important observations that counter the one-dimensional Western perception of a Balkan city torn apart by ethnic conflict. Three of her points are specifically useful in understanding the complexities of Sarajevo. Firstly, she stresses the secular, multicultural aspect of Sarajevo and Bosnia that was intrinsic to the city's historical identity rather than a manufactured construct of Tito's Yugoslavia. Her account of working in Sarajevo counters Western perceptions of the war in Yugoslavia rooted in the long-established notion of the Balkans as a place of 'elemental and irreconcilable racial enmity' (Keyserling, *Europe*, p. 319) animated by ' the spirit of eternal strife' (*Europe*, pp. 321–2). Sontag writes:

> Did I have a multi-ethnic cast, many people have asked me. And if so, was there conflict or tension among the actors, or did they, as someone here in New York put it to me, 'get along with each other'?
>
> But of course I did – the population of Sarajevo is so mixed, and there are so many intermarriages, that it would be hard to assemble any kind of group in which all three 'ethnic' groups are not represented – and without ever inquiring who was what, it was by chance that I eventually learnt that Velibor Topić (Estragon I) had a Muslim mother and a Croat father, though he has a Serb first name; while Ines Fančović (Pozzo) had to be Croatian, since Ines is a Croatian name, and she was born and grew up in the costal town of Split and came to Sarajevo thirty years ago. Both parents of Milijana Zirojević (Estragon II) are Serb, while Irena Mulamuhić (Estragon III) must have had at least a Muslim father. I never learnt the ethnic origins of all the actors. They knew them and took them for granted because they are colleagues – they've acted in many plays together – and friends.
>
> Yes, of course, they got along.
>
> ('*Waiting for Godot* in Sarajevo', pp. 92–3)

Secondly, Sontag de-exoticizes Sarajevo's actors and audiences by stating that 'just as good actors still live in Sarajevo, so do members of this cultivated audience' ('*Waiting for Godot* in Sarajevo', p. 88). She describes both the extremely difficult circumstances under which she and her actors (Illustration 15) worked as well as the more typical ups and downs that are part of the creative process everywhere. Thirdly, she understands the existential need for continuity amidst violent rupture and the chaos of destruction, even if it comes at a great risk. For Sontag, as for many theatre makers and theatregoers in Sarajevo at the time, to put on a play was an 'expression of normality' ('*Waiting for Godot* in Sarajevo', p. 91). She points out that this expression of normality was a means for the citizens of Sarajevo to reclaim their dignity. It was also a means of collective self-preservation, of salvaging, reshaping and keeping strong the identity of the city in the eye of systematic destruction.

Illustration 15 Susan Sontag and the cast of *Waiting for Godot*, photo courtesy of 'Friends from Sarajevo'

In short, the citizens of Sarajevo greatly appreciated Sontag and she offered some valuable insights into the besieged city while posing complex questions concerning artists/intellectuals and political engagement. Why my continued uneasiness with *Godot*, then? Firstly, despite Sontag's best efforts, the discourse created about and around *Waiting for Godot* in Sarajevo reiterates the notion of the city as a passive, lethargic and depressed dystopia of Balkan multiculturalism. Secondly, Sontag's directing of *Godot* in Sarajevo emerged as *the* key moment of cultural intervention and as a symbolic political intervention, rather than as one of many already existing 'expressions of normality' in the city. In the following discussion, my aim is neither to discredit Sontag's contribution to the cultural life of the besieged city, nor to deny the suffering of Sarajevo and its citizens, but to offer a more contextualized, and hopefully multifaceted, reading of both *Godot* and the city.

In 1998, scholar David Toole published a book entitled *Waiting for Godot in Sarajevo: Theological Reflections on Nihilism, Tragedy, and Apocalypse*. His book was inspired in great part by Sontag's account of her experience of staging Beckett's play in Sarajevo. This particular staging, however, is not the only reason why Toole uses Sarajevo to symbolically frame his refutation of 'the Enlightenment dream of a universal humanity endowed with a single reason, embodying a single morality' (*Waiting for Godot in Sarajevo*, p. 3). He is upholding a common notion amongst historians that the twentieth century actually began in Sarajevo in 1914 when Gavrilo Princip's assassination of Archduke Franz Ferdinand incited the Austro-Hungarian monarchy to declare war on Serbia, quickly inflaming the whole of Europe, and escalating into the four-year-long carnage of the First World War . As the end of the twntieth century approached, Toole revisited this historical trope of Sarajevo only to find that history had come full circle. In 1992, the city that had epitomized all the hopes of the Enlightenment, where Christians (Orthodox and Catholic), Muslims and Jews co-existed peacefully and productively, was ravaged by civil war. For Toole, Sontag's article served as a portal to the city and a lens through which Sarajevo was mediated. It enabled the author to formulate the key questions of his study: 'What does the fate of Sarajevo – as the city that has come to symbolize both the atrocities and the hopes of our century – say about the future?' (*Waiting for Godot in Sarajevo*, p. xiv). Or, perhaps more pertinently for our discussion, what does it mean to live a life of dignity in a world of undeniable suffering? Toole writes:

> By staging *Godot* in Sarajevo and then writing an account of that event, Sontag has given me at least an initial tether between text and world. When she says that *Godot* has been written for and about Sarajevo what she means, it seems to me, is that the circumstances in Sarajevo in July 1993 were such that to stage the performance of *Godot* then and there allowed for a remarkable convergence of text and world. To begin by *Waiting for Godot* in Sarajevo, then, is to begin both with a reminder of the suffering that holds a central place in our world and with a reminder of the relationship between this suffering and any attempt to think seriously about this world.
>
> (*Waiting for Godot in Sarajevo*, p. 4)

In Toole's and Sontag's discourse, Sarajevo clearly emerges as a synecdoche of suffering. What about 'dignity' and performance? Tool writes:

> In the summer of 1993, Susan Sontag travelled to the besieged and battered city of Sarajevo to stage the production of Beckett's play *Waiting for Godot* [...] As it turned out, the prospect of staging a play in a city that had at once become a battlefield and something of a concentration camp presented unique difficulties. [...] perhaps it *should* seem odd – that Sontag spent more than a month in Sarajevo

> putting together a performance of *Waiting for Godot*. Why did she risk not only her own life but the lives of actors and spectators alike to, of all things, stage a play in a war zone? [...] Does not such an action founder precisely on its impractical nature, not to mention its insensitivity to the horrors of genocide?
>
> (*Waiting for Godot in Sarajevo*, p. 2)

Waiting for Godot has emerged as a key event that allowed for the 'remarkable convergence between the text and the world', between suffering and dignity, and between rupture and normalcy. Although Sontag touches on other cultural activities in the besieged city, Toole's text does not provide any context or insight into local cultural life. Sontag's opening comments about her Sarajevo experience include her recollection of some of the other cultural events that were being offered in the city: Haris Pašović's two productions (a devised piece, *City*, and Euripidus's *Alcestis*), the musical *Hair*, daily rehearsals of the String Quartet, and varied projects of a film production company. In that sense, coming to stage *Godot* in Sarajevo was not only a way of foregrounding the seriousness of the humanitarian crises in Sarajevo, but a way to be actively involved in broadening the cultural offerings to citizens who were hungry for food as well as for the sustenance of normal, dignified urban life. And how hungry Sarajevo's theatregoers and theatre makers in 1993 were! Nevertheless, I would argue that this hunger – physical and existential – was a driving force for an incredibly rich repertoire of performances that took place during the three-year-long siege of the city.

The status of *Waiting for Godot* changes significantly when one compares Sontag's impressions of cultural life in Sarajevo during the siege with local theatre archives, documentations and eye-witness accounts. In the introduction to his collections of testimonials about theatre in Sarajevo during the war (*Teatar u ratnom Sarajevu: 1992–1995*), Darko Diklić provides a summary of the cultural activities during the siege:

> [...] in this period 3,102 artistic and cultural events took place or on average 2.5 events per day! The Sarajevo Philharmonic orchestra performed 48 concerts in Sarajevo and in Europe. On 5 February, when 66 people were killed and 199 wounded in the Markale massacre, the Sarajevo String Quartet performed its hundredth concert and continued performing until the end of the war. Yahudi Menuhin, Zubin Mehta, Jose Carreras [...] gave guest performances. Fifteen writers were killed during the war, while, at the same time 263 books were

> published. Although 18 visual artists were killed, exhibits were taking place all the time during the war – a total of 177 in six city galleries and in a number of improvised venues. [...] Despite the fact that ten filmmakers were killed, 156 documentary and short films were produced during the war. Almost at the very beginning of the war MESS (*Male i eksperiemntalne scene Sarajeva*) inaugurated the Sarajevo Film Festival. (When a foreign journalist asked Haris Pašović 'Why a film festival during the war?', he would answer: 'And why a war during the film festival?!'). In Sarajevo theatres, 182 performances premiered and over two thousand shows were performed that half a million people saw. There were also countless other artistic and cultural events, the festival *Sarajevo Winter* (*Sarajevska zima*), *Fama, La Benevolencia* etc.
>
> (*Teatar u ratnom Sarajevu 1992/1995*, p. 10)

This account contradicts the depiction of Sarajevo as a city of passive suffering where very little was going on aside from destruction and the day-to-day struggle for survival. Although Sontag's visit to Sarajevo happened in the relatively early days of the siege, which, to some degree at least, might account for the difference between her tally versus the local archives, the impressive amount of cultural activity clearly shows that *Waiting for Godot* was more than an isolated phenomenon outside the context of the overall cultural production in Sarajevo during the war. Even if Sontag's staging of *Waiting for Godot* is used as a metaphor to unpack various aspects of moral philosophy, this contextualization is crucial. Nevertheless, neither the works that critique Sontag's project, nor those inspired by it, such as Toole's study, suggest that she was invited to direct a play within an existing cultural infrastructure with its production logistics already adjusted to the impossible circumstances of war. In other words, Sontag's 'impractical project' as Toole described it, was not a novelty. Rather, it was one of many creative projects, each one no more and no less 'impractical' than another, created during the siege of Sarajevo.

Sontag's narrative, as well as a number of subsequent scholarly and journalistic texts on the subject, spread the word that her production of *Waiting for Godot* was single-handedly responsible for shaping the cultural, political and symbolic resistance of the city. This not only canonized a single project led by a Western intellectual while simultaneously minimizing the immensely rich local cultural production, but also established Sontag's view as the dominant narrative about the city in general. As a celebrity intellectual writing in the dominant language of the Western world with access to leading American and European publications, Sontag's assessment became the 'privileged interpretation' (Butler, *Bodies that Matter*, p. 108). Her interpretation, albeit well-intended, not only failed to fully describe the rich cultural life in Sarajevo but imposed suffering as the dominant trope and prevented the emergence of a more heteroglossic narrative of the city.

Sontag's account of the staging process of *Waiting for Godot* is dominated by a first-person narrative where the authorial/directorial 'I' is seldom replaced by the more participatory and collective 'we'. In other words, the discussion regarding all the dramaturgical and directorial decisions is dominated by her first-person singular narrative. On the other side of this personal narrative, are Sontag's descriptions of the malnourished and desperate actors whom she directed. Veteran actress Ines Fančović, who played Pozzo in Sontag's *Godot*, offers her account of working on this project:

> She [Sontag] had her own concept. I think she set a very difficult task for herself that she couldn't fully complete. She wanted to have three couples of Estragon and Vladimir to allude to the three constituent nationalities of Bosnia; but that was making it too literal. She was struggling a lot with her three couples and with how to divide the text. Atko (Admir Glamočak) and I were left to work on our own. I was working a lot on my role often at home, at night in total darkness. When we finally got to work on my scene, she told me that I had already done a brilliant job with it. This role has become one of my favourite and perhaps one of the best performances I ever gave. It probably came from the extra energy, that not only I, but the whole group had. It was unbelievable.
>
> (quoted in Diklić, *Teatar u ratnom Sarajevu*, p. 80)

This account shows a more energetic, creative, collaborative, and pro-active approach in the process of staging *Godot* and working with Sontag. It offers a respectful, but not uncritical insight into the creative process, painting a more complex and more interesting picture of *Waiting for Godot* in Sarajevo.

Conversely, Sontag's account reiterates the trope of passive suffering in a city whose physical survival necessitated the support and intervention of US politicians (Sontag and the actors often dubbed *Waiting for Godot* in Sarajevo 'Waiting for Clinton'), while the spiritual/cultural survival of the city desperately required aid from Western liberal intellectuals and artists. Certainly, art was as important to Sarajevo's vitality

Illustration 16 *Waiting for Godot*, photo courtesy of 'Friends from Sarajevo'

as humanitarian aid but there was one major distinction: humanitarian aid of any kind necessitated help, that is, external intervention, while cultural production was inextricably linked to an internal process of resistance through which the city's identity was shaped and preserved. Thus, the impetus for the city's cultural production could only come from its citizens: artists and audiences alike (Illustration 16).

'The most real place in the world'

The testimonies of citizens/artists, even when documented, were written in a 'minority' language and published in books like Diklić's *Teatar u ratnom Sarajevu* that have remained relatively obscure even within the wider Balkan context, let alone the international scene. Sontag's agency gave voice to a good cause, but it did not offer space, through translation and publication in more prominent media outlets, for local voices to commingle with the voices of international celebrity intellectuals and artists. In fact, Sontag's staging of *Waiting for Godot* generated more publicity than any other theatrical event during the Sarajevo siege by local artists and international guests alike. Both Sontag's and the actors' accounts of the process mention numerous press conferences and the large number of foreign journalists who frequented the rehearsals. 'The rehearsals were unusual – we never knew if we would have ten or fifty journalists at a rehearsal; if we were going to rehearse or spend more time being photographed' (*Teatar u ratnom Sarajevu*, p. 91), observed Glamočak. Sontag's international profile certainly generated large-scale media interest, but why was it that local actors/artists were often photographed but seldom addressed? Why were the journalists so lacking in curiosity about other events in the city?

Sontag's perception of the suffering city that struggled for its dignity made the drama of Sarajevo easily accessible and smoothed over any contradictions and ambiguities. In her transition from mere witness to active participant in the life of the city, she failed to notice or record one of the key features of Sarajevo – its sense of humour. In the imaginaries of ex-Yugoslavians and among local inhabitants, the spirit of Sarajevo is often described as a paradoxical *joie de vivre* – a mixture of humour, resilience, irony and nihilism – that enabled projects such as the *Sarajevo Survival Guide* to be published locally in 1993. In it, images of death and destruction are mixed with pseudo-tourist advertisements of the city – as the ideal place to lose weight and to get fit, for example, since there is no food and one needs to run through the streets to avoid sniper fire. This spirit, even if somewhat limited as all cultural imaginaries are, enabled the proverbial Bosnian jokesters, Mujo and Haso, to emerge from the rubble and despair of the besieged city with darkly funny jokes about the war. It also enabled the city to live its possible contradictions to the fullest. As many accounts of life and theatre in Sarajevo at that time confirm, one often needed to pass dead bodies in the street on the way to the theatre. There was no heating, no electricity, no running water, yet, as Glamočak asserted, it was never more wonderful and more important to do theatre. Descriptions of life in Sarajevo at the time often involve back-to-back accounts of seeing someone's brain spilled on the pavement and attending fantastic parties where people sang and danced all night. The suffering of Sarajevo was undeniable and easy to understand, anticipate and feel. Its 'normalcy' and its pleasures were much harder to fit into Western imaginaries of a suffering city. Commenting on Sontag's description of Sarajevo as 'the most real place in the world', Elin Diamond writes:

> I am interested in underscoring the identification fantasy of a lifelong New Yorker who can transform the political and social calamities of a Balkan city into the 'most real place in the world.' What would the most real place in the world look like? Clearly only Susan

> Sontag knows. Her real is the fantasy of the real, which reflects well on her efforts and obscures the differences and dissent of others.
>
> ('Blau, Butler, Beckett and the Politics of Seeming', p. 41)

The city seen through Sontag's experience can be understood, imagined and mourned. In the city that Admir Glamočak remembers, there were dead bodies on the streets, but there were also great parties. Such a paradoxical mixture is much harder to translate across cultures and the identification fantasy is not readily available. Although Sontag's account of the besieged city, like many others, reinforced the trope of suffering, it needs to be said that she, more than most, provided a deeper insight into life in Sarajevo during the war. The majority of the encounters between the citizens of Sarajevo and foreign artists, intellectuals and journalists were, as Dževad Karahasan has characterized one such meeting with a French journalist, 'elevated and graced by beautiful, noble feelings' (*Sarajevo, Exodus of a City*, p. 62), but also accompanied by preconceived notions. Karahasan further points out that their 'attempt to communicate was similarly founded on an entirely sincere effort to understand each other, and to agree', yet the meeting did not go as well as they had hoped (*Sarajevo*, p. 62). Besieged Sarajevo, pieced together through news reports and images, entered our living rooms and our imaginations. It was so easy to 'know' the city and its suffering without understanding either the city or the war that was tearing it apart. I am not trying to suggest that this city and the war in the Balkans would be impossible to grasp without some exclusive, esoteric experience and insight into the region. The feud of the Balkans, of which Sarajevo was one of the biggest and most iconic victims, was not beyond comprehension to foreigners, as some local imaginaries about the region suggest. The issue is the media's need to summarize complex conflicts by presenting the suffering of others in the clipped and clinically-informative language we have come to call news that is channelled into the comfort of our living rooms. In its translation of complex events onto two-dimensional screens and pages, many valuable layers are inevitably lost. When these two-dimensional translations replace the multifaceted original, they often become axiomatic even in other forms of expression that have traditionally allowed for more in-depth coverage. Two-dimensional translations become our points of entry into the worlds of others because they require less time and effort and because they fuel our imaginaries more easily than the chaotic original. Thus, even in an actual, physical encounter, a place is seen through one's preconceived knowledge of it, which makes it easy to know but hard to understand.

No wonder, then, that the encounter between the writer, Karahasan, and the French journalist did not go as well as both men had hoped:

> Well, my guest from France observed me, but could not believe me, because he could not hear what I was telling him. What was I talking about? In his view, the cause of my suffering lies in the fact that he thinks I suffer, because the fact that he observes me and thinks about me proves that I exist. For him, I am a victim because he thinks that I am a victim, and so on...
>
> (*Sarajevo*, p. 66)

Encountering the *Other* is easy; shattering one's own imaginaries is not.

In his 1994 article for *Liberation*, 'No Reprieve for Sarajevo', Jean Baudrillard foregrounded the political and ethical traps of Sontag's kind of activism:

> It was Susan Sontag who came to have 'Waiting for Godot' played in Sarajevo. Why not bring 'Bouvard & Pecuchet' to Somalia or Afghanistan? But the worst is not about this cultural soul-boosting. It is about the condescending manner in making out what is strength and what is weakness. They are strong. It is we who are weak and who go there to make good for our loss of strength and sense of reality.

The comparison between Beckett's play and the nineteenth-century epic novel by Gustav Flaubert is somewhat puzzling. Is Baudrillard falling into his own trap, making a cultural assumption while criticizing Sontag's activism? *Bouvard and Pecuchet* is an episodic, picaresque, satirical novel, often considered to be a precursor to semiotic and postmodern thinking. Unlike *Godot*, it is not as widely known outside France as are some of Flaubert's other novels. Baudrillard's ironic comment suggests that Flaubert's novel would have no relevance in a different cultural context – that it would be an absurd imposition of a cultural canon that is in fact not shared. He might be right about *Bouvard and Pecuchet*. The critique and comparison between the staging of *Godot* in Sarajevo and the hypothetical export of Flaubert to Afghanistan, assumes that the Balkans have a culture that is very different from Western European culture – that *Godot* in Sarajevo would be an imposition of Western, self-indulgent intellectual preoccupations. Like others, Baudrillard overlooks the particular cultural context – not only the cultural production in Sarajevo during the war, but the more general cultural make-up of the former Yugoslavia, including its strong European aspects. The first regional performance of *Waiting for Godot* took place in Belgrade in 1954 and since then the play has had numerous productions across the former Yugoslavia, securing an honoured place on academic reading lists. The play has long been 'domesticated' within the local culture through varied and at times even difficult performance circumstances – from its Belgrade premiere in 1954 in the atelier of a famous modernist painter, Mića Popović, when the Ministry of Culture did not allow its public performance, to *Waiting for Godot* in Sarajevo. Although the analogy between *Waiting for Godot* and waiting for the end of the siege might come across as somewhat tautological, the text was certainly not alien cultural material. On the contrary, it was precisely their familiarity with the play that allowed the audience to contemplate the staging interventions made by Sontag and others.

Although Baudrillard's critique of Western intellectual cultural and other assumptions may not have wholly escaped his own preconceptions, he is not entirely inaccurate in detecting a certain self-indulgence that unwittingly emerges in humanitarian cultural missions. In his essay, 'Tales from the Wild East', playwright Goran Stefanovski makes a point that supports Baudrillard's critique:

> It does take a lot of courage to stay alive and make ends meet under the everyday pressure of that 'historical soap opera'. This courage can't be appreciated from the outside. The Western observer pretends to know exactly what could be done in the situation, how these wrongs could be made right, and how this drama could be powerfully dramatized. (It's like watching football on TV and knowing how to score every time.)
>
> (http://www.eurozine.com/articles/2009-03-24-stefanovski-en.html)

In this light, the ironic mentioning of Flaubert's novel makes sense, even if not exactly in the way Baudrillard intended. *Bouvard* and *Pecuchet* are two office clerks who leave their job in pursuit of adventures. Not unlike some of the engaged Western intellectuals and journalists, they go to different places and have a lot of exciting, at times dangerous, encounters, but they do not know how to 'read the signs'. Hence, they return home and back to their old lives not learning from their adventures as much as they could have.

5
City-as-Body

All we have left is the place, the attachment to the place
we still rule over the ruins
of temples spectres of gardens and houses
if we lose the ruins nothing will be left
(Zbigniew Herbert, 'Report from the Besieged City')

The first theatre production that opened in Sarajevo during the siege was called *Grad* (*City*). It premiered in 1993 under Haris Pašović's direction. The performance script of *Grad* – a collage of various texts including the poetry of Zbigniew Herbert – was performed on the intimate, rink-shaped stage of Kamerni Teatar 55 – a courtyard building in the heart of Sarajevo's city centre. Kamerni 55, tightly encircled by private apartments, provided a sheltered space for *Grad* and other performances to carry on during the siege. A recording of the performance shows a bare, candle-lit stage where a group of actors are chanting, singing and uttering the lines of Herbert's poetry. The audience sits near the stage and the small auditorium is packed. The atmosphere is peaceful, meditative and almost ritualistic. Even the two-dimensional recording of the event manages to document moments of profound togetherness between actors and spectators – 'a theatre in which the activity of the actor and the activity of the spectator were driven by the same desperate need' (Brook, *The Empty Space*, p. 60).

The theatre becomes a physical shelter from the almost constant shelling of the city and a symbolic space 'where a greater reality could be found' (Brook, *The Empty Space*, p. 49). The city appears as the central trope of the performance; the barren, theatrical space emerges as its synecdoche. Yet this minimalism is not about the disappearance of place – a mere illustration of *urbicide* – nor is it about blind escapism into theatrical illusions. Rather, the performance emerges as a means of asserting and affirming the city in the face of its systematic annihilation. Given these particular circumstances, the gathering of actors and audience members surpasses the theatrical event and becomes a congregation of citizens – a direct communication and a collective meditation on the city. The performance of *Grad*, simple and elegant on the bare stage of Kamerni 55, recalls Peter Brook's notion of *holy theatre* where the actors have no other choice but to create out of their deepest need and in response 'to a hunger' (p. 49): 'This theatre is holy, because its purpose is holy; it has a clear defined place in the community and it responds to a need the churches can no longer fill' (p. 67).

Director Pašović comments about *Grad* in the following way:

> A group of actors and I put the show together very quickly, in only one week and it was actually quite good. This was a collage based on meditations about the city. The city was the focus for all of us, and the world was talking about Sarajevo – the city under siege. What is a city actually?
>
> (in Diklić, *Teatar u ratnom Sarajevu*, p. 203)

A good deal if not all of the outstanding cultural production in Sarajevo during the siege sought answers to similar questions: What makes a city a *city*? How does a city under siege, reduced in most parts to rubble and ruin, continue to figure as such? What does it mean to be a citizen in a city under siege?

In less extreme circumstances, Situationists and, more generally, psychogeographers, have claimed that 'the self cannot be divorced from the urban environment' and that 'it had to pertain to more than just the psyche of the individual if it was to be useful in the collective rethinking of the city' (Simon Sadler, *The Situationist City*, p. 77). The case of Sarajevo makes this connection painfully and somewhat paradoxically obvious – the individual psyche, the collective self and the city are all intrinsic parts of a fragile ecology that depend on each other for survival. Here the city-as-body is exposed, ravaged, yet resilient. This resilience has its source in the attitude of a collective rethinking that emerges as a reaction to violence. In order to sustain the individual self, the collective and the city, this rethinking quickly morphs into action – it becomes a performance. There is no room for detachment, every bit of the experience is embodied, even phenomena that involve distancing as a core strategy, such as humour and irony. The rethinking and the performance are vital to the point that they almost become matters of life and death. To rethink, perform and re-perform everything from the rituals of daily life to theatre-making is a way of sustaining the idea of the city – its role and its cultural function – and it becomes a mode of being a citizen.

Lucky the city

'I'm performing the city.' This is how actor Admir Glamočak described his performance of Lucky in Susan Sontag's *Waiting for Godot* in Sarajevo (Illustration 17). Glamočak explains:

> I told Susan Sontag, who had her own vision of this character, that by performing Lucky, I will be performing the city. She replied that that could not be played, but I knew and felt that Lucky as a victim had tragic dimensions in common with Sarajevo. For me, Lucky sublimated what I was experiencing and what I was seeing and hearing: he was my child, my spouse, my friend – in short, my city. In a condensed and simplified way, he was, thus, the expression of Sarajevo. That's why Lucky has been one of the best roles I've ever played. Lucky was the metaphor of Sarajevo and its citizens.
>
> (in Diklić, *Teatar u ratnom Sarjevu*, p. 93)

Illustration 17 *Waiting for Godot*, photo courtesy of 'Friends from Sarajevo'

What does this notion of Sarajevo as Lucky tell us about the besieged city? What did Glamočak mean when he maintained that he was 'performing the city'? Reading Sarajevo through both Beckett's text and through Glamočak's contextualization of Lucky, reveals some key features of the besieged Sarajevo.

1. Sarajevo, like Lucky's festering body sores, is a city that has been wounded:

   Estragon: What ails him?
   Vladimir: He looks tired.
   Estragon: Why doesn't he put down his bags?
   Vladimir: How do I know? (*They close on him.*) Careful!
   Estragon: Say something to him.
   Vladimir: Look!
   Estragon: What?
   Vladimir: (*pointing*) His neck!
   Estragon: (*looking* at the neck) I see nothing.
   Vladimir: Here.
   (*Estragon goes over beside Vladimir.*)
   Estragon: Oh, I say!
   Vladimir: A running sore!
   Estragon: It's the rope.
   Vladimir: It's the rubbing.
   Estragon: It's inevitable.
   Vladimir: It's the knot.
   Estragon: It's the chafing.
   (*They resume their inspection, dwell on the face.*)
   Vladimir: (*grudgingly*) He's not bad looking.

   (*Waiting for Godot*, pp. 17–8)

2. Like Lucky, who painfully attempts to recreate meaning from the garbage heap of language, the city tries to survive through the alchemical process of turning rubble into urban art. That is, even though Lucky's speech is nonsensical, it makes a statement about the inadequacy of language and representation.
3. It is an impossible and dangerous, yet absurdly vibrant place. Despite everything, Lucky exercises his ludic urge to perform and the performance is painful for Pozzo his master and tormentor.
4. It is a resilient city. Vladimir kicks Lucky to see if he is dead, but Lucky is alive and Vladimir hurts his foot.

Lucky conveys the notion of city-as-body: wounded yet resilient.

In his book, *Art and the City*, Nicolas Whybrow comments on the notion of city-as-body in the context of the rapidly changing modern city:

> bodies can be said to both *produce* and *be produced by* the city. And whilst cities obviously contain bodies, bodies also contain cities. In fact, the city itself functions as an 'ecological' body, one that *facilitates* the circulation of particular socio-economic and cultural discourses whilst also *delimiting* them.
>
> (p. 8)

In his understanding of the city as an 'ecological' body, Whybrow works with Henri Lefebvre's notion of the production of space, suggesting that it is not only the activities of bodies that shape the city-body but that the process is a two-way street. Moreover, the paradigm of city-as-body allows us to move beyond the mutual shaping and reshaping of the city-body duality and to consider one as an integral part of the other. The notion of city-as-body foregrounds the hybrid body of the city and the perpetual process of its transformation – of turning flesh into stone and stone into flesh – that could be realized only through, and as, performance. Sarajevo was a unique and extreme case of the city-as-body notion: it was the ravaged, wounded, tormented body, but it was also a body that revitalized itself – the body that never stopped performing. It was, indeed, Admir Glamočak's Lucky in *Waiting for Godot*.

The perspective from above

How did Sarajevo become Lucky or how did Lucky become Sarajevo? I would argue that it was a process that happened through different, opposing and clashing forces that could be reduced to two basic categories: violence and resistance. These two categories involve two different perspectives – the view from above and the view from below – both, in their opposition, foregrounding the notion of the city-as-body. The former is the perspective of the aggressor; the latter, the view from within the city. In the case of Sarajevo, this configuration of perspectives is both literal and symbolic. It not only symbolizes the dynamics of power and violence but also conveys the spatial anatomy of Sarajevo. Historically, the heart of the city lay in the valley, surrounded by mountains, but the war changed the relationship between the city and its mountains: the hills turned into military strongholds of Serbian forces from which the city was shelled and its citizens picked off by snipers. In both Dževad Karahasan's writing, and in the *Sarajevo Survival Guide*, this change has been duly noted. Karahasan, who depicted Sarajevo as an 'inwardly' turned city, described the mountains as part of the city's metaphorical identity:

> It was built in the valley (that of the Miljacka river) surrounded by hills which screen and isolate the city from the world, shutting it from everything external and turning it completely on itself. The commercial centre known as 'Čaršija' (the equivalent of the 'city' in contemporary European towns) was built in the flat valley bottom, while the residential quarters called *mahalas* spread over the inner slopes of the hills surrounding the valley floor. In that way the centre of the city is in fact doubly shut off from the world – by hills surrounding the city and by the *mahalas* which, because of the configuration of the terrain and the urban plan, and because of their relation to the centre, function like a protective shell secreted by the centre of the town to defend it from everything external, just as a snail or a shellfish is protected by its casing.
>
> (in Labon et al., *Balkan Blues*, pp. 89–90)

Karahasan's portrait of the city is rooted in this inward/outward and inside/outside configuration of Sarajevo's anatomy that has shaped its various aspects – from everyday life to its imaginaries. The hills, *mahalas* and the city centre (Čaršija) emerge as an integral, organic whole, where one is defined and protected by the other. The war ruptured this wholeness geographically, physically and metaphorically. The notion of the city surrounded by hills has changed its meaning – from being encircled in a protective shell to being besieged – from being sheltered to being trapped. The *Sarajevo Survival Guide* describes this violent reconfiguration in the following way: 'Sarajevans once loved their hills and the fact that the city was like a bird in a green nest. In the war these hills are the sites where the death of Sarajevo is being engineered and spread around, daily' (p. 75). Karahasan sees in this violent reconfiguration a reduction of complex, layered, metaphoric identity of the inward city into a banal description of its entrapment – of the siege: 'In this way, Sarajevo, which was an inward city in the sense attributed to that word by the Esoterics, that is in a non-literal sense, is now becoming so literally, so stupidly literally inward. And that literalness hurts, believe me' (in Labon, *Balkan Blues*, p. 103). One might add that in these reconfigurations of territories, concepts and meanings, the duality of inward/outward – city and mountain – had degenerated into a binary of inside-outside, centre-periphery, below-above, victim-aggressor, demos-ethnos and them-us.

Moreover, this violent reconfiguration played out the simplistic scenario of the military conflict, while, on a more complex level perhaps, its specific symbolic and geographical binary – the position that granted the perspective from above and the condition of the view from within – resembled some of the sadistic dynamic of the Lucky-Pozzo relationship. From both perspectives, albeit for different reasons, the city was perceived as a *precarious body*, which Judith Butler, from whom I have borrowed the term, explains in the following way:

> The precarity of life imposes an obligation upon us. We have to ask about the conditions under which it becomes possible to apprehend a life or set of lives as precarious, and those that make it less possible, or indeed impossible. Of course, it does not follow that if one apprehends a life as precarious one will resolve to protect that life or secure the conditions for its persistence and flourishing. It could be, as both Hegel and Klein point out in their different ways, that the apprehension of precariousness leads to a heightening of violence, an insight into physical vulnerability of some set of others that incites the desire to destroy them.
>
> (*Frames of War*, p. 2)

When targeting a multi-ethnic city such as Sarajevo, the leaders and soldiers on the hills knew that they were not killing only the ethnic other, the proclaimed enemy of their national and ideological project – the Bosnian Muslims. Indeed, Serbs in central Sarajevo have died of Serbian snipers from the hills as well. What made this city *other* was not its homogenous ethic profile, but its multicultural fabric that rendered national concepts and ideas of ethnic purity absurd. In his reaction to the destruction of Sarajevo and other cities in Bosnia and Croatia, Serbian architect and, at one time, mayor of Belgrade, Bogdan Bogdanović wrote:

> What I sense deep in the city destroyers' panic-ridden souls is a malicious animus against everything urban, everything urbane, that is, against a complex semantic cluster that includes spirituality, morality, language, taste and style. From the fourteenth century onward the word 'urbanity' in most European languages has stood for dignity, sophistication, the unity of thought and word, word and feeling, feeling and action. People who cannot meet its demands find it easier to do away with it altogether.
>
> ('The Ritual Murder of the City', p. 55)

The desire to destroy the city, however, had no singular source – ranging from both symbolic and actual strategies of realizing ethnic/ national imaginaries and territorial aspirations to the lucrative war economy that the siege had enabled. The city itself was the enemy, the city as ecosystem, as a whole where bodies and buildings, flesh and stone, epitomized this singular precarious body – precarious enough to be destroyed. The struggle over the city was a struggle over a precarious body, one that those in the hills *above* wanted to destroy for the same reasons that those *within* wanted to preserve. Following Butler's line in reading the city as a precarious body, 'there is no thinking of life that is not precarious – except, of course in fantasy, and in military fantasy in particular' (*Frames of War*, p. 25). The perspective from above – of the Serbs bombarding Sarajevo from the hills – was indeed fuelled and sharpened by national and military fantasies. And although the distinct anatomy of Sarajevo gave some unique features to both methods of aggression and forms of resistance, the perspective from above – the military fantasy – was enabled through a generic framework that Butler calls a 'differential distribution of precarity' (*Frames of War*, p. 25), which is 'at once a material and perceptual issue, since those whose lives are not 'regarded' as potentially grievable, and hence valuable, are made to bear the burden of starvation, underemployment, legal disenfranchisement, and differential exposure to violence and death' (p. 25) At the root of military fantasies is a generic frame through which the perspective from above is constructed. In the early 1990s, this frame enabled the Serbs on the hills surrounding the city to turn Sarajevans into military targets. Likewise, a more recent frame-construction has cast the lives of Iraqi civilians, or the body of the Libyan dictator's baby grandson, as less grievable and more valuable as military targets.

Citiness/wilderness

In his seminal work *Flesh and Stone: The Body and the City in Western Civilization*, Richard Sennett understands the city through its relationship with the body. He points out that the key aspect in the relationship between urban space and the body in modern cities is the experience of speed. Sennett argues that this experience has made the body passive and turned space into a 'means to the end of pure motion' (p. 17) as we 'now measure spaces in terms of how easy it is to drive through them, to get out of them' (p. 18). For Sennett, the distinctive feature of a modern city that sets it apart from the urban spaces of our ancestors is the ease with which we move through the urban environment:

> Navigating the geography of modern society requires very little physical effort, hence engagement; indeed as roads become straightened and regularized, the voyager need account less and less for the people and the buildings in order to move, making minute motions in an ever less complex environment.
>
> (*Flesh and Stone*, p. 18)

For a city in extreme circumstances like the besieged Sarajevo, the relationship between the body and the urban environment was foregrounded, but in the exactly opposite way. The physical effort of navigating the urban environment still remained one of the defining features of Sarajevo *in extremis*. Yet unlike other modern European and American cities, the relationship between body and space in Sarajevo was marked by an extreme difficulty of navigation. The violence and destruction of war stripped the place of all features – positive and negative – of a modern European, Balkan city. It excised both the comforting and the commodifying dimensions of Sarajevo's *citiness*.[1] The siege imposed on the city a *modus operandi* of daily survival that constantly challenged its identity as an urban environment. This imposition of an opposite dynamic, of a counter-arrangement, so to speak, reinforced by the increased mediation of Sarajevo through news reports, turned the city into a heterotopia of violence.

Nevertheless, Sennett's notion of the physical effort involved in navigating a city as a feature of modernity and urbanity is not evoked solely to diagnose the obvious destruction of Sarajevo – to pronounce the act of *urbicide*. The correlation between the physical effort of navigating through Sarajevo and its identity as a city offers a lens through which to view this heterotopia of violence in its full complexity. In the case of Sarajevo, the dialectic relationship between the city and the body is heightened. It is a relationship of struggle and difficulty that paradoxically marks a wounded urban identity on the brink of extinction, while at the same time foregrounding the effort of sustaining the *citiness* of Sarajevo.

The film *Dnevnik Reditelja* (*Diary of a Director*), by Mirza Idrizović, one of Bosnia's leading directors, depicts this complex relationship between the body and the city. It features the war-torn city over four seasons and through several thematic segments entitled 'Window', 'Water',

'Letter', 'Assassination', 'Fire' and 'Stop'. In the film, urban, quotidian life seems both familiar and uncanny as the camera captures unremarkable, everyday moments in an environment that is made extraordinary and dangerous. For instance, in the opening segment called 'Window', Idrizović appears to be fixing a broken window in his stylish, tastefully furnished flat. A close-up reveals that he is actually trying to cover a gaping hole in the window frame with a piece of transparent nylon. An exterior shot of a beautiful apartment building from the period of the Austro-Hungarian monarchy follows; all the window panes, smashed from shelling, have been replaced with nylon.

The most pronounced aspect of the film, however, is the difficulty of navigating the city. Whether it is the daily routine of fetching water or the occasion of visiting a friend's grave, walking through the city becomes the central activity of the film. At one point during the segment entitled 'Water', Idrizović walks through debris and over the remnants of a destroyed bridge in order to get water for his family in the heat of summer. He walks slowly until gunshots are heard at close range at which point he accelerates his pace. The camera follows him in long shots conveying the duration of the walk and foregrounding the physical effort the body is making to safely reach the other part of the city. The footage is accompanied with two alternating soundtracks – a solemn piece of classical music and a well-known traditional Bosnian love song (*sevdalinka*) that contains the following refrain: 'Kad ja podjoh na Bem Bašu, na Bem Bašu na vodu...' ['When I went to fetch water on Bem Baša...']. The song – that both contrasts and illustrates, at face value, the filmed images of the city and its citizens, navigating through ruins to secure their water supplies – works as an ironic estrangement device and affirms the legendary sense of humour of Sarajevans. His laboured and dangerous walk through central Sarajevo casts him in a role that is part Camusian Sisyphus, part Beckettian clown.

In another segment called 'The Letter', Idrizović walks through the city and into an apartment building to deliver a letter. The camera follows him as he enters the hallway and climbs the stairs; the sound of gunfire is heard. Both the exterior and the interior of the building have been ravaged, making it hard to fathom how someone could even enter, let alone live in the building. Then the camera takes us outside again, capturing an elderly woman peacefully absorbed in gardening the plot in front of the building. The ordinary, life-affirming normalcy of the everyday appears surreal and invincible amongst the city's ruins. Filmic juxtapositions and associative editing further reinforce the notion of life in the besieged city as a simultaneous mixture of the uncanny and the familiar.

The relationship between the body and the city in the film emphasizes the urban landscape in extreme crisis where *citiness* – as a distinct, yet generic, quality that makes a city a city – is brought into question. *Citiness* is on the verge of turning into its opposite as the siege changes the features of the city, turning the place into a *wilderness*. During his long walk in search of water, Idrizović's citizen/protagonist is exposed to the relentless pounding of summer heat. In another segment entitled 'Stop,' he hitchhikes in the city on a blustery winter's day. Cars are few and far between and nobody stops. After some time, Idrizović gives up and continues on foot to his destination. In both instances, there is a heightened awareness of being exposed to elements associated more often with wilderness than with an urban environment where opportunities for shelter are normally possible. In another segment called 'Fire', Idrizović reveals an absurd urban-wilderness when he films his wife as she walks through the snow-covered ruins of the city searching for twigs. In this environment where there were no trees and where most of the time there was no electricity, heating and cooking during the cold winter months was impossible. Similarly, the *Sarajevo Survival Guide* uses bitter humour to depict the sense of an urban wilderness:

> Tree-cutting
>
> An entirely new city discipline. Tools for this sport are an electric saw and axes, small and big. One gets trained by cutting, trimming, splitting and piling the wood on the balcony or in the room, where they don't suffer so much humidity. Wood is stacked in the bedroom, hall, living room, in the next apartment whose owners have left or disappeared.
>
> (p. 51)

In order to survive, citizens are often forced to 'use' the city as if one were in a wilderness. Instead of meandering in and out of shops and cafes, these citizens venture out on a dangerous quest for even the barest of essentials – water and fire. The complexity, modernity and a certain degree of excess that have shaped the notion of the contemporary city are reduced and replaced by another set of imagery: flesh, debris and the basic elements – water, fire, air and earth. Both the film and the *Sarajevo Survival Guide* document the transformation of ways of *being* in the city as a direct consequence of violence inflicted upon the city and its citizens. Both Idrizović's camera and the *Sarajevo Survival Guide* adeptly capture the sharp, almost painful contrast between the documentary footage of the quasi surreal, post-apocalyptic landscape that Sarajevo had become and the resilient, familiar routines of everyday life.

Framing and breaking-out

The section of Idrizović's film entitled 'Assassination' mixes archival footage of a vibrant and lively Sarajevo from the 1980s with images of its destruction ten years later. Focusing on the grandeur of the historic building that housed the Sarajevo library, the film juxtaposes the beautiful architectural features of the edifice and its devastation after being attacked by the Serbian army. The segment also presented archival footage of the assassination of the Archduke Ferdinand in a silent montage sequence of city images, past and present, ending with the sound of Gavrilo Princip's gun-shot that killed the Austrian monarch and symbolically announced the beginning of the First World War. Idrizović depicts the city reduced to rubble, while still elevating it above the desperate conditions of the present moment that have all-but-stripped the city of its identity. In other words, the two-dimensional image of the suffering city has been deepened by reasserting the notion of Sarajevo as a palimpsest, where beauty is trapped in recurring cycles of violence and destruction. Idrizović resituates the city – previously reduced to the heterotopia of violence – in history.

The film reminds us that Sarajevo, like any other city, is a palimpsest. In doing so, it allows the victimized, ravaged body of the city not only to speak viscerally through its violation – where wounds are the only evidence of its existence and the only way to produce some kind of claim – but to re-enter logos, to take part in the discourse. Hannah Arendt wrote: '[…] violence, as distinguished from power, is mute; violence begins when speech ends' ('Essays in Understanding', p. 308). In *Regarding the Pain of Others*, Sontag draws from Simone Weil when she asserts that 'violence turns anybody subjected to it into a thing' (p. 11). The city-as-body does not only unfold through the dynamic of movement and stasis and through the ambiguity of living and lifeless, it also speaks. Beckett's Lucky, too, attempts to re-enter discourse, to *mean* something. Even if Lucky only serves to point out the impotence of this endeavour, his attempt, on some level, unequivocally counteracts inarticulate, mute violence. Unlike Lucky – whom Pozzo orders to put on his thinking hat – the possibility of speaking was not granted to the city by the master/oppressor but was reclaimed by the citizen/artist.

In her play, *Credible Witness*, playwright Timberlake Wartenbaker coined the term *historical paralysis* – to describe how war trauma has displaced her characters not only from any stable sense of place and identity, but also deprived them of the possibility of making meaning out of their suffering.[2] *Historical paralysis* is the inability to speak, act, and/or bear witness to one's own experience – a physical manifestation of silencing. The conditions of wilderness imposed on the city and the constant death threats that the citizens of Sarajevo experienced were also tactics of silencing. The making of Idrizović's film, like the stubborn persistence of Sarajevans to maintain the cultural life of their city, was a cry for help, an ethical challenge for its potential audiences and a mode of witnessing. Equally, if not more importantly, it was a speech act.

Performative utterances of the city become a form of activism, similar to what Butler has described as 'breaking out' of the frame in her analysis of the circulation of images of torture at Abu Ghraib and the poems by the prisoners of Guantanamo:

> The conditions are set for astonishment, outrage, revulsion, admiration, and discovery, depending on how the content is framed by shifting time and place. The movement of the image or the text outside the confinement is a kind of 'breaking out,' so that even though neither the image nor the poetry can free anyone from prison, or stop a bomb or, indeed, reverse the course of the war, they nevertheless do provide the conditions for breaking out of the quotidian acceptance of war and for a more generalized horror and outrage that will support and impel calls for justice and end the violence.
>
> (*Frames of War*, p. 11).

Cultural production in Sarajevo was a form of *breaking out* of the confinement that the siege had imposed both literally – central Sarajevo and some other parts of the city were sealed off – and metaphorically. Showing how power manipulates the terms of appearance, Butler compares the notion of 'breaking out' both to a prison break and in relation to the concept of 'frame' – meaning both the context within which a content is organized and in the sense of being framed – 'to be subject to a tactic by which evidence is orchestrated so to make false accusation true' (p. 11) and/or to impose a certain way of seeing the subject. Sarajevo appeared under several competing and contesting frames that imposed a certain *a priori* judgement of the city.

One of the most blatant examples of the 'framing' of Sarajevo was the political instrumentalization of the Markale massacre that took place on 5 February 1994 in an open market in central Sarajevo, when a grenade killed 67 people and injured 142. The Bosnian government immediately used the massacre to justify its plight. Bosnian Serbs, who had held the city under siege for 300 days at the time of the massacre, defended themselves with a conspiracy theory, according to which the Bosnian government orchestrated the tragedy to push its own agenda since the massacre coincided with Geneva peace talks that were to be held a few days later. This was not the first time that Bosnian Serbs had accused the other side of fabricating victims. Not surprisingly, the state-run media of Milošević's Serbia was always ready to back the leaders of Bosnian Serbs.[3] The Bosnian Serb side needed a perpetual reproduction of the frame whereby the city would be perceived as guilty. The media machinery of Milošević's Serbia produced a slightly different frame. According to them, not only were most of the injuries that the city suffered self-inflicted (and if they were not, claimed Belgrade's state media, the majority of victims turned out to be Serbs), but the siege itself was next to non-existent. This framing was not so much about controlling the perception of the war as it was about cultivating a logic of oblivion which enabled the appearance of 'normal life' in places like Belgrade, as discussed earlier in this book. In his analysis of the Markale incident via theatrical frames, Branislav Jakovljević notes:

> Before the crater made by the shell in the pavement at Markale had time to cool, United Nations Protection Forces (UNPROFOR) representatives, politicians, and journalists, first domestic and then foreign, swarmed the market. The investigation of the crime scene, the broadcasting of images around the globe, the charges and counter charges of responsibility for the massacre and the high-level political negotiations all began at the same time. As all these processes were evolving, the victims of the massacre were gradually replaced by their images.
>
> ('Theatre of Atrocities', p. 1816)

For Jakovljević, the term 'theatricality' has a different meaning than my own use elsewhere in this book. Whereas I use the word 'theatricality' to describe subversive, performative and political strategies and a meaning-making device in both theatre and everyday life, Jakovljević's use of the term has the opposite (i.e., negative) connotation. More specifically, for Jakovljević, theatricality denotes the point of non-distinction between reality and fabrication – the domination of the frame (i.e., in Butler's sense of the term) over the materiality of the event. Butler's 'framing' also requires a certain detachment, one that in Jakovljević's context of theatricality, replaces bodies with images, and, one might add, makes lost lives less grievable. Butler asks:

> We read about lives lost and are often given the numbers, but these stories are repeated every day, and the repetition appears endless, irremediable. And so we ask, what would it take not only to apprehend the precarious character of lives lost in war, but to have that apprehension coincide with an ethical and political opposition to the losses war entails?
>
> (*Frames of War*, p. 13)

To some extent, Jakovljević also talks about framing when asserting that 'the employment of theatricality survived the war in Bosnia' through Belgrade's tabloids that ascribed similar 'conspiratorial staging of atrocities' to other subjects (i.e., Kosovo Albanians).

Jakovljević reads Markale via Lyotard's concept of *disreality*, by which he means not 'a non-reality or fantasy, but a principle that corrodes what we commonly refer to as reality and the discourses that surround it. Disreality is the essence of war and its continuation by other means' ('Theatre of Atrocities', p. 1819). I would argue that Lyotard's disreality is embedded in Butler's frames of war and implicitly linked to her notion of the *grievability* – that 'precedes and makes possible the apprehension of the living being as living being, exposed to non-life from the start' (*Frames of War*, p. 13), but also has implications in producing 'iconic versions of populations who are eminently grievable, and others whose loss is no loss' (*Frames of War*, p. 24). In a way, Jakovljević also establishes a correlation between disreality and grievability when he concludes his Markale article in the following way: 'The site of atrocity becomes the motor of theatricality only insofar as its meaning as a site of pain is erased' ('Theatre of Atrocities', p. 1819).

Pain, however, plays one of the central roles in another dominant framework in the perception of Sarajevo as a site of suffering and as a site of sacrifice. Western media depicted the city through their endless replays of images of violence and destruction. The city became framed as a site of passive suffering, mute and frozen in its *historical paralysis*, while mediated through voices of politicians, journalists and Western intellectuals. Paradoxically, elements of suffering and pain were also present, albeit perversely, in some of the most racist framing of the city and the Bosnian war. For instance, an official document on the Markale massacre issued by the Serbian Ministry of Information claims that suffering and sacrifice is engrained in the Muslim mentality 'that starts from the axiom that it is an honour to die for Islam' (in Jakovljević, 'Theatre of Atrocities', p. 1818).[4] As asserted earlier, although the suffering of Sarajevo is undeniable, it is important to foreground the necessity of *breaking-out*, whether the imposed frames tended to vilify the city, justifying its destruction, or to work in favour of its survival – the perspective from above needs to be counteracted by alternative frames from below.

Moreover, instances of *breaking-out* that most resisted the erasure of pain from the site of violence were often neither violent nor painful in themselves. In his introduction to the *Metastases of Enjoyment*, Slavoj Žižek calls for an expansion and alteration of the frame within which the tragedy of Sarajevo has been read and understood in a manner that is akin to Bulter's notion of *breaking out*:

> [...] reporters compete with each other on who will find a more repulsive scene – lacerated child bodies, raped women, starved prisoners: all this is good fodder for hungry Western eyes. However, the media are far more sparing of words apropos of how the residents of Sarajevo desperately endeavour to maintain the appearance of normal life. The tragedy of Sarajevo is epitomized in an elderly clerk who takes a walk to his office every day as usual, but has to quicken his pace at a certain crossroads because a Serbian sniper lurks on the nearby hill; in a disco that operates 'normally,' although one can hear explosions in the background; in a young woman who forces her way through ruins to the court in order to obtain a divorce so that she can start to live with her lover; in the issue of the Bosnian cinema monthly that appeared in Sarajevo in 1993 and published essays on Scorcese and Almodóvar...
>
> (p. 2)

The film *Diary of a Director*, like numerous other examples of life in besieged Sarajevo – from cultural events to weddings – does not show mere violence and destruction, but rather, as already pointed out, the struggle for normalcy – for simple performances – whether private or public – of everyday life in the city. In the 'Fire' segment of the film, a woman comes home, uses the twigs found in the rubble to light a small, improvised stove and makes some coffee. Idrizović, his wife and a couple of other people sit in the kitchen and drink the coffee. This simple daily ritual of having a cup of coffee with a friend, a neighbour, a family member – common in the Balkans – temporarily recuperates a sense of place and community. It is almost a moment of regaining a degree of freedom and safety, however fragile, within an extreme environment that in many ways resembles a ghetto. Simple, daily acts of salvaging normalcy not only reveal a private/public dichotomy of what it means to dwell in an extreme city, but also offer a point of entry for us – *its intimate outsiders*. The 'Fire' episode ends with a long shot of the woman smoking and drinking her coffee – a stand-alone moment when the outside world is shut out. This small, daily pleasure is extraordinary for two reasons. First, because it could have happened almost anywhere, or at least in any Balkan city, at that given moment – I might have had a cup of coffee and a cigarette at the same time in my flat in Belgrade. Second, because it could happen, and indeed was happening, in besieged Sarajevo in 1992. This moment also allows entrance into the city by means of identification with a daily ritual – a tiny bit of shared experience with an urban environment transformed by war from a vibrant Balkan city into a heterotopia of violence. Yet it also forces us to comprehend the difference. Moments of small, shared experiences enable a better understanding of the extreme suffering within which small pleasures have carved their place. This comprehension of someone else's pain – through a dialectics of both identification and difference – corresponds to Luc Boltanski's critique of the politics of pity invoked in Jakovljević's article and to Hannah Arendt's writings on understanding and imagination. Following Boltanski, and applying the politics of pity to the initial investigation and subsequent interpretation of the Markale massacre, Jakovljević writes: '[...] compassion is religious, pity is political: whereas compassion require proximity, pity establishes distance, and while compassion is particular and practical, pity is general and spectatorial' ('Theatre of Atrocities', p. 1816). While Markale epitomized contesting frames of war constructed through theatricalization (in Jakovljević's sense of the term) and the politics of pity, the images of everyday life captured in Idrizović's film enable a breaking-out of the frame. In other words, they offer a possibility for Boltanski's compassion to take place. Idrizović's camera depicts everyday life in the city through his own personal perspective. The film is both a document and a meditation on the city, with shots that are mostly silent, unrushed – allowing the viewer to stay with the images for some time, to take them in, to feel the close proximity of people and furniture in Idrizović's kitchen as coffee is being made, to imagine what it might be like to live that reality. This is the same kind of imagination that Arendt finds crucial in critical thinking:

> [By] force of imagination it makes the others present and thus moves potentially in a space which is public, open to all sides; in other

> words, it adopts the position of Kant's world citizen. To think with the enlarged mentality – that means you train your imagination to go visiting.
>
> ('Appendix/judging, p. 257)

Breaking out of the frame is a provocation and a challenge to the politics of pity. *Diary of a Director* enables the spectator to become an *intimate outsider* who understands the suffering of the other by force of her imagination and relates to the other through compassion. The provocation is in the film's intimacy where compassion needs to become a mode of ethical practice and where imagination, as a force of critical thinking, carries responsibility – the responsibility for the other that, one might argue, also lies at the core of Butler's concept of the precariousness of life:

> the very idea of precariousness implies dependency on social networks and conditions, suggesting that there is no 'life itself' at issue here, but always and only conditions of life, life as something that requires conditions in order to become liveable life and, indeed, in order to become grievable.
>
> (*Frames of War*, pp. 22–3)

Hence, cultural production during the 'impossible' circumstances of the siege also answered the ethical dilemmas posed from the distance of intellectual salons that was touched upon earlier in this book: Is it ethical to sing, dance, paint, make films, play, stage shows in a city ravaged by war? The question about the ethics of performing in a city under siege could only be asked by outsiders – in a frame constructed through the politics of pity. For the citizens of Sarajevo, confined between the deafening sounds of artillery and the silence of dead bodies, to re-enter the discourse – to put on Lucky's thinking hat – could only be an act of subversion and bravery. This act (or series of acts) of breaking out of the frame(s) of war brought the city back from its absurd state of wilderness into history (not necessarily a better place, but certainly a more meaningful one).

Anthropomorphic city

> if someone, somewhere, somehow were to build a totally new city on the grand scale of cosmos to man and cosmos to the human cell, then that city's external form would represent an ideal diagram

> of the universe in miniature while concealing the contours of the human within. Think of the vibrant, beautifully ordered mind necessary to envisage the city as a humanoid construction, a construction-as-paraphrase.
>
> Is it a mere chance? The map of the ravaged Sarajevo, as well as it can be pieced together from television clips, resembles nothing so much as a man who has toppled into a cauldron and is struggling to raise his head above the surface.
>
> (Bodanović, 'A Human Sarajevo', *Balkan Blues*, p. 69)

The poster for the 1994 Sarajevo Winter Festival (Sarajevska zima) featured cellist Vedran Smajlović wearing a black tuxedo, sitting with his instrument in the midst of the ruins of the National Library, his hands on his face in a gesture that reads simultaneously as mourning and as prayer (Illustration 18). Although the scene was staged, the idea came from an actual activity that took place daily from the beginning of the siege. For three years, Smajlović played his cello every day in various locations throughout the city – from the promenade and cultural landmarks to ruins and graveyards. Always dressed in a black tuxedo, Smajlović performed his outdoor concerts even when there was no audience and when his music had to compete with the sound of gunfire. More than a piece of Festival memorabilia of Sarajevo under siege, however, the poster of the cellist is a document that depicts a performance in which the very use of space was a political act.

It is in the act/image of Smajlović performing amidst the ruins of the Sarajevo library that versions of both Michel Foucault's concept of *heterotopia* and Edward Soja's *Thirdspace* emerged within the palimpsest of the city. Foucault describes libraries and museums as heterotopias of time in which 'time does not cease to accumulate' ('Of Other Space', p. 355). Sarajevo's ruined library, where hundreds of invaluable medieval manuscripts now lay entombed in ashes, adds a somewhat paradoxical twist to Foucault's point. The ruined library, however, does not necessarily embody the erosion of time as a direct opposite to Foucault's functional *heterotopia*. Rather, the ruins continue to signify the meaning and the memory of the space, even if both the shape and function of that space has been transformed. Moreover, Smajlović's performance on the library ruins confirmed the primary function of the destroyed building – its role as a cultural institution. The image, nevertheless, reveals other layers of this *heterotopia*, established through a violent insertion of another spatial and temporal dimension – the condensed present tense of the war zone.

Illustration 18 The Sarajevo Cellist, photo by M. Evstafiev

The ambiguity of this space is evident in the contrast between the 'setting' and the person – the cellist performing on the ruins of a bombed-out city, dressed as if he were playing in a concert hall. The city is at the same time a cultural centre and a war zone. Its libraries, museums, mosques and churches, buildings and streets are – in the moment of Smajlović's performance – both repositories of cultural memory and death traps. Contrasts that render the performances of the Sarajevo cellist somewhat surreal also subvert expectations and make the familiar strange by inserting into the iconography of a war zone the images and sounds of a concert hall. Through the act of performing, Smajlović temporarily produced an alternative space. The performance established Soja's notion of *Thirdspace* – a space of intervention and resistance through a symbolic act that subverted the finality of destruction. In Soja's and Lefebvre's terms, the performance produced an alternative to both *First Space* – a site of erasure where all that remained of the National Library was rubble – and *Second Space* – the representational, ideological and symbolic dimensions that the ruin evoked. *Heterotopia* here emerges as a space of defamiliarization and resistance, since the performance of the cellist produces an 'other' space at the very moment when 'otherness' and difference – whether it be ethnic, political or cultural – is met with gunfire. The production of *Thirdspace* through performance asserts the idea of continuity, or in Sontag's words, the 'expression of normality', into a context where rupture and destruction have been the norm and *modus operandi.*

Flesh into stone/stone into flesh

The cellist of Sarajevo, who subsequently inspired Steven Galloway's novel of the same name, was an icon of the city's anthropomorphism, which emerged during the war as a unique preservation strategy. The anthropomorphism of Sarajevo is not embodied in its architecture per se, but in the citizens performing the city. Since most of the cultural institutions where either ruined or too dangerous to use, local artists, like Smajlović, persisted in performing the function of artistic venues and cultural sites even when they were reduced to rubble. They performed on the ruins of libraries and in theatre basements, exhibited in hallways of apartment buildings, made installations of debris, thus salvaging and rebuilding the city's culture with any means left. Citizens performed the cultural life of the city, turning various performance practices into urban, communal rituals of survival.

The anthropomorphism of Sarajevo is not only about re-humanizing the devastated city and breathing life into the ruins, it is a more ambiguous and dialectical affair of turning flesh into stone and stone into flesh. This anthropomorphism stands between two forces that destabilize the relationship between a human being and an object – between living and lifeless – theatricality and violence. In his article 'Man and Object in Theatre', Czech Structuralist Juri Veltruský wrote that in theatre a lifeless object can be perceived as a performing subject, and conversely, a live human being may appear as an element completely without will:

> The function of each component in the individual situation (and in drama as a whole) is the result of the constant tension between activity and passivity in terms of the action, which manifests itself in a constant flow back and forth between the individual components, people and things. It is therefore impossible to draw a line between subject and object, since each component is potentially either.
>
> (p. 90)

Veltruský starts with the premise that in reality the relationship between the animated and the lifeless is a stable one, whereas theatre has the potential to destabilize this relationship, creating a 'dialectic antinomy' between the human body and the object on stage.

Nevertheless, everyday life in besieged Sarajevo unfolded theatrically, almost resembling the body-object relationship that Veltruský ascribed almost exclusively to the theatrical stage. Violence itself often involves a similar kind of dialectic antinomy between living and lifeless, which 'turns anybody subjected to it into a thing' (Sontag, *Regarding the Pain of Others*, p. 11). Yet this dialectic antinomy is ingrained in the anthropomorphism of Sarajevo in a more complex way. It, too, manifests itself through ambiguity between passivity and activity: the passivity of the vulnerable body becoming an object, a target for the sniper, and the activity of the body in its daily acts of survival. It is the body that walks several kilometres to fetch water, but afterwards takes pleasure in a cup of coffee prepared on a makeshift stove. It is the body that runs through back alleys of the city to escape sniper fire, making its way to a theatre show. Performances in extreme circumstances that involve a high degree of risk, like Smajlović's concerts on the city ruins, foreground the symbiotic and anthropomorphic link between bodies and buildings. In other words, such performances stress the high degree of identification between person and space/object – between flesh and stone.

In Galloway's imagining of the Sarajevo cellist, the identification between flesh and stone is almost palpable when he writes:

> When the mortars destroyed the Sarajevo Opera Hall, the cellist felt as if he were inside the building, as if the bricks and glass that once bound the structure together became projectiles that sliced and pounded into him, shredding him beyond recognition. He was the principal cellist of the Sarajevo Symphony Orchestra. That was what he knew how to be. He made the idea of music an actuality. When he stepped on stage in his tuxedo he was transformed into an instrument of deliverance. He gave the people who came to listen what he loved most in the world.
>
> (*The Cellist of Sarajevo*, p. 4)

Like Glamočak's Lucky, who felt that he was the city, the protagonist of Galloway's fiction experienced the Opera Hall building as part of his own body. Galloway's fiction imagines very precisely the specific ambiguity between the citizen and the city as a constantly shifting relationship – a dialectic antinomy between flesh and stone. In Smajlović's real-life performances, the ambiguity between living and lifeless was played out further through its unique paradoxes: the live performance on library ruins and graveyards reanimated these spaces, while in return, the presence of the live performing body on the ruins foregrounded the void, the loss, the violence – almost trading places with the lifeless. Indeed more often than not, Smajlović played for the dead.

The anthropomorphic nature of Smajlović's performance at the same time resists and echoes Balkan myths of the ritual sacrifice of humans in order to sustain a city. One of the most famous myths is depicted in a medieval Serbian epic poem called *Zidanje Skadra* (*Building of Skadar*).[5] In the poem, people try to build the city of Skadar, but no matter what they erect during the day, a malevolent fairy destroys overnight. The fairy is building her own city in the clouds and she will not be satisfied until she has received a human sacrifice. The citizens sacrifice a young mother, burying her alive in the city walls, and the fairy, finally, leaves the city in peace. In the context of Bosnian conflict, this myth could in part be read as an allegory where Skadar stands for the besieged Sarajevo, while the city in the clouds that the cruel fairy builds shares a common logic with narratives of the imagined community of Serbian nationalism. My main interest here, however, is the relationship between the live body and the building as in the iconic performances of the Sarajevo cellist. There is an element of sacrifice in the cellist's performance as far as the risk of playing outside, even during the severest attacks on the city, is concerned. In Galloway's fictional rendering of this iconic figure, there is a scene where a Serbian sniper is about to kill the cellist, but gets so enchanted by the music that he stops and listens. However, the notion of sacrifice does not go further than the risk factors involved in the performance of the cellist, and in other similar acts, including audiences who braved their way to concerts and theatres. The performance rituals that established the unique anthropomorphism of Sarajevo are anti-sacrificial in nature. In this case, to save the city from destruction – to reanimate the buildings – it is crucial that the citizen/artist survives its own act of sacrifice. These counter-sacrificial rituals are based on the relentless repetition of performing the city and for that it needs bodies that act and move. The counter-sacrifices emerge as acts of alternative reconstruction.

Spoliation

Historian of architecture, Amra Hadžimuhamedović writes:

> To destroy a city does not always mean to demolish an entire built environment. Destruction of a city takes place when its memory is destroyed and when landmarks within the structure of a city are demolished that have through history been identified as its architectural heritage.
>
> ('Grad Razdrag', p. 114)

Hadžimuhamedović views war as a mass ritual of sacrifice, which had its full expression in the Balkans on the cusp of the twentieth and twenty-first centuries and is most visible through rituals of demolishing cultural and historical heritage. Through this destruction of the *Other*, a cultural aspect that has also 'shaped the identity of the destroyer, becomes extinguished' (p. 114). According to Hadžimuhamedović, temples of the *other* have been one of the key targets of military actions from ancient times to the Balkan conflict. She uses the word 'temple' as 'a mental map, which determines the structure of every city' (p. 114). In a sense, the destruction of the temple is closely related to the destruction of a community – erasing the centre that symbolically, culturally (not necessarily religiously) structured the city and its daily life. Hence, we might add, the notion of 'mental map' with the temple as its focal point, implies a broader understanding of the temple – not only and always as a building of sacred architecture, but an urban landmark that is also a repository of cultural memory (i.e., the Sarajevo library). Hadžimuhamedović recognizes four phases in the ritualistic process of destruction: (1) de-sacralization of space; (2) destruction of the sacral shape (building); (3) destruction of memory (taking the remains away); and (4) giving new meaning to the space (i.e., building a parking lot on the grounds where the sacred building stood). Against this backdrop of ritualistic destruction the anthropomorphism of Sarajevo – understood through performances about the city, in the city, and on the ruins of the city – could be read as a counter-ritual – as a performance of alternative reconstruction. In other words, performance practices in Sarajevo during the war were a means of keeping the identity of the city, of salvaging the focal points of its structure, and of preserving its mental map. These urban practices that managed to maintain the mental map of the city could be described through the architectural concept of *spoliation* as a form of alternative reconstruction.

Spolia, from Latin (spoil), the reuse of earlier building material in a new monument has the following meanings: (1) literary, displaying the spoils of war that were in ancient Rome used to decorate the houses of warriors; (2) a Latin term for skinning; (3) reviving the past in the present, by inserting an old building, or its elements, into a new one; (4) finally, in the legal context, spoliation of evidence means the withholding, hiding or destroying of evidence. Hadžimuhamedović points to the connection between these meanings when she writes: 'destroying of monuments and building their remains into an entirely different context represents a way of skinning the city of its layers'('Grad Razgrad', p. 119). Etymological roots of the term spolia/spoliation, thus, highlight at least two opposing tendencies – destruction and preservation – that reveal a peculiar paradox. Both tendencies – to destroy/erase and to preserve – imply change. In order to destroy the *other* culture its rubble is used in a different context through which its original meaning and history becomes erased; while in order for the structure to be preserved, its rubble is reused to preserve the meaning of the structure by building in additional elements.

On the one hand, spoliation is about violence and erasure of *the Other* – destruction, appropriation and altering the meaning of the ruined whole and even altering the meaning of the rubble. On the other hand, it also means a selective reconstruction of the past, building the past into the present – reviving the ruin by building it into a new structure. Hadžimuhamedović defines spoliation as 'a kind of alternative reconstruction, which in some instances can become its own opposite' ('Grad Razdrag', p. 119). She problematizes the notion of reconstruction and questions its possibilities of preservation through building and architectural projects based on recycling destroyed historical buildings and monuments. She traces the notion of spoliation from the medieval period – in relation to which the term has most often been used – where remains of Roman buildings were built into Christian temples representing the triumph of Christianity over the pagans, to the recent reconstruction of mosques in the Bosnian towns of Banja Luka and Foča after the war. In all these instances, she argues, spoliation has been more successful at erasing or manipulating the memory that the recycled debris conveyed, rather than salvaging it.

I would like to look at performance interventions in Sarajevo, such as the ones by the famous cellist, as alternative reconstructive strategies that operate within the framework of spoliation. Unlike most of the architectural projects that Hadžimuhamedović criticizes, *performative spoliation* has the potential to truly emerge as a form of resistance against destruction and the erasure of memory. As with other instances of spoliation, performative interventions of this kind are a form of alternative reconstruction that modifies the debris to greater or lesser extent. In the daily concerts of the Sarajevo cellist, spoliation repeatedly unfolds in the ephemerality of performance. The performance on the Sarajevo library ruins symbolically reconstructs the notion of a cultural institution from the amorphous rubble, but through a different usage of the space. The ruins are, and are not, the library. It is impossible to engage in the space as if it were still a library, but it is possible to treat the ruined building as a cultural space, where one might perform a concert. Thus the performance both mourns the destruction and the void that the ruin stands for and, at the same time, reconstructs the library itself – as a repository of cultural memory in the mind-map of the city and also as an actual and functional cultural space. Given that the spoliation emerges in the here and now of the performance, it is impermanent and performative in nature. Yet, the repetition of the performance – the cellist plays everyday in different locations – still functions as a reconstruction ritual that not only preserves the memory of a historical building, but keeps the ruins alive.

While performances on top of ruins, or within semi-destroyed cultural institutions, such as Smajlović's concerts or the daily rehearsals of the Sarajevo String Quartet, reasserted the identity of the building/object, projects such as collages made of rubble by artist and filmmaker, Nedžad Begović, offered a different version of *performative spoliation*. In his documentary, *War Art*, we follow Begović as he wanders through the deserted streets of Sarajevo rummaging though rubble and collecting bits and pieces of objects that have lost their identity – pieces of metal from burned vehicles and streetcars, broken glass and pieces of wood from the shattered windows of houses, the remains of everyday objects that seemingly do not play an important part in the palimpsest of the city. Once in his studio, Begović transforms the remains of the city, devoid of their function and meaning, into new objects. In his collages, rubble turns into figures of birds, horses, plants. Exhibiting his art in Sarajevo's makeshift galleries, Begović, like Smajlović, contributes to the preservation of the city's mind-map. Although there is no resemblance between the collages and their original material, this process – in the given circumstances – also works as a form of alternative reconstruction. Begović uses the word alchemy to describe his strategy of transforming the spoils of war into artistic objects. Moreover, by working with fragments of everyday objects that by nature are far less subjected to big historical narratives and claims, Begović is able to subvert the finality of destruction by entirely changing the meaning and function of the destroyed objects.

Both Smajlović's concerts and Begović's alchemical process of turning rubble into art – represent a new aspect of spoliation that emerges through the movement and performance of live bodies in space. This kind of spoliation has, of course, a different temporality than relatively permanent, architectural and recycled reconstructions. Unlike the architectural and building projects of spoliation, performance interventions, temporally located in the here and now, have the possibility of resisting the imposition of fixed meanings. *Performance as spoliation* can neither fully represent the triumph over destruction nor perform the kind of selective erasure that victors' reconstruction projects often do. Whenever Smajlović came out to perform in the streets of besieged Sarajevo, the tension between erasure and preservation, between violence and resistance, was played out. In other words, the ruins and graveyards of the city became heterotopic performance spaces – both places of death and sites of unique live performances. Performance interventions, viewed as a specific kind of spoliation, are palimpsest-making processes that embody the layers of the city that has been *skinned* through violence and terror.

6
Theatricality versus Bare Life

Haris Pašović asserts that the cultural production in Sarajevo 'was not some unique feature of Sarajevans and that it would have happened in other places since this is a human reaction to dehumanized circumstances. Primarily, it is an anthropological dimension rather than a special trait of our people' (quoted in Diklić, *Teatar u ratnom Sarajevu*, p. 205). He points out common traits in the cultural activity of Sarajevo during the war with the recent history of other cities including the Leningrad siege and the Warsaw ghetto during the Second World War. One might also add the Theresienstadt concentration camp where inmates, most of them highly educated, were given some resources and a certain degree of freedom enabling a form of urban life and activity to flourish under extreme circumstances, until most of the inhabitants got deported to the death-camps. Although the comparison between Nazi concentration camps and the Sarajevo siege is, as Pašović himself admits, limited and problematic for a number of reasons, it is relevant to our attempt to grasp how theatre, performance and overall cultural activity in the besieged city shaped the meaning of being a citizen. Why is it possible to talk about theatre, performance and rich cultural production in the context of Sarajevo and Theresienstadt, for example, but much less so in the context of, say, Auschwitz? The answer inevitably brings Giorgio Agamben's notions of bare life and the camp into discussion. To what extent did the besieged Sarajevo embody Agamben's concept of the camp and to what extent was life in the city a bare life?

Bare life

In formulating his notion of bare life, Agamben's point of departure is the Ancient Greek distinction between *Zoë*, 'which expressed the simple fact of living common to all living beings (animals, humans or gods), and *bios*, which signified the form or manner of living peculiar to a single individual or group' ('Form-of-Life', in *Means Without Ends*, p. 3). He then identifies his notion of a naked life as a 'presupposed common element that is always possible to isolate in each of the numerous forms of life' ('Form-of-Life', p. 3). This possibility to isolate the axiomatic bare life from other forms of life is, in some instances and on its political level, akin to Butler's concept of framing, discussed earlier, through which some lives appear less grievable than others. As Agamben illustrates, drawing from Ancient Greek and Roman law, a bare life is one that can be taken but cannot be sacrificed – in other words, a life framed so that it appears devalued in all its aspects except as confirmation of the political power that rules over it. Agamben writes:

> The state of exception, which is what the sovereign each and every time decides, takes place precisely when naked life – which normally appears rejoined to the multifarious forms of social life – is explicitly put into question and revoked as the ultimate foundation of political power. The ultimate subject that needs to be at once turned into the exception and included in the city is always naked life.
>
> ('Form-of-Life', pp. 5–6)

The street scenes from Sarajevo that regularly appeared in media reports and that constituted the everyday reality of the city, illustrate to a great extent what bare life looked like. Hungry people and stray dogs wandering through city ruins in search of food always under the watchful eye of the enemy sniper; water queues, filth and stench, and spilled brains on the pavement – all suggest life reduced to literal survival in Agamben's terms:

> Biological life, which is the secularized form of naked life and which shares its unutterability and impenetrability, thus constitutes the real forms of life literally as forms of survival: biological life remains inviolate in such forms as that obscure threat that can suddenly actualize itself in violence, in extraneousness, in illness, in accidents. It is the invisible sovereign that stares at us behind the dull-witted masks of the powerful who, whether or not they realize it, govern us in its name.
>
> ('Form-of-Life', p. 8)

In these images from Sarajevo, one can clearly see the actualization of naked life through political violence. As other bodies in extreme circumstances that are both physical and political, the suffering bodies of Sarajevans remind us of the intrinsic link between biological life and politics, since even the tendency to separate the body from its political dimension is essentially about power. Hence, even if we talk about biological life as a secularized naked life, we are still, following Foucault's line of reasoning, talking about a form of biopolitics.

For Agamben, inasmuch 'as its inhabitants have been stripped of every political status and reduced completely to naked life, the camp is [...] the most absolute biopolitical space that has ever been realized – a space in which power confronts nothing other than pure biological life without any mediation' ('What is a Camp?', in *Means Without Ends*, p. 41). A camp is the materialization of the state of exception that is often invoked through a rhetoric of protection from a threat that needs to be isolated. In this sense, the rhetoric of protection is the common denominator in a variety of historically very different camp contexts – from colonial wars to Nazi death-camps, and from the camps of the most recent wars in the Balkans to Guantanamo. Agamben somewhat provocatively points out that 'we will have to admit to be facing a camp virtually every time that such a structure is created, regardless of the nature of the crimes committed in it and regardless of the denomination and specific topography it might have' ('What is a Camp?', pp. 41–2). Aspects of Sarajevo, a city that clearly had features of a camp, resembled Theresienstadt. According to the argument of Bosnian Serbs, the three-year-long siege of the city, an invocation of a state of exception, was justified in order to protect its folk from the Muslim population that was perceived as both a physical and a political threat. The material conditions of the siege, more often than not, reduced life to mere survival.

On the one hand, the images and footage of Sarajevo that were widely circulated through media outlets often epitomized bare life. Indeed, we saw starved, wounded, suffering bodies of Sarajevans, like all other suffering bodies, used in a variety of political scenarios but stripped of any political status. On the other hand, Sarajevo could not be fully reduced to the notion of city-camp space inasmuch as the life of its citizens was not a naked life at each and every moment of the siege. All the examples of cultural production, and some aspects of everyday public and private life in the city, could be read as forms of resistance to naked life. Sarajevo was a place of tension and ambiguity rather than a mere embodiment of political violence. The city was and was not a camp; life in Sarajevo was and was not naked. That is what makes Sarajevo truly interesting as a case study. The inhabitants resisted the violence of naked life in a variety of ways – from performing civic roles and duties and maintaining social rituals such as weddings and funerals, to vibrant cultural production. The possibility to counteract naked life with other forms of life enabled Sarajevans to have agency – to find ways to assert their rights and responsibilities as citizens.

It goes without saying that the possibility of resistance and ambiguity could never have emerged in Sarajevo without a certain degree of freedom, individual autonomy and safety. These are the axiomatic minimal conditions without which resistance to bare life would be impossible. Whereas these axiomatic conditions existed in Sarajevo and Theresienstadt enabling a communal life, including various forms of performances and cultural activity, they were fully revoked in places like Auschwitz. Haris Pašović also talks about the physical circumstances without which theatre in the city would not have been possible:

> If it wasn't for those defending the city we wouldn't be able to perform downtown, because the *chetniks* would have physically entered the city [...] This was one set of circumstances. Otherwise they would have come into the city and made us leave as had happened in Prijedor, Banja Luka, Srebrenica, etc. [...] Thus our audience was in a way also these fighters who defended the city. In the morning they would be on the front line, in the afternoon they would come to see our performances – not all of them, but quite a good number. In that sense, our audience enabled us to perform.
>
> (quoted in Diklić, *Teatar u ratnom Sarajevu*, pp. 201–2)

In the ecological triad of individual psyche, collective self and the city, there is a direct relationship between physical space and freedom. The axiomatic condition for theatre and performances to take place in the city was essentially based on relative degrees of physical distance from the forces that invoked the state of exception. In some parts of the city, the proximity between a person running down the street and the hillside sniper fire was no more than 50 metres – close enough to have to run for your bare life but far enough away to have a chance to escape. Although the siege imposed some aspects of the camp onto the city, the state of exception was never fully materialized. Back alleys, basements, secluded courtyards and gardens, tucked away houses, apartment-building corridors and underground spaces enabled a city-within-the-city to sustain itself more or less under the radar of sniper-fire and mortar shells. Even under siege conditions, the city asserted itself in opposition to the camp status. It emerged as an ambiguous space – at one and the same time controlled and uncontrollable. In his novella, *Apocalypse from the Recycling Bin*

(*Apokalipsa iz recycle bina*), poet, writer and former soldier in the Bosnian Army, Faruk Šehić, describes his encounter with Sarajevo in December 1995 when, with a group of soldiers, he entered the city:

> It felt as if life here doesn't exist at all. Only grey buildings dotted with shrapnel, grey pavement, grey streetcar tracks. Ghastly was the feeling of standing in the street in the hope of seeing something alive. The silence that filled the Sarajevo air was worse than all the fighting I went through as a solder of the 5th corpus. Desolation was getting into my sleeves like the winter cold. What I saw and felt was surrealism in the real world, escaped from within book covers, painting frames, and film screens. In that moment I had only one wish, to get on a bus and out of this dead city.
>
> The first place where I encountered a living soul was the coffee house Cinema. Here the colour black was intimate and warm. [...] Then I discovered the true image of the city, hidden and vibrant in secluded coffee houses and clubs where everything unfolded as if the outside world did not exist. In addition to the Cinema, Obala, Kuk, and Lisac were also open and many more invisible ghettoes. If any city lived its underground life, it was Sarajevo during the siege. The entire city was a vast underground gallery with an astonishing instinct for life and joy. There was no anger and no anxiety, we were all still embalmed[1] by the war, when life is celebrated most.
>
> (pp. 263–4)

This description captures what it was that made Sarajevo different from Theresienstadt: the latter, despite its cultural activity and some degree of internal autonomy, remained a strictly controlled space – a camp. In contrast, the Sarajevo siege – justified by the political and military enforcement of a state of exception – never truly materialized as a camp. In the case of Theresienstadt, a minimal axiomatic degree of freedom and safety was temporarily granted to the inhabitants by the sovereign power (following Agamben's thought, a 'sovereign' is the one who authorizes a state of exception) and subsequently revoked. Although Theresienstad mimicked a city in its layout and in its cultural life, its inhabitants were no longer citizens – they were inmates. In the case of Sarajevo, the physical and political circumstances were very different as central Sarajevo was besieged, but not occupied.[2] In the 'underground life' of the city, which could never be fully contained by the state of exception, the inhabitants alone reclaimed their safety, freedom and agency, asserting their status and role as citizens.

Theatricality

In opposition to his concept of bare life, Agamben sets up the notion of *form-of-life* to describe life as that which 'can never be separated from its form, a life in which it is never possible to isolate something such as naked life' ('Form-of-Life', in *Means Without Ends*, p. 4). According to Agamben, intellectuality and community are intrinsically linked to life being constituted as a form-of-life: 'Intellectuality and thought are not a form of life among others in which life and social production articulate themselves, but they are rather *the unitary power that constitutes the multiple forms of life as form-of-life*' (p. 11). In her critique of the refugee figure, which plays a central role in Agamben's discourse on naked life and camp, scholar Patricia Owens turns to Hannah Arendt and to performance practice. She suggests that the possibility of resistance is not in the effort to reclaim 'bare life', but is:

> [...] wholly dependent on the ability to forge a public realm grounded on the appropriate distinction between nature and political artifice, between human life and political world.
>
> ('Reclaiming "Bare Life"?', p. 569)

Naked life presupposes the collapse of private and public spheres into one another, while the notion of form-of-life necessitates the opposite – a formation of public sphere. Throughout the siege, Sarajevans reclaimed the public sphere in a multiplicity of ways including theatre productions, performances on the ruins of cultural institutions, publishing the newspaper *Oslobodjenje* and radio-programmes such as *Zid*. When public institutions had either been destroyed or deemed unsafe, the public realm moved to private spaces. Filmmaker Nihad Kreševljaković reminisces about the *mobile university* that often took place in his own backyard:

> Lectures and discussions took place under an apple tree in our garden where there is a gorgeous view of Sarajevo. A few American and local professors gave lectures in a variety of disciplines including art, architecture, history, etc. Everything started within the project 'Beba Univerzum' organized by MESS and FAMA.[3] Suada Kapić[4] had an idea to create a mobile university where university lecturers would go to various locations to give accessible, public lectures in their areas of expertise. Tvrdko Kulenović[5] gave a lecture in Svrza's house, while all the other lectures took place in ours because it was easier to organize

> them. Behija Zlatar, Boris Minavić, and Mila Kuposović talked about the history of Sarajevo. Dževad Jezbašić talked about railways, Professor Numić lectured on ancient philosophy. William Hunt's lecture was on the Vietnam War; while John Fine and Robert Donia[6] talked about the medieval Bosnian state. All these lectures included discussions where both experts and the wider public participated. Erika Munk gave a lecture,[7] and Vanessa Redgrave talked about her life and acting in general. More than 200 people came, filling every bit of space in our garden. All of this happened in '94 in the midst of the besieged, bombarded, and tortured city.
>
> (quoted in Diklić, *Teatar u ratnom Sarajevu*, p. 145)

This example illustrates Arendt's and Owen's notion of resistance by which '*bare life* is repudiated and a new, worldly community is formed around resistance to injustice: that is, when individuals *begin to create public space between them*' (Owens, '"Reclaiming 'Bare Life"?, pp. 577–8). I would argue that in the case of Sarajevo, both the creation of the public sphere and Agamben's 'intellectuality as antagonistic power and form-of-life' ('Form-of-Life', p. 11) more often than not sustained itself through communal theatricality. This theatricality encompassed different aspects – from putting a performance on stage to everyday communal encounters where people used jokes, jests and occasional enactments to give both meaning and distance to their situation. Theatricalization of everyday life – as self-conscious framing of behaviour for viewing by others – emerges as a means of making and maintaining a public sphere. Theatricality, both as a communal experience of some form of theatre and performance and as the theatricalization of everyday life, was a way of meaning-making – of inserting thought into the violence of naked life.

Nihad Kreševljaković's film, *Do You Remember Sarajevo?* clearly depicts the role of theatricality as a means of resistance to bare life. It is a deliberately rough cut documentary that features various episodes from everyday life in the city during the siege with commentary from the author's friends, neighbours and family. The film starts in the early days of the war and captures a voice from Sarajevo television calling for citizens to film the reality unravelling around them as a mode of witnessing. Kreševljaković's camera bears witness to first attacks on the city and to the confusion and dismay of the citizens. It depicts the siege from the perspective of citizens as they watch grenades fall on the city from their apartment windows or, as they squat, panic-stricken, in underground shelters. The footage from the early days of the siege is often shaky as the filmmaker moves quickly to safety or to film another attack. Voices around him are shouting: 'Look what they are doing to the city!', 'It hit Hotel Europe! Hotel Europe is burning… .' Kreševljaković continued to film the city and its citizens throughout the siege and edited the film after the war was over. As the siege wore on, however, the life that the filmmaker was documenting was no longer solely epitomized by looks of fear, panic and bewilderment. It becomes apparent that the inhabitants are no longer completely caught in their altered reality, but rather are able to step back and comment on their situation with a sense of distance, often with dark humour. Distance and humour are particularly important here as they not only become strategies of reflecting on the given conditions, but also presuppose a choice of frame within which the reality is represented.

The film depicts the Sarajevo siege from the perspective of the besieged, and although the subjects are at times simply caught on camera, they also often address the camera or perform for it – to some degree choosing the frames and strategies of their own representation. Most of the interviewees have an almost gestic approach to Kreševljaković's camera as they offer surreal reflections on the city or dead-pan commentaries. One of them, called Ibro, appropriates a mock attitude of a wise-elder of the community when talking about life in the besieged city: 'It's nice to be without anything, we have no worries. We are relieved. I recommend to everybody: don't accumulate too many things. And always have a bag with the most necessary things ready in case someone chases you out one day… .' The documentary also depicts kids playing joyfully amongst the ruins, the opening of the Sarajevo film festival and a wedding. In the wedding sequence, the expected wedding imagery is mixed with some extraordinary elements in which this civil ritual takes place. It is a modest affair, but everybody is nicely dressed and the guests enjoy the party very much, singing *Guantanamera* to the accompaniment of a guitar player. When the elegant and cheerful group passes by shattered buildings and façades pockmarked by shrapnel, one of the guests looks slightly alarmed. Another reassures him: 'Don't worry, there are no snipers here, just grenades!' Everybody bursts out laughing. In another wedding scene, one of the guests takes both a bouquet of flowers for the newlyweds and a first-aid kit out of the trunk of his car. Lifting the first-aid kit in front of the camera, he grins and says: 'Just in case.' Perhaps more than bearing witness to the atrocities of war, this film shows how theatricality and performance became a vital part of the relationship between public and private realms, not only through various forms of cultural production, but also as aspects of daily life.

In this context, humour emerges as a means of distancing and a vital strategy of meaning-making that necessitates some degree of theatricality in everyday life. Nikolai Evreinov, a member of Russia's avant-garde who was interested in the theatricality of everyday life, ascribed to it the somewhat anthropological traits ingrained in a shared impulse or will to play. Interestingly, Evreinov's notion of theatricality as a necessity, no different from the need for food and water, is not that far removed from Pašović's:

> It wasn't at all extraordinary that we made theatre during the war. It was extraordinary that the siege lasted as long as it lasted or whatever it was that was happening. It was extraordinary to bomb a city, to kill people. That was extraordinary. Making theatre and making bread is nothing out of the ordinary. That's normal for people to do.
>
> (quoted in Diklić, *Teatar u ratnom Sarajevu*, p. 205)

Kreševljaković, too, makes a similar observation that has somewhat anthropological roots:

> In a sense, there was no distance between the stage and the audience in theatre. Of course, if a performance was put on in a theatre there was physical distance between the stage and the auditorium. But there was this feeling of community that has blurred all the divides. Everybody was a participant and we all felt safe although more often than not this was an illusion. In general, I think that theatre, for reasons unknown to me, has a specific power that became particularly evident during the war. For example, in my neighbourhood children gathered and started making performances. Nobody brought them together or asked them to do it. They decided on their own to play theatre.
>
> (quoted in Diklić, *Teatar u ratnom Sarajevu*, p. 142)

Evreinov emphasized that the notion of transformation lies at the core of theatricality. It is a rejuvenating principle that restores the sensation of life. He urges us not to be ourselves, and goes back to a pre-theatrical time when 'primitive' people realized that in addition to the conscious, waking *I*, there was a second *I* that existed in dreams. 'Without seasoning, without the salt of theatricality, life was a dish we would only eat by compulsion' (in Golub, *Evreinov*, p. 52). Cultural production in the city, performances in theatres, dark humour and the theatricality of everyday life enabled this transformational potential of theatricality to take place.

The case of Sarajevo offers a possibility to rethink the notion of reclaiming Agamben's bare life through two seemingly disparate, but essentially linked spheres – the public realm (Arendt, Owen) and theatricality (Evreinov). Theatricalization becomes an integral part of the public sphere and, thus, a means of counteracting the reduction to bare life where all forms of life become only one – survival. A sequence in Kreševljaković's film, *Do You Remember Sarajevo?* depicts an utterly surreal scene from daily life: a young man in full skiing gear, glides masterfully through the streets of Sarajevo. His skiing through the city is both a practical way of getting around and a commentary – a unique site-specific performance of navigating the streets of a city left without public transportation and under the always-watchful eyes of enemy snipers. The next scene takes place in a private home with two friends. They announce that this was a skiing championship and that their friend – whom they decide to call Alberto Tomba, after the famous Italian ski champion – is the winner. As a reward, he gets half a kilo of powdered milk, while the runner up is awarded a half-eaten piece of feta cheese. When one of them asks: 'Where is the second runner-up?' they look around before quickly remembering 'he is dead of course'. Finally, the three young men pretend to stand on a pedestal while singing the Italian anthem. Their short, dead-pan improvisation instantly reverses the situation they are in – and the absurdity of their existence in besieged Sarajevo has at least temporarily lost its hold over them. In other words, by performing the absurdity of life in Sarajevo, they reclaim the imposed condition, albeit temporarily, and place it under the control of theatricality.

On an individual level, which clearly influences the public realm, there is a certain kinship between the three young men who turned their experience of a snow-covered, besieged Sarajevo into a home-made show about a skiing competition, and a seemingly very different example, Christoph Schlingensief's opera-oratorio, *The Church of Fear* (2009), where the famous German director staged and performed his own terminal illness. Both performances are made in circumstances where individuals are threatened by the imposition of bare life. Moreover, in both cases the resistance emerges through invoking a kind of public realm and through the interplay of theatricality and performativity. By bringing the process of his own illness and death to centre stage, Schlingensief masterfully blurs the lines between reality and performance. In this case, he also inserts the private into the public, not so much to blur the lines, but to create a shared communal experience as a means of reclaiming life as a form-of-life. The three young men in

Sarajevo theatricalize their daily navigations through the besieged city by staging a mock public event – the skiing competition – in their own living room. Through theatricalization, they transform an everyday episode into a commentary on their own existence in the city. Using dark humour, they also make a sophisticated and painful link to Sarajevo's past identity in the global context – as the host city of the 1984 Winter Olympic games. The absurdity of this performance lies largely in its enactment of a grand, public event in a small living room – seemingly without the public. But we must not forget Kreševljaković's camera that bears witness to this performative commentary and eventually brings it back to the public realm.

Through this possibility to comment, which lies at the core of the concept of public sphere, *Zoë* is distinguished from *bios*, and the resistance to naked life takes place. In a sense, bare life could be understood as a form of life deprived of its impulse to theatricality, stripped of its ability to play (in Evreinov's sense of the term). It is a form of life that is denied the possibility of commenting on its own situation – deprived of the distancing through which life acquires meaning. Through both performance-making and through the self-fashioning of daily life, theatricality in Sarajevo became a means of individual and collective commentary – a transformative self-reflection and a form of agency. Agamben writes:

> human beings – as beings of power who can do or not do, succeed or fail, lose themselves or find themselves – are the only beings for whom happiness is always at stake in their living, the only beings whose life is irremediably and painfully assigned to happiness. But this immediately constitutes the form-of-life as political life.
>
> ('Form-of-Life', p. 4)

In another sequence of Kreševljaković's film, a young man stands in a sun-filled street of besieged Sarajevo, looks into the camera and says the most unexpected thing: 'Sometimes, I'm so happy'. I believe him.

7
Theatre as Ideal City

Throughout this book, I have put forward another reading of the besieged Sarajevo and its performances in an attempt to counteract some of the predominant Western imaginaries of the city. Consequently, I have focused my attention on those performances that might be seen to redress the trope of suffering. In so doing, I am aware that my concentration on notions of resilience and ambiguity runs the risk of replacing one set of imaginaries with another. So far, citizens/artists have been the main protagonists, through whose performances I have tried to understand both the suffering and the resilience of Sarajevo. However, they were not the only players in the scenario of the Sarajevo siege and they certainly did not take the centre stage.

In this section, I will look at the place of theatre and performance from two perspectives: (1) within the broader context of the war in Sarajevo and (2) against the backdrop of post-war Sarajevo. It goes without saying that to understand Sarajevo is to be aware of its particular context of suffering and resistance. It also requires recognition of the crucial role that imaginaries play in comprehending what Sontag has called the 'pain of others'. At the very least, imaginaries work in two ways. They can simplify, frame, inflate and construct realities to bring their meanings closer to the outsider's preconceived notions. Or, exercised differently, they can be vital components of contextualization that encourage us to consider the allusive and complex identities of diverse places that we do not know, or think we know but do not fully grasp. Imaginaries are *not* intrinsically inauthentic. Moreover, the process of their construction and deconstruction has its own epistemological potential – a dialectic of learning and unlearning. This final glance at theatre and performance in besieged Sarajevo does not intend to do away with imaginaries altogether, but rather add to their complex layering. Looked at from another perspective, that is, as resistance rather than as suffering, the performance that took place in Sarajevo during and after the war requires the contemplation of another set of imaginaries, one that can enrich our current understanding of how in a particular time period, a city under siege and its art were so inextricably entwined.

Theatre and performance in Sarajevo during the siege was both an extraordinary phenomenon and a pedestrian, easily explicable activity. Pašović argues that the cultural activity in Sarajevo was part of the city life and that it should not be romanticized or singled out from other daily activities such as going for water or collecting twigs to make fire. He writes:

> [...] Theatre was neither less nor more important than anything else. Everything that takes place in a big city was taking place during that time as well. As far as the theatre is concerned, let's not mystify the matter, most of the time there was no electricity, there was no television, no cinema, or very occasionally if a generator was found, or during short periods when there was electricity. People were bored. Among other things, theatre was one of the very few forms of entertainment left. It wasn't like you could go home, eat a big dinner, lie on the sofa and flip through TV channels. No. First, you could not have a big meal, second, you could not watch TV since there was no electricity [...].
>
> (quoted in Diklić, *Teatar u ratnom Sarajevu*, p. 202)

Kreševljaković's explanation of the phenomenon of theatre and cultural activity in Sarajevo is more ambiguous:

> It is true, however, that many other activities were a matter of physical survival and therefore necessary like going for water, looking for food and fuel, etc. Theatre didn't belong in this category and yet people were risking their lives to attend a show. People were also risking their lives to go to their neighbour to borrow a book. My mother suffered a terrible shock when she witnessed one of the massacres in Sarajevo and from then she refused to go out. The first time she left the house again during the war was to attend the opening of the Film Festival. Hence, it could be said that for a certain number of people in Sarajevo, culture was as important for their spiritual survival as water and food were necessary for their physical survival.
>
> (quoted in Diklić, *Teatar u ratnom Sarajevu*, p. 142)

During the war, the majority of theatre in Sarajevo was produced by one of three companies: Kamerni 55; Youth Theatre (*Pozorište mladih*), under the artistic direction of Nermin Tulić; and *SARTR*, an acronym for *Sarajevski ratni teater* (Sarajevo War Theatre) that was formed during the siege by playwright Safet Plakalo. Their repertoires were varied and included both performances that addressed the war through complex analogies and metaphors, like Pašović's *Alceste* and Sontag's *Godot*, as well as those like the musical *Hair* – arguably, the most popular show in the besieged city – that made easily accessible and literal analogies to the current situation. The war repertoire also included light, escapist comedies and pieces such as *Bešeskija, san o Sarajevu* (*Bešeskija, Dream about Sarajevo*) – a take on eighteenth-century Sarajevo based on the real life of local historian, *Bešeskija*. To some extent, this production foregrounded the city's Islamic tradition, but more than that, it dealt with the destiny of ordinary people in turbulent times. Whether aiming to reflect on the extreme circumstances of the city or to offer a temporary escape from reality, whether set in the contemporary context or uncovering the city's tradition and heritage, these performances had one thing in common – they never involved any aspect of war propaganda. My research into the repertoires of these theatres, based on numerous conversations with theatre makers in Sarajevo, found no examples where theatre was used as a means of reinforcing nationalism, promoting particular political and religious views or calling for action against another ethnic group. In his contribution to the *Teatar u ratnom Sarajevu* collection, actor Admir Glamočak further testifies to this claim:

> Another interesting thing about theatre during the war was the genre diversity of shows that were staged. [...] We played *Richard III*, *Alcestis*, *Waiting for Godot*, we staged Chekhov and Ionesco, we staged a couple of plays by writers from the former Yugoslavia and some pieces by local playwrights, etc. Nothing was put on to satisfy any agendas outside of our artistic choices. Politics was not meddling into theatre, except in some very marginal ways, which was fantastic. Nobody was pushing us to make a performance so somebody could appear on stage in a friar's habit or wearing a hijab.
>
> (quoted in Diklić, *Teatar u ratnom Sarajevu*, p. 99)

Clearly, theatre in besieged Sarajevo served several purposes. Sometimes it was offered as pure entertainment, a simple means to overcome boredom as Pašović claimed. Other times it provided a communal ritual, a means of sustaining the collective and individual identity of the citizens. It became a way to preserve the cultural mind-map of the city even when its main architectural landmarks had been reduced to rubble. The fact that theatre (and other forms of performance) was never used as a tool of propaganda allowed the integrity of the theatre to remain intact and the cultural integrity of the city to be preserved.

Theatre reflected the notion of a multicultural Sarajevo (and Bosnia) that the war had attempted to eradicate. The ethnic diversity of the cast of *Godot*, described by Sontag, was far from unique. On several occasions during the siege, with the help of international artists such as Peter Brook and Liv Ullman, to name only two, Sarajevan theatre productions were invited to make guest appearances in cities like London and Paris. During press conferences, artists were regularly asked about the ethnic make-up of the cast, an assumption they found offensive in its implication that the demographic of Bosnian theatre ensembles had to reflect the ethnic and religious divide of the conflict. Responding to these queries, they proudly explained that the situation was exactly the opposite: theatres in Sarajevo had retained their multi-ethnic identity even (and especially) during an era of various nationalist and religious agendas. Although invitations to other cities provided artists with a golden opportunity to leave Sarajevo and claim their right to refugee status elsewhere, in fact few artists did so with most of them opting to return to Sarajevo. During a guest performance in Paris, Glamočak spoke of his strong attachment to Sarajevo:

> In 1994, I was performing in a show in Paris. Someone who at one point visited Sarajevo during the war, invited me to come and do a show in Paris. The reason I'm mentioning this is to say that my stay and work in Paris didn't matter that much, especially in comparison to the work I was doing in Sarajevo in that period or when we took our local shows to other parts of Bosnia or abroad. I spent the time in Paris like a mad person, constantly phoning Sarajevo to find out what was happening there and counting the days until my return, especially as the rumours about lifting the siege started to circulate... I couldn't imagine not being in Sarajevo on that day, without my wife and child and without my theatre. This might sound absurd from today's perspective, but I've never regretted staying in Sarajevo. I'm only sorry that now, after the war, it has all been quickly forgotten...
>
> (quoted in Diklić, *Teatar u ratnom Sarajevu*, pp. 94–5)

Through its amazing cultural production, theatre in the besieged Sarajevo emerged as an ideal city. Theatre and performance activities strengthened the sense of a multi-ethnic community and its ethics and were part of a larger civic support network. They helped Sarajevo retain its 'it' factor regardless of how absurd this might seem in the context of the siege. Theatre – from the staging of plays to performances of everyday life – established the city-within-the-city not only as resistance to undeniable suffering, but also as *a better place* amidst the blatant criminalization of the city and its concomitant murky economic and political dealings. In other words, theatre as the *ideal city-within-the-city* epitomized yet another version of the *utopian performative*.

Back-stage actions

> I won't let you spoil my war for me. Destroys the weak, does it? Well, what does peace do for'em, huh? War feeds its people better.
>
> (Bertolt Brecht, *Mother Courage*)

The city-within-the-city ideal that kept itself alive through theatre and other cultural activities was rooted in a relatively small section of central Sarajevo. Artists tried to travel to other parts of the city, but the main cultural action took place in the city's compact centre. It was increasingly difficult to connect various parts and neighbourhoods through usual urban routines such as walking or using public transportation. The latter did not exist during the siege, while one had to be both cautions and economical with walking. Often small distances took hours to cover as the only relatively safe routes were the long wayward ones and every outing was indeed a risk. Since the near-by hillside suburb of Grbavica, controlled by Bosnian Serbs, overlooked the downtown strip that became known as 'sniper alley', from the start Sarajevo was a divided city both spatially and politically; the front line and sniper alley cut off the Muslim held Dobrinja neighbourhood from the city centre and the old town.

In his illuminating book, *Blue Helmets and Black Markets*, Peter Andreas applies Erving Goffman's tropes of 'front-stage action' and 'back-stage action' to illustrate how the media manipulated the perception of Sarajevo and the war in Bosnia. More specifically, Goffman's concept of 'back-stage action' gave Andreas the conceptual tool to look beyond the undeniable but often simplified 'front-stage action' of suffering and ethnic violence. By including the concept of 'back-stage action', Andreas was able to explore key aspects of the siege, such as the war economy and the incipient criminalization of the city that the mainstream media (local and global) so deftly sidestepped. Against the dominant trope of suffering and ethnic strife, the resilience of the city, that is, its *normalcy*, its cultural production and its performances in everyday life were also relegated to the back-stage domain. Rarely, if ever, were they granted the media spotlight. Andreas is interested in other aspects of the back-stage action though, which still implicitly foregrounds the notion of theatre as the ideal city-within-the-city. This back-stage action is constituent in creating what Andreas calls the siege-within-the-siege:

> The siege of Sarajevo was actually two sieges: one external, the other internal. The internal siege was made possible by the external siege, and helps to explain how the interests of some players within the city were served by the siege conditions even as the majority of the population suffered. The siege provided an opening and cover for the abuse of power and a rational for tolerating such abuses; [...] it created enormous economic opportunities for theft, war profiteering, and redistribution of wealth while most of the city's residents struggled to simply survive.
>
> (Andreas, *Blue Helmets and Black Markets*, p. 90)

At the onset of the siege, local gang leaders and ex-convicts became engaged in the defence of the city and soon formed their own military units. This was of course not unique to Sarajevo and to the Bosnian army. Serbian paramilitary forces were made of the same kind of fighters, including the infamous *Tigers*, responsible for numerous atrocities during the wars in Croatia and Bosnia, led by the notorious gangster, with close ties to Yugoslav State Security and Secret Police, known as Arkan.[1] The main difference was that in the case of Sarajevo, it was believed that these ex-convicts were instrumental in defending the city, especially in the earlier period of the siege. The Sarajevo government was unprepared for the war, believing that more overt war preparations would be interpreted as provocative. As a result, they somewhat naively counted on international military support in case war broke out. Although the Sarajevo government announced the formation of the Bosnian Army on 15 April 1992, it took months for it to grow into a serious military structure. In the meantime, Sarajevo's criminal underground stepped in. In Kreševljaković's film, a Sarajevo police official talks about how known criminal gangs volunteered to save the besieged city and joined forces with the Bosnian police and the army. Andreas explains:

> What Sarajevo lacked was not manpower but rather arms, organization, coordination, and initiative in setting up the basic elements

> of a perimeter defence. The city's criminal gangs – teamed up, ironically, with police forces and local residents defending their homes – were relatively well armed and well organized, providing some semblance of cohesion that initially substituted for a formal military structure. Their leadership role at the start of the siege also had a huge psychological effect, providing Sarajevans with a much-needed boost of optimism and sense of defiance in the face of military encirclement. Indeed, some of Sarajevo's criminal defenders became instant heroes – embraced and celebrated as a kind of 'patriotic mafia'.
>
> (*Blue Helmets and Black Markets*, p. 28)

Gradually, this 'patriotic mafia' grew out of control, stealing and terrorizing the citizens.

The key mafia figures and their armies split the control of the city and its main checkpoints through which food and other supplies made their way into the city. Acts of saving the city quickly turned into strategies of war profiteering that often involved lucrative trading deals with the enemy from the surrounding hills. In his book on the Bosnian war, entitled *The Serbs*, Tim Judah writes: 'After the first few hellish months of war, Serbian cigarettes and fresh produce such as tomatoes began to appear in city markets. They arrived courtesy of the mafia connections of some of the men who were organizing the frontlines' (p. 251). They were also, however, responsible for the oppression and violence against Serbs who decided to remain in the city. In his book, *The Fixer: A Story from Sarajevo*, journalist and artist Joe Sacco, famous for his graphic non-fiction, profiles the leading underground figures who became prominent and powerful while defending the city during the war. Like Andreas, Sacco points out that most of the key figures of the 'patriotic mafia' did not recognize any military authority above their own and 'not only ignored the chain of command but often flaunted their disdain for it' (Andreas, *Blue Helmets and Black Markets*, p. 92). Some of the journeys of these fighters and ex-convicts were truly paradoxical. Juka Prazina, for instance, one of the most well known criminal/defenders of the city grew so blatantly out of control that a warrant for his arrest was issued in 1992. Fleeing Sarajevo for nearby Mount Igman at first, Prazina was able to control the most important access road in and out of the city. Even though he had promised to liberate Sarajevo and return to the city on a white horse, he abruptly switched his allegiance after being defeated and expelled by the Bosnian army and joined the Croatian forces in Mostar (Andres, *Blue Helmets and Black Markets*, p. 92, Sacco,

The Fixer, p. 69). In 1993, Juka's body was found dumped at a rest-stop in Belgium. Not unlike their counterparts on the enemy side – the 'patriotic mafia' that came to fight on the side of Bosnian Serbs – the criminal defenders of Sarajevo by and large met their end in clashes with the Bosnian army and others – some were arrested, others were killed in circumstances that typically have remained unresolved. This has left room for speculative theories according to which these fighters, at the upper end of the chain of command, knew too much and perished just in time – before they could be brought to the War Tribunal in The Hague to testify.[2]

Journalist David Rieff, Susan Sontag's son, covered the Bosnian war extensively and subsequently wrote a book about Sarajevo. Looking back, he admits:

> Those of us [among the foreign press corps in Sarajevo] who were convinced of the rightness of the Bosnian cause tended to underplay the corruption of Bosnian political elites, who, throughout the war, even in Sarajevo, were making fortunes off the conflict, doing private deals with the Serbs, and placing family members, friends, and mistresses in cushy jobs abroad. We also wrote less then we should about the relationship between war and crime on the front line, where the black market flourished even in the worst moments of the fighting.
>
> (Rieff, 'Murder in the Neighbourhood', p. 47)

In their heyday, the 'patriotic-mafia' were key players in a siege economy where both sides across the front line profited. As Andreas points in his study, the siege of Sarajevo was porous. The two main routes in and out of Sarajevo were the tunnel running underneath the city airport and the airport itself. As *The Sarajevo Survival Guide* explains, UN convoys provided another means of entry and/or exit:

> Convoy is the term which equals organized exit, a ticket with no return. For all such journeys there are lists, and there is time spent waiting, filled with uncertainties. [...] Discretely, but to no one's surprise, the City was left by wives, children, parents and friends of various officials, illegal channels were used, starting in Stup, Ilidža, Kobiljač. From there, to Kiseljak – a Hong Kong of Sarajevo – if heading West. To Pale, if going East. On each of these starts, there was a 'connection', a guy dealing with the formalities which basically means exchanging tangible hard currency for the invisible bus ticket.

> Starting fee is 100 to 200 DM. Additional amounts were supplied by Muslims, for they often needed false documents.
>
> (p. 79)

In addition to the business of smuggling people out of the city, then, an even more lucrative business was keeping them in the city and 'managing' the siege.

In the summer of 1993, the Sarajevo government completed an 800-metre tunnel linking the Butmir area (where the airport was located) with the suburb of Dobrinja. This made it possible to reach nearby Hrasnica – an outpost of the Bosnian government beyond the parameters of the siege – and to go further, via Mount Igman, to the Bosnian-held towns of the Neretva river valley southwest of Sarajevo. Both Hrasnica and the towns in the Neretva valley were sources of relatively cheap goods that could be resold at extortionary prices in the besieged city. Various points of this smuggling route were controlled by different players in 'back-stage' scenarios of the Sarajevo siege – from the army to the criminal defenders of the city. Permission to use the tunnel, it should be noted, was strictly controlled by the Sarajevo government.

Similarly, when a year earlier the UN had brokered an agreement with Bosnian Serbs to reopen Sarajevo airport for humanitarian aid to enter the city, it became both a lifeline for the suffering citizens and a lucrative enterprise for those controlling access. The Serbian side regularly received its cuts for making this allowance while the leaders of the Bosnian Serbs may 'have begun to realize that the prolonged siege offered promising commercial opportunities' (Fawcett and Tanner, 'Birth of the Aid Juggernaut' in Andreas, *Blue Helmets and Black Markets*, p. 36). Both the UN airlift and the grounds of the airport were used to smuggle everything from food to weapons. As smugglers became more and more creative in getting goods past the UN forces that controlled the airport into the city, allegations emerged implicating some of the peace-keeping troupes in war profiteering.[3] *The Sarajevo Survival Guide* offered tips on how to use the airport runway:

> The runway is equipped with photo-cells and sensors which detect anyone who might be walking by. This trap, installed by UNPROFOR, may surprise you with alarms or spotlights which go on immediately after you are spotted. Different divisions of the UN force – the Blue Helmets – react in accordance with their national, regional and personal sense of humour. The French are amused by our wit. Ukrainians are made nervous by our stubbornness, but they can be talked into a

> deal. The best guys are the Egyptians. They are running after the old lady who is smuggling bananas from Hrasnica to Dobrinja. They forgive the guy who is running with crutches. One such guy was forced to return no less then eight times; the ninth time he wrote his own obituary in French. Since the French have respect for the dead, he left the city on the air-transport. All sides catch smugglers, but also those who managed to crawl across half the runway. In short, the journey is hard, but once the basics are completed, and you are on the right side, everything is a matter of superstructure – skill, papers, money. It is no secret that for 1000 to 2000 DM one can fly out on a humanitarian aid plane. The only drawback is that there are no guarantees at which airport you are going to land.
>
> (p. 81)

The siege economy also provided a certain infrastructure, albeit a fragile one, that made the city both more accessible and more manageable than any other location during the Bosnian war. As Andreas suggests, accessibility may have played a key role in Sarajevo's iconic status in the world media:

> [...] UN control of the airport not only drew media attention to the airlift but also greatly facilitated the influx of foreign journalists into the city, who would conveniently fly in and out to nearby Germany, Croatia, and Italy via the airlift. The opening of the airport turned a city under the siege into the most accessible war zone in Bosnia. This partly explains why Sarajevo was transformed into a global media spectacle, becoming the most familiar face of the war.
>
> (*Blue Helmets and Black Markets*, p. 38)

Clearly, Sarajevo was not the only place in Bosnia that endured siege conditions. The town of Mostar, located about 130 kilometres from Sarajevo, was seriously devastated as the Croatian siege sealed its eastern part of town. Conditions in Mostar and the close-range fighting on its streets made it more difficult and dangerous for TV crews to enter the city and provide footage than was the case in Sarajevo. Consequently, the suffering of Mostar took place away from the gaze of the world media and went largely unnoticed.

Although it was a UN-designated safe area, the Muslim enclave of Goražde was also surrounded by Serbian forces and suffered heavy attacks during the three and a half years of war that left the town on the brink of obliteration. Its fate turned out to be somewhat less grim than that of other 'safe areas' of East Bosnia, Srebrenica and Žepa. When UN forces abandoned these areas in the summer of 1995, the Bosnian Serb army and the paramilitaries entered Srebrenica and Žepa and committed horrendous massacres. At the point that British and Ukrainian peacekeepers pulled out of Goražde, the inhabitants feared the same fate would befall them. Fortunately, following the NATO bombing of the Bosnian Serb positions, and the cease-fire and peace talks that ensued, the town was spared. Alongside its new relative safety came a degree of short-lived media interest. In *Safe Area Goražde*, Sacco depicts his visit to the town in 1995 that took place while Slobodan Milošević, Bosnian President Alija Izetbegović and Croatian President Franjo Tudjman were sitting in Dayton, Ohio, negotiating the peace agreement:

> We'd barely stepped out of our vehicle when the red carpets started rolling out, criss-crossing left and right! [...] Oh, they were happy to see journalists in Gorazde, to see us, to see me, to see *anybody*. [...] Gorazde! Which has just wrested the spotlight from the media darling Sarajevo! Gorazde! Which was getting CNNed! NPRed! BBCed! But its proverbial 15 minutes were ticking away! Pretty soon no one will remember Gorazde! Gora-wuh? Hunh?
>
> (pp. 5–6)

Sacco was right. The 'it' factor of the provincial Bosnian town evaporated before the global village had even learned how to pronounce its name.

Political scientist Stathis Kalyvas argues that the coverage of contemporary internal wars is predominately focused on urban centres. He talks about 'urban bias' and claims that the war in Bosnia was 'mostly covered from Sarajevo' (*The Logic of Violence in Civil War*, pp. 39, 41). Historian Robert Donia also describes how Sarajevo dominated the war coverage in Bosnia. In his biography of Sarajevo, he suggested that although the city was, of course, very dangerous, it still provided enough safety and accessibility for the 'privileged observer':

> The daily violence was conducted under the scrutiny of international civil servants, aid workers , 'peacekeepers', journalists, and scholars (including this author) who could travel with relative ease on conveyances not available to the local population. Sarajevo was the lens through which most outsiders viewed the conflict; the agony of Sarajevo became the embodiment of the Bosnian war's savagery and senselessness. At most times, the army of privileged observers could

> get into and out of the city, stay in relative comfort at the Holiday Inn (the sole hostelry that functioned throughout the war), ride in armoured vehicles along the city's most dangerous routes, and send dispatches to the outside world using the latest communication technology.
>
> (*Sarajevo: A Biography*, p. 287)

Sarajevo was embraced not only for what it was but for what it was not. It became a surrogate for less accessible, less equipped and less attractive, yet, arguably, more dangerous locales of the Bosnian war. Suffering, danger, deprivation and atrocities, as well as strategies of resistance and self-preservation, were varied and conditioned by different factors. No matter how iconic Sarajevo was, it simply could not stand for it all. Nevertheless, the special place of Sarajevo in both the world media and in the context of Yugoslavia's downfall is important. The iconic city became a lens that magnified the complexity and tragedy of the conflict and brought clarity to the brutality and the banality of the war.

Unveiling the back-stage actions of the Sarajevo siege engages dialectically and critically with two dominant tropes of the city – the trope of suffering and the trope of Bosnia (and more widely the Balkans) as the locus of age-old ethnic strife. Reducing Sarajevo to its undeniable suffering becomes a form of romanticization of the Balkan conflict. The counter-discourse of resistance through cultural production, humour, performances of every day life, and an assertion of 'normalcy' in extraordinary circumstances, runs the risk of committing the same kind of fallacy. The trope of ethnic hatred casts an Orientalizing view on the Balkans, in Edward Said's sense of the term, as a place of primitive *Others* who, on the cusp of the twentry-first century, continue to fight their medieval battles. This view is dangerous not only because it is ahistorical and ignores the inherent and somewhat inevitable multiculturalism of the Balkans, but because it also undermines the complicity of international politics in the latest Balkan war scenarios. There is a more pessimistic and ironic aspect to the city where everybody – from bloodthirsty *chetniks* that kept it under siege to ex-convicts that defended it, from local politicians to UN peacekeepers – fought for their share in a murky war game. This forces us to view the besieged Sarajevo beyond the binaries of suffering and resistance, beyond the geography of inside-outside and, equally, beyond relatively simple images of this part of the Balkans, 'such as fault lines, ancient hatreds, and powder kegs that offer the advantage of beguiling simplicity to those confronted with Balkan history' (Goldsworthy, 'Invention and In(ter)vention', p. 28).

The examination of the 'back-stage' and 'front-stage' dialectics of life in Sarajevo reveals a frequently overlooked dimension – the implication of the international community in the local conflict. Within this complex, ambivalent and, above all, obscure and dangerous setting, the ideal city-within-the city – carved out by theatre and cultural production in Sarajevo – emerges even more strongly as a remarkable phenomenon. Although Beckett's *Waiting for Godot* came to represent the main theatrical metaphor of living in besieged Sarajevo, Brecht's *Mother Courage* might well have been more appropriate. In its messy mixture of tragedy and resistance, humour and violence, profiteering and survival, courage and criminality, the dialectics of front-stage and back-stage action of the siege makes a perfect setting for Brecht's play. The scenarios of being and acting in the besieged Sarajevo belong to the world of *Mother Courage* as they embody the workings of the war economy, showing, with defamiliarizing clarity, how everyone becomes complicit in war-time – warmongers, peacekeepers, army commanders and even the international press corps.

Postscript: the multicultural subconscious of the city

In 2009, when I visited Sarajevo's *Kamerni Teater 55*, theatre had re-emerged as a vast improvement on the actual, if not yet quite ideal, city. *Kamerni*'s artistic director, Zlatko Topčić, proudly talked about the ethnic diversity of his ensemble, pointing out that the theatre's demographic resembled the pre-war census of Sarajevo. The actual city demographic, however, had changed from the last pre-war census in 1991 to the first post-war one in 2002.[4] Sarajevo, like other capitals of the new nation-states emerging from the disintegrated Yugoslavia, became less multicultural than it had been before the war. Given that the wars of the former Yugoslavia were in many ways about national secession, reinforcing the imagined communities of ethnic homogeneity, this does not come as a surprise. However, the multicultural mind-map of the city, which Karahasan identified as a microcosm of multiple coexisting worlds on the crossroads of East and West, has been key to its identity. Arguably, more than in other regional capitals of the former Yugoslavia, multiculturalism was woven into the fabric of everyday life in Sarajevo and was integral to its identity. Bosnia, especially Sarajevo, was the most ethnically-mixed part of Yugoslavia with no ethnic majority group and with the highest percentage of citizens who, before the war, chose to self-identify as Yugoslavs thus avoiding singular categories of national identity.

According to the Federal Office of Statistics of Bosnia and Herzegovina, located in Sarajevo, the 1991census states that 49.4 per cent of the city's population identified itself as Muslim.[5] In 2002, 79.6 per cent of Sarajevo's population self-identified as Bosniac. The number of Serbian inhabitants of the city dropped from 29.8 per cent in 1991 to 11.2 per cent in 2002; the number of Croats remained relatively stable – 6.6 per cent in 1991 to 6.7 per cent in 2002 – while the number of Sarajevans who identified themselves as *ostali* (other) dropped from 3.6 per cent in 1991 to 2.5 per cent in 2002. Last but not least, in 1992, 10.7 per cent of the citizens identified themselves as Yugoslavs while in the 2002 census, this category no longer existed. Moreover, the category *ostali* (other) included Jewish and Roma inhabitants of the city, for instance, whose statistically decreasing numbers significantly altered the subjectivity of the city. In lamenting the exodus of Sarajevo Jews from the besieged city, Karahasan depicts the loss that statistical data could never capture, even when it had the numbers to prove it:

> In April 1992 the Jewish graveyard became involved in our deaths as well. The snipers of the Yugoslav People's Army opened precise and deadly fire upon Sarajevo's citizens from the graveyard hill. Is that proper and just? And in accordance to what principles, if it is?
>
> I know that it happened in accordance with the same principles that caused the attack on Sarajevo to begin precisely in the year of our Jewish community's observance of its 500th anniversary of their exile from Spain. Half a millennium of common life was observed in the encircled city, semi-destroyed and surrounded by heavy artillery, so that not even a bird could enter. Yet it was commemorated decorously and sadly, in the only way the anniversary of an exile can be observed [...].
>
> (*Sarajevo, Exodus of a City*, p. 94)

> Less then twenty days after that observance nearly the entire Jewish community left the city, heading for a new exile. Perhaps ten odd fanatical lovers of their homes and the city stayed on. The same principles that involved our Jewish graveyard in our deaths for the first time, the same laws that willed our Jews to commemorate five hundred years of exile, the same laws that caused their city to disappear gradually in front of their very eyes – these laws caused Sarajevo to be left without its Jews, a community whose arrival made Sarajevo a complete world in miniature, the planet's little heart, and the community that profoundly determined the city's physiognomy.
>
> (pp. 95–6)

In changing the demographics, the exodus from the besieged city presumably determined a subtle, but deep change in the city's identity, culture and everyday life. In post-war Sarajevo, this appears as a recognizable shift from multicultural and multi-ethnic principles towards ethnic ones – a shift that could be recognized, in different variations, throughout the entire region. It is, however, not simply the result of various instances of exile that took place during the war and of the ethnic conflict itself, but also of a constitutional system that redefined the parameters of being a citizen of Sarajevo and Bosnia and emphasized homogenous ethnic particularity on account of the city's multicultural history. In her study of multiculturalism in post-war Sarajevo, anthropologist Fran Markowitz points out that '"citizens" subjectivities and the demands of the state are coalescing into what is increasingly experienced as the "natural" way of defending self and others' (*Sarajevo: A Bosnian Kaleidoscope*, p. 78). Sarajevans are encountering 'new demands from the Bosnian state to think and act in terms of tripartite citizenry comprised of members of one and only one of the Bosniac, Croat, or Serb constituent nations' (p. 78). In Sarajevo, where mixed marriages and multiple ethnic identities are very common, this becomes particularly problematic. Instead of 25 categories used in the national census of 1991, the post-war one had only three named categories: Bosniacs, Croats and Serbs, while 'all the other nationalities that were part of Bosnia's ethnoscape had simply vanished' (*Sarajevo: A Bosnian Kaleidoscope*, p. 82).

Avdo Mujkić, a professor of political science and ethics at the University of Sarajevo, coined the term *ethnopolis* to describe a kind of paradoxical *ethno democracy* that he traces back to the Dayton Peace Agreement on which the Constitution of Bosnia and Herzegovina is based.

> Even a superficial look at Bosnian political practice forces us to conclude that the obvious lack of the main ingredients of constitutional liberalism in the vague provisions of its Constitution – a document that elevates the collective rights of ethnic groups above those of individual citizens – has pushed Bosnia's so-called 'democracy' ever deeper into the quicksand of discriminatory, illiberal politics and social practices. [...] The constitutional framework laid out in the Dayton Agreement encourages procedural democracy only among the political representatives – or better, the ruling oligarchies – of the various ethnic groups.
>
> ('We, the Citizens of Ethnopolis', p. 112)

Mujkić examines the Dayton Constitution against the backdrop of Habermas's notion of tripartite citizen recognition (1. individual, 2. member of a cultural or ethnic group, 3. member of a political group). He identifies only one of the parameters: 'a citizen of Bosnia and Herzegovina is recognized only as a member of an ethnic group, and only through this recognition is he or she recognized as a member of a political community' ('We, the Citizens of Ethnopolis', p. 113). The term 'constituent people' – meaning a group that belongs to a particular national identity, rather than a *populous* or a sum of individuals that together comprise the citizens of a state – is the keyword not only in the context of Mujkić's Bosnian ethnopolis, but in relation to the ethno-politics of the entire ex-Yugoslavian region. The term 'constituent people' was first used, just before the downfall of Yugoslavia, in the Republic of Serbia's official submission to the Arbitrational Commission of the European Community that asked: 'Does the Serb population in Croatia and Bosnia and Herzegovina as constituent people of Yugoslavia enjoy the right to self-determination?' (quoted in Mujkić, 'We, the Citizens of Ethnopolis', p. 114). According to Mujkić, the term was used in the peace talks and documents during the war in Bosnia and 'was finally introduced into the fundamental legal document, the Constitution of November 1995' (p. 114). It has also served as a basis for Mujkić's definition of *ethnopolis*, a concept that is akin to the phenomenon that Roger Friedland defines as *religious nationalism*:[6]

> *ethnopolis* puts forward a particular ontology of power, an ontology affirmed and revealed through its politicized practices and the central object of its political concern, practices that locate collective solidarity in ethnic affiliation tied to particular religions, as opposed to contractual and consensual relations between individual citizens.
>
> ('Religious Nationalism', p. 116)

Mujkić's *ethnopolis* describes the post-Yugoslavian ethos–demos divide not only in Bosnia, but applies fully to other ethnocentric nation-states in the Balkan region that have emerged during and after the war. *Ethnopolitics* is based on the reduction and simplification of a complex multiethnic fabric to homogenous national identities of the 'constituent peoples'. Nevertheless, Sarajevo again emerges as a site – a microcosm or a heterotopia – where the practice of the ethnopolis is confronted with other practices in the public sphere of the city.

Recent debates show a struggle between two contrasting approaches – one deeply rooted in the religious nationalism of the ethnopolis, the other eager to begin the journey towards a secular, modern democracy. The film by Jasmina Žbanić, *Na putu* (*On the Road*) made in 2010, epitomizes this tension between religion and secularism in its central protagonists – a young, modern Sarajevo couple. At the beginning of the film, they are very much in love and want to have a child. After a chance encounter with an old wartime friend who has become increasingly religious, the husband's interest in religion is piqued. He becomes a practising Muslim and subsequently joins the conservative Muslim sect, Vahabije. This gradually changes the couple's everyday life, eventually putting an insurmountable strain on their relationship. The wife is unable to except the strict rules of the Muslim sect and is particularly uncomfortable with the position and role of women within the sect. Finally, she confronts her husband and asks him to choose between religion and family. To some extent, these protagonists are meant to be read as allegorical figures reflecting the notion of Bosnia in transition – an unfinished journey that comes to a fork in the road. The metaphor is clear, as is Žbanić's preference.

A need to negotiate histories and identities of the city and the region also appeared in the new play *The Time Tunnel*, written by Nenad Veličković. The play was directed by Admir Glamočak (who played Lucky in Sontag's *Godot*), and premiered in the spring of 2007 at the Youth Theatre in Sarajevo (Pozorište mladih). The starting point of the play is satirical: three students venture into an underground tunnel – a space between a Bosnian version of the Pyramid of the Sun and the Sarajevo Tunnel, the access route in and out of the city during the siege – and journey through different historical periods of the region. The protagonists encounter a variety of historical figures including Alija Sirotanović, who was part of the socialist-realist iconography of Tito's Yugoslavia. Well-known in Yugoslavia as the heroic miner who made a record mining achievement way above his work norm, Alija Sirotanović's face appeared on the Yugoslav ten dinar banknote. He was the symbol of the communist work ethic and its celebration of the working class. Farther along, the youths encounter Gavrilo Princip, the assassin of Grand Duke Ferdinand, followed by the Islamic cleric Bešeskija, who was already featured as a protagonist in another project at the Youth Theatre; a Bosnian poet, Aleksa Šantić, and his muse; as well as the soldiers who controlled the tunnel underneath the airport, and others. In one way or another, each encounter invokes a political crisis. The production notes state that although the circumstances and characters that the protagonists encounter belong to different historical moments, they are examples of recurring instances of the trope of crisis:

> [...] the essence of Bosnian instability remains the same throughout the ages and this instability is, to an equal extent, a consequence of both international influence and aspiration, as well as of local indifference and lack of education.
>
> The situation and personalities they confront effect our heroes as well, and they begin to wonder how much they themselves are victims of inherited suffering and misconceptions, and how much they are in fact contributing to the ethical and political collapse of their native country.
>
> The play was written and directed primarily for the younger generation, with a hope and a wish that they will recognize its story as 'their own', if not for its political effort in the breaking of epic, patriarchal and ideological stereotypes, then certainly for the humour that is interwoven in this journey.
>
> (http://www.pozoristemladih.ba/eng/prede.asp)

The play's satirical journey into the past becomes an epistemological strategy of defamiliarizing the historical narratives of the region and its heterotopias of crisis in order to negotiate a better deal for the present and for the future. I saw the dress rehearsal of the play on the first night that the actors were able to work with the set. Although it appeared somewhat oversized for the stage of Pozorište mladih, I have never learned if that was a deliberate attempt to create a visual metaphor or just a result of imperfect measurements. In any case, for me the uneasy fit between the set and the stage and between the set and the actors was telling. It reflected a difficulty that became almost physical in negotiating the competing and contrasting histories that the protagonists passed through. Yet, the actors found their way through the overwhelming set and the tunnel of history that it represented.

Like the journey staged by the makers of the *Tunnel*, Sarajevo, through its layout and architecture, represents a similar kind of palimpsest of competing and contrasting histories. In the introduction to her book on Sarajevo, Markowitz offers a vivid and evocative perception of the city, another testament of its charisma:

> I love that the arches and domes of Turkish stone buildings, the ornate facades commissioned by Austrian capitalists, and mega-sized concrete structures of socialist modernism stand side-by-side;

> that the sacred and profane transgress into each other's space; that government-produced apartment blocks, private places of purchase, houses of worship, and people's homes rub up against each other. I relish the variety of Sarajevo's built environment that provokes the imagination with a long list of possibilities for being in the world. The churches, mosques, and synagogues speak to the Abrahamic faiths, each to its own although they share a progenitor as well as urban space. [...] These styles of the city, carved in stone, and painted or printed on canvases and billboards, signs and menus, postcards and currency, speak to multiple histories and inspire imaginaries of possible futures in the present continuous of Sarajevo's motile public culture.
>
> (*Sarajevo*, pp. 6–7)

Within a radius of some 15 to 20 metres, the main pedestrian street, Ulica Maršala Tita, turns into Ferhadijina Street. Thus, a part of the pedestrian zone has kept the name previously shared with most of the main streets in the cities of the former Yugoslavia. In most of the other places of the region, Maršala Tita Streets have been deliberately renamed in a series of symbolic and normative gestures of throwing 50 years of communist/socialist legacy out the window. In most post-Yugoslavian cities and towns, the streets were renamed to demonstrate the freshly resurrected monarchic, religious or nationalist traditions. This ritual of political exorcism indiscriminately cleansed the region of all the bad along with all the good things communist ideology had fostered including its multicultural and internationalist ethos. I have never found out why Sarajevo's city officials decided to keep the street named after Marshall Tito but the name is certainly telling. It foregrounds a layer of history of the place that cannot be erased, it brings about the sense of Yugo-nostalgia, it points to the relationship between communism/socialism and ethnicity, and provides a link between past and present. In Sarajevo, the main street is split between two names Maršal Tito and Ferhadijina – which is the name of two mosques, one in Sarajevo and one in the town of Banja Luka, itself a Serbian stronghold during the war and a centre for Bosnian Serbs afterwards. The sixteenth-century mosque in Banja Luka, although under UNESCO protection, was partially destroyed in 1993. The reconstruction of the mosque is ongoing and has remained a controversial and inflammatory subject for both Bosnians and Serbs in the region. Thus, the part of the street named in honour of the mosque is not only juxtaposed to evoke Yugoslavian history in the name of Marshall Tito, but is also a momentum memorial to the most recent destruction and war in Bosnia. The name Ferhadijina evokes the beautiful Banja Luka mosque that was destroyed, but also the mosque as a site of both the past and of the ongoing tensions in contemporary divided Bosnia. At the confluence of Maršal Tito and Ferhadijina Streets, the palimpsest of the city is further reinforced by other features: the Yugoslav memorial Vječna vatra (Eternal Flame), lit in 1946 for the first anniversary of the city's liberation from Nazi occupation, to honour the military and civilian victims and fighters in the Second World War. The inscription on the memorial states its dedication to all the peoples and ethnic groups of Yugoslavia and their struggle against the Nazis. Since 1946, throughout the war in the early 1990s and to this day, the Eternal Flame has remained lit. Across from it stands the more recently opened Iranian Cultural Centre – a post-1990s war institution established as the Bosnian government's expression of gratitude to the Republic of Iran for its support during the war for Bosnian independence. This spot, in the very heart of the city, embodies the tension, or rather the need to reconcile different, painful yet intertwined histories of the city – the legacy and imprint of Yugoslavian multiculturalism with the reassertion of Bosnia's Islamic identity. In spite of the semiotics of this city strip that foregrounds tension and contestation, everyday life makes these signs rather playful. From the war images of the cellist Vedran Smajlić performing his concert in front of Vječna vatra during the worst attacks on the city, to the street's post-war transformation into a lively, bustling centre, the point where Maršal Tito and Ferhadijina Streets meet reads more like a place of possibility for more convivial publics to emerge.

In spite of the ethno-politics that still dominate Bosnia and the rest of the ex- Yugoslavia region, the layout, architecture and some of the practices of everyday life in Sarajevo reveal a phenomenon that I will call *the multicultural subconscious of the city*. The way that the city operates, moves and performs itself through the layers of its past and into the present moment has its own rhythm and even its own ethos. It reflects and inscribes the politics of the place, but simultaneously goes against the political current. Markowitz uses the metaphor of the kaleidoscope to suggest that:

> along with the shattering experiences of war and the constitution that enforces the entrenchment of either or national(istic) belongings, the cityscape of Sarajevo and the long-term experiences of its residents serve as constant reminders of compatible ethnic, confessional, and philosophical trajectories and the pleasure of cosmopolitanism.
>
> (*Sarajevo*, p. 13)

The varied and diverse architectural features of the cityscape of Sarajevo also play into its *multicultural subconscious* where reminders of Ottoman rule and the grandeur of Habsburg Empire buildings mingle with the minimalist and somewhat ascetic architecture of post-Second World War socialist realism.

Sites that dominate the heart of the city include the famous Baščaršija, of course – the old Islamic part of the city and its magnificent Gazi-Husrev Begova Mosque dating from 1530. Yet only a short walk away one can find the old Orthodox church, the Cathedral of Jesus's Heart (Katedrala Srca Isusova), also dating from the sixteenth century, and the synagogue. On the Trg Oslobodjenja – Alija Izetbegović (Liberty Square – Alija Izetbegović) overlooking the old Orthodox church, stands the sculpture of *Ecce Homo*, dating from the 1984 Winter Olympics. The sculpture, by Francesco Porilli, is also called *Multicultural Man* and it features the following inscription: 'Multicultural Man will build the world' ('Multikulturalni čovjek izgradjivaće svijet'). *Ecce Homo, Multicultural Man*, stands in the middle of a globe-like structure, surrounded by iron doves and holding the left and right sides of the circle/the world in his hands (Illustration 19). The sculpture is encircled by the busts of leading literary figures from the region dating from the period of the Socialist Federation of Yugoslavia. In the square's rose garden, old men play chess while in front of the square, street vendors sell all kinds of things: Muslim prayer books, mats and beads, lighters with Marshall Tito's face painted on them, red stars and partisan hats from the Second World War, mannequin heads (pictured on the cover of this book), and pirated DVDs of the latest Hollywood blockbusters. The spatial multiplicity of histories makes it impossible for a city like Sarajevo to be defined by the imposed mode of homogenous and singular ethnic consciousness. The city, through its performance of everyday life, reacts to this imposition of singularity, acting out its *multicultural subconscious*.

My colleague Milija Gluhović, whose own research is engaged with the performance of religion, has generously shared a story of his recent walk through Sarajevo. A friend, who served as Milija's guide, claimed that this walk, which included visits to three different religious shrines, had the ritual power of wish fulfilment. The walk leads across the Gavrilo Princip Bridge to the tomb of Seven Brothers. It is there that the first prayer and a small donation are made. At the site there is a covered structure (*turbet*) with seven windows for each of the seven men buried there. As belief has it, throwing a coin through each of the windows will make your wish come true regardless of one's religious orientation. Standing in front of the Seven Brothers, Milija noticed that

Illustration 19 The *Multicultural Man*, photo by S. Jestrovic

the people around him belonged to different religions. Some performed a Muslim prayer, which would have been expected given that the shrine was a mosque, but others uttered a Christian one. The next stopover was St Ante, the Catholic church, then back across the bridge to the old

Orthodox church on Baščaršija. The ritual of prayer, in any of the three religions, was repeated at each place. On their pilgrimage of mapping multi-ethnic and multi-religious Sarajevo, my colleague and his friend added a fourth destination to the map – the Synagogue.

Although the walk is rooted in Sarajevo's multi-ethnic and multi-religious civic legacy, its scenario seems to be a post-war invention. I found a newspaper article from 2008 that describes the route of this new pilgrimage to different religious places in Sarajevo. It quotes the old Orthodox church leader who confirms that he often sees people of different religions praying in his church and it delights him. The article points out that citizens profess beliefs that are often different from the normative ones, describing them as 'Sarajevo beliefs'. The vicar of the Catholic church shares a similar story: 'As a born and bred Sarajevan, I remember that old Muslim women used to come to the church, kissed the statue of St Ante, prayed and lit candles. That has remained to this day. One of the reasons is the belief that St Ante has healing powers' (Stojaković, 'Three Shrines for One Wish'). The author of the article claims that among those who most frequently perform the walk linking the three shrines are pupils and students who hope to do well in exams, but also 'gamblers and football fans'.

Regardless of the individual and collective political rationales and agendas, the *multicultural subconscious of the city* is ludic and finds a way to perform itself through both the profane and sacred life of the city. The citizens know, sometimes even without fully apprehending their own embodied knowledge, that the ethos and *modus vivendi* in a city like Sarajevo lies in its eclectic multicultural practices – where Christians pray in front of a mosque, Muslim women kiss the statue of a Catholic saint, and atheists walk from shrine to shrine in the hope that their wishes will be granted.

Part III
City of Exiles

> *I am looking at my Yugoslav passport. It has a red cover with 'SFR Jugoslavija' inscribed on the front, as in 'Socialist Federal Republic of Yugoslavia'. The country, my country, does not exist anymore. The passport was issued in 1991 and even at the time Yugoslavia did not exist.*
>
> *So, what is this red booklet? A membership card of the League of Expatriates. An ID from Atlantis. A one-way ticket to fiction.*
>
> (Dragan Todorović, *The Book of Revenge*, p. 377)

During the 1990s, both Belgrade and Sarajevo were cities of exile. Both had an influx of refugees displaced from various parts of the Balkan wars. Both had established their own inner exilic spaces – their city-within-the-city – to preserve and protect a form of urban life that had been threatened. Finally, both cities had their itineraries of departure – places where one would go when one wanted to leave. I have already mentioned the itineraries of physical exile from Sarajevo – the airport, the Tunnel, and the UN convoy routes. In 1993, the United Nations imposed economic sanctions on Serbia and Montenegro (the last two remaining republics under the umbrella name of Yugoslavia), since they had been deemed most responsible for the bloodshed in the fall of Yugoslavia. This included an embargo on international flights from Serbia. One of the main city squares, Slavija, located in the heart of Belgrade, became a designated point of departure for all those who felt that years of anti-regime activism had proven ineffective. For them, leaving war-mongering Serbia was the only thing left to do. The buses usually left Slavija Square late at night in order to reach the Budapest airport by early next morning. From there, new exiles would get on a flight towards a place they hoped might one-day become their new home. On departure evenings, Slavija Square was unusually populated with people and luggage. Family members and friends waved long, teary goodbyes and remained on the pavement long after the bus had disappeared into the misty, Belgrade night on its route to Budapest and beyond. On several occasions, I was amongst those standing in Slavija Square, waving to friends as their faces in the bus window became smaller... and then indistinct.

In April 1995, I, too, became one of the passengers struggling with oversized bags full of clumsily selected items. Like everyone else, I believed that the content of my luggage was exactly right. It included practical things along with a few, less necessary trifles – the bare minimum needed for an identity to be transplanted and take root in a foreign landscape. A stringent paring down was *de rigeur* since all of the settings, and most of the props and costumes with which our identities had been interwoven, could not fit into the stipulated allowance of two suitcases per person. The best we could do was to take a few objects – the smallest, lightest and most telling details of our individual settings that we were about to leave behind. Metonymic objects – tiny scenic synecdoches – were wrapped in old newspaper, stuffed into the sleeves of folded sweaters, and tucked into the corners of our suitcases of various shapes and sizes.

In my own case, I left Belgrade to immigrate to Toronto in the spring but my suitcase was disproportionately packed with a number of warm sweaters and socks, as if the long and harsh Canadian winters might never actually end. Some of the other objects in my luggage included three cookbooks, several souvenir mugs bought a year earlier during a visit to Prague, and a set of crocheted coasters made by a family member that in the end remained unused. I have never been able to fully decode the logic behind my choice of items, yet when I packed, I must have believed that through them my world would be reconstituted somewhere else. The semiotics of my hand luggage was more easily readable. Aside from the almost useless Yugoslavian passport that a Canadian landed immigrant visa suddenly turned into a viable travelling document, I was carrying my Bachelor of Arts degree from the University of Belgrade, its English language transcript, and a copy of my new play that I planned to translate into English as soon as I arrived in Toronto. Carefully protected in the inside pocket of my bag was a bright red Easter egg. It is part of our tradition to colour the first Easter egg red and to keep it safe throughout the year until the following Easter – the belief being that the egg protects the home and the family. My documents and even my new play were personal talismans chosen in the hopes that they would open doors, from my entry into the new country to the opportunity to preserve a kind of professional identity that I had just started to establish. The egg was there to turn the bland, rented, one-bedroom apartment in the high-rise on the corner of Yonge and Isabella Streets into home. All these objects scattered in my handbag and in my suitcase were there to secure continuity – the illusion of an uninterrupted journey where everything would be a matter of simple and straightforward translation. My play, written in Serbian, would quickly find its English equivalent; my identity as an ex-Yugoslavian would be efficiently exchanged for my new status as a landed immigrant in Canada.

Of course, not all departures were the same. My cousin Željko had far less luggage when he left Sarajevo. In late March of 1992, when the first signs of unrest in the city started, he sent his wife, two young children and his father-in-law to visit their family in Belgrade. They had planned to be away for a week, two at the most, until things calmed down a bit. Convinced that there could be no war in Sarajevo, they packed only what they thought would be needed for a week's visit. Željko stayed in Sarajevo to keep their penthouse apartment safe. A few days later, the first grenades started falling on the city and air-raid sirens alerted the citizens to move to the nearest shelters. From the initial attacks on Sarajevo, Željko spent his nights with his neighbours in the communal shelter in the basement of his building. One evening, as he was descending the staircase to the shelter, a deafening, violent thud shook the entire building. Everyone stayed awake trying to figure out what and where the grenade had hit since they had never experienced such a powerful detonation. In the morning, when the air-raid sirens announced that it was safe to leave, Željko climbed the long flight of stairs to his apartment. When he reached the top of the stairs, he found a gaping whole in the place where his home used to be.

The war in the former Yugoslavia displaced about 2 million people. It also triggered the largest brain drain in the history of the region, based on intellectual unemployment and the lack of prospects, but even more so on political disagreement with the dominant power structure of the time. Some, like myself, had a choice, and even a place to return to, even though the relationship to it was geopathological. But there were many, like Željko and his family, who could not return: 'they had, quite literally, lost their place in the world, bombed and burned out of existence by an opposing faction' (King, 'Migration, globalization and place', p. 26).

The circumstances of departure differed but there were several popular, or rather possible, destinations that were relatively open for exiles from the Balkan wars. Although a large number of refugees and other émigrés from former Yugoslavia made their way to Western Europe, especially the United Kingdom, the Netherlands, Germany and others, in the 1990s, 'many governments [have] stiffened their procedures on admitting refugees, looking for loopholes in UN guidelines in order to screen applications more severely. The refugees streaming out of former Yugoslavia discovered this hardening attitude on the part of the "West"' (King, 'Migration, globalization and place', p. 26). Canada, Australia and New Zealand still openly accepted refugees and landed immigrants from the former Yugoslavia. This, of course, involved an application and selection procedure and a hefty fee, given the economic context. Some countries, Australia, for example, had a more Draconian, point-based application process but even so, there were never any guarantees. Official approval for refugee or landed immigrant status, depending on one's circumstances, meant legal entry into the country and a secure work permit. Canada, with its reasonably high application approval rates, became one of the favourite destinations for exiles from the former Yugoslavia.

A few months after a grenade had decimated his apartment, my cousin Željko managed to get out of the besieged Sarajevo and to reunite with his family in Belgrade. Shortly afterwards, they were accepted to Canada as refugees and moved to Toronto. After a number of friends, acquaintances and friends of friends went through the application process and, with or without documents, were dispersed, throughout North America, Western Europe, Australia and other places, I, too, submitted my landed immigrant visa application to the Canadian embassy. Several months later, in spring of 1995, I was a landed immigrant in Toronto. Željko, his wife Pejka, their children and their grandfather (my great uncle), had already settled there. It had been two years since they had arrived in the city and their place felt like home. I listened to their story and told them mine, we talked about job hunting and about the best and the cheapest places to live in the city. We started to share our immigrant life in Toronto, swapping stories and recipes over comforting winter dinners and summer barbecues. Toronto became our true meeting place, where our different stories – previously set in Sarajevo and Belgrade – came together, and where we began to relate to each other more than we ever had as members of a large, extended family in former Yugoslavia.

8
In the Comfort of Non-Place

> *The identities of places are a product of social actions and of the ways in which people construct their own representation of particular places. It is people themselves who make places, but not always in circumstances of their own choosing.*
>
> Pat Jess and Doreen Massey, 'The Contestation of Place', p. 134

The exilic city implies a certain perspective, a way of seeing – it is articulated through both representation and spatial practice. *Exilic city*, reveals a specific *sense of place* unfolding through 'the focus of personal feelings' (Rose, 'Place and identity', p. 88), which are not seen as trivial. The *sense of place*, shaped through connection between place and people, 'is more than one person's feelings about a particular place; such feelings are not only individual, but also social' (Rose, 'Place and identity', p. 88). In the phrase *exilic city*, the attribute *exilic* immediately, although vaguely, invokes a social feeling and the perspective of the individual figure – through whose eyes, experience and urban practice – the city is lived and mediated. This also charts an alternative map of the city, whose signposts and landmarks do not necessarily match those of the official map.

At one of our many gatherings, Željko, whose stories about Sarajevo, the war and immigrant life were captivating, described his first encounter with Toronto:

> 'On my first day, I got on the subway and rode to the very last stop, to the edges of the city. At the last stop, I got off and I slowly walked back to the city centre.'

'Why did you do that?' – we asked.
'To see how big it was, to measure what I was up against.'

Željko's walk was an act of shaping the *exilic city* – of mapping an urban landscape through the immediate experience of a recent immigrant. The map that he drew by walking started at the centre of the city and moved to its margins on the outskirts, before making its way back to the city centre. Russian writer and émigré to Berlin, Wladimir Kaminer, wrote a satirical city guide entitled *Ich bin kein Berliner: A travel guide for lazy tourists*, where he depicts the city through the eyes of a foreigner. Some of his city tips and suggested itineraries are directly linked to immigrants' mappings of the city. For instance, Kaminer suggests an alternative itinerary for the visit to Alexanderplatz, the landmark site of Alfred Doblin's classic *Berlin-Alexanderplatz*. The first stop is the Police Headquarters on Alexanderplatz, where asylum seekers and other immigrants apply to remain in the country and to get work permits. The next stop is a tiny inn – a place to have a beer. Finally, Kaminer recommends trying the old fortune-telling machine – dwarfed by the famous TV tower that marks Alexanderplatz – which regular tourists usually fail to notice.

When I first arrived in Toronto, a number of friends and acquaintances from Belgrade and other parts of the former Yugoslavia were already there. Every one of them took me on a tour of the city. On these outings, we talked far more about the practicalities of everyday immigrant life than we did about Toronto. The only time that our conversation switched gears was when we reached Yonge Street – the main city artery that begins downtown on the shores of Lake Ontario and stretches past the city's northern limits to Lake Simcoe, a gateway to the wilderness of the Upper Great Lakes. On reaching Yonge Street, each of my immigrant city guides would knowingly pronounce: 'This is Yonge Street. The longest street in the world.' Some even added: 'It's in *The Guinness Book of Records*.' The street that incorporated the varied and colourful cityscape in front of our eyes was not the Yonge Street of our exilic imaginaries. Our Yonge Street was a long, clean, straight line – its everyday life, a simple geometry, its history, written in kilometres.

The term *exilic city* describes one of several transient identities of the city. It unfolds horizontally through space, rather than vertically through time. In the familiar cities that we had left, like Belgrade and Sarajevo, each street had layers that hid old names, demolished buildings, recently plastered shrapnel holes, long covered-over graffiti. For us, every street in Belgrade and Sarajevo was a palimpsest, each one cutting vertically through time leading into a tunnel (or, rather, the abyss) of history. In our exilic city, Yonge Street was simply the longest street in the world. Its designation was both childishly amazing and strangely comforting. For us, its identity was summarized as an entry in *The Guinness Book of Records* – measurable in kilometres and representable with connecting dots on the map. At first, Yonge Street was not a place, but a signpost. The ability to locate it easily provided physical and existential reassurance that one would not get lost in the *exilic city*. In this context, Toronto's Yonge Street became an *exilic non-place*. Hence, to pass the knowledge of this signpost to a fellow immigrant was a way to reiterate the new and still fragile relationship with the city. More than that, it was an act of sharing *the comfort of the exilic non-place*.

For a recent exile, the history, politics, complexities, density and diversity of the new place are too much to grapple with. The city confronts the newcomer with a multitude of new signs – from the imposing cityscape and complicated legal and administrative systems to subtle social signs and cultural codes. At first, they are all difficult to navigate and read. Thus, it is not in the multiple identities of the exilic city that the newcomer seeks refuge and finds identification, for they are indeed overwhelming, but in its *non-places*. The map of one of Toronto's non-places – the subway lines – largely shaped Željko's itinerary and first encounter with the city. In order to be confronted, walked through and conquered in about a day on foot, the entire *exilic city* must first become a non-place in Marc Augé's sense of the term.

In his notion of non-place, Augé takes de Certeau's distinction between space and place as a point of departure, asserting that some of the same parameters apply to non-place as to place. He further explains how non-places never exist in pure form:

> places reconstitute themselves in it; relations are restored and resumed in it; the 'millennial ruses' of 'the invention of the everyday' and 'the art of doing', so subtly analysed by Michel de Certeau, can clear a path there and deploy their strategies. Places and non-place are rather like opposite polarities: the first is never completely erased, the second never totally completed; they are like palimpsests on which the scrambled game of identity and relations is ceaselessly written.
>
> (Augé, *Non-Place*, pp. 78–9)

Augé does not define non-place with the same oppositional relation between space and place as de Certeau does, rather he points out that: 'in the same way that the geometrical figure is opposed to movement, the unspoken to the spoken word or the inventory to the route: it is a place in the established and symbolized sense, anthropological place' (*Non-Place*, p. 81). For Augé, the term *non-place*, unlike de Certeau's *space* with which it shares some traits, does not imply the negative quality of place as 'an absence of place from itself' (p. 85) and as embodied in the contrast between the 'symbolized spaces of place' and 'the non-symbolized space of non-place' (p. 82). He points out that those non-places still mediate 'a whole mass of relations, with the self and with the others, which are only indirectly connected with their purpose' (p. 94).

The exilic experience presupposes a heightened involvement with the phenomenon of non-place and offers its own taxonomy of *non-places*. The transient quality of non-place, in the context of exile, fully reveals its two-fold character, described by Augé in the following way: 'Clearly the word "non-place" designates two complementary but distinct realities: space formed in relation to certain ends (transport, transit, commerce, leisure), and the relations that the individuals have with these spaces' (*Non-Place*, p. 94). On the one hand, *non-places* include transitional spaces that constitute the connecting points of a journey. One passes through them, but presumably does not dwell there long enough to make their transitional quality more ambiguous. Some are traveller's spaces, which Augé recognizes as the archetypes of *non-place*s (p. 86), such as airports, border crossings and hotels; others are more specifically exilic, like refugee camps, detention centres or immigration offices. On the other hand, the exilic experience also involves different kinds of *non-place* in which the transient quality is not realized through constant movement – a ceaseless passing through – but by dwelling in a space. Hence, the taxonomy of exilic non-places includes both public and private spaces. One category of the public places involves the aforementioned *non-places* that Augé also lists. Despite their symbolic dimensions, these *non-places* share an aura of uniformity. The other category involves places such as Yonge Street that become temporarily cast as a *non-place*, not necessarily because of its uniformity and movement, but through an immigrant's *sense of place* informed by a heightened experience of *placelessness*.

Theatre scholar Dragan Klaić left the country and his professorship at Belgrade University in the early 1990s and settled in Amsterdam. He became Director of the Dutch Theatre Institute and subsequently one of the leading European cultural policy experts. In addition to his scholarly work, he wrote an exilic memoir, *Exercises in Exile*, and a number of essays on this topic, including 'The Post-Yugoslav Exile: An Interim Account' from which the following quotation has been excerpted:

> The simple experience of moving with my wife and daughter into a completely empty apartment, carrying a few suitcases and nothing else, starting a new household from scratch after 15 years of living together was even liberating. True, a good many of my books were afterwards sent on from Belgrade, together with a few items of artistic or sentimental value, and that helped the domestication a bit.
>
> (p. 41)

In this passage, Klaić describes the private space of a recent immigrant as a non-place. When I first moved to Toronto, my apartment looked like most of the other homes of recent immigrants I have visited. Our places were alike – the architecture of the cement-block high-rises, the layout of their compact rooms, the colours on the walls and even the omnipresent 'ex-YU lamp'. The latter item was a lighting fixture of modern, nondescript design, available for an extremely low price in Dollar Stores all over Toronto, which most of us found quite agreeable. Almost every household of recent immigrants from the former Yugoslavia had one; hence, it acquired its own code name within our communities. As the years went by and the first immigrant household was abandoned for an even cheaper dwelling, or, as was often the case, for a mortgaged property, many of these 'ex-YU lamps' ended up in garage sales and gradually disappeared from immigrants' domestic spaces.

Homes of recent immigrants are *private non-places* because of their emptiness and uniformity and because of their somewhat transient nature – new immigrants do not usually stay too long in their first dwellings. Yet, what gives these homes a *sense of non-place* are the furnishings that provide the instant illusion of a fulfilled need and even a certain lived-in quality. Essentially, though, they lack context or connections to memory as well as any metaphoric and symbolic dimension. Somewhat paradoxically, the uniform items and furnishings that turn immigrants' private non-places into instant homes become codes – the 'ex-YU lamp,' for instance, was a sign of shared experience among ex-Yugoslavian immigrants in Toronto. The sight of certain Ikea tables and chairs in the photos of friends scattered across Western Europe and North America elicited a similar recognition of the shared experience of immigration and of a certain paradoxical comfort we all found at one point or another in the settings of globalized non-places.

After some time has passed, immigrants' non-places become more ambiguous as they enter a process of *domestication*. Private non-places, some complete with furnishings and accessories, that at first foregrounded the placelessness of the immigrant's domestic space, change their meaning as a different kind of ownership is established – not of the place or of an object, but of the unique symbolism shaped through the immigrant's prolonged personal relationship with it. Klaić's memoir, *Exercises in Exile,* is subtitled 'the reshaping of an expat at the Ikea table'. In the book, the Ikea table becomes both an iconic and a symbolic object connecting different themes and various stages of the author's immigrant life. In a way, it first appears as a feature of an exilic non-place – of the empty Amsterdam apartment. Gradually, it becomes a gathering point for the family and their numerous friends from all over the world. This nondescript item is both a connection to the exilic non-place of the early days of immigration and a metaphor of its domestication – its transformation into a *Lived Space*.

Several years ago, not long after I had read *Exercises in Exile,* I visited Dragan Klaić at his home in Amsterdam. Along with some of Klaić's Dutch colleagues, expats from the former Yugoslavia and immigrants from other parts of the world, we formed an eclectic group of guests. The year was 2004 or 2005, and the home of the Klaić family could not be further from an *exilic non-place*. Paintings and photographs of ex-Yugoslavian and international artists, plants, books and mementoes of Klaić's frequent trips casually arranged on the shelves, gave this domestic space a unique personality. We sat down on either side of a long, dining table and there it was, under the linen tablecloth, covered with a colourful display of delicious foods and wines – the Ikea table. It was an ambiguous item – a metaphor of exilic experience and a metonymic object of an exilic non-place. The Ikea table, that in a way became the protagonist of Klaić's exilic memoir, could have been easily replaced, but it was deliberately kept and preserved. Just as the little items in the suitcases of departing emigrants were a means of connecting to the memories and metaphors of the places left behind, so Klaić's Ikea table preserved the connection and memory to the exilic non-place. Through creative intervention and the practices of everyday immigrant life, a bland and branded product was appropriated and turned into a comic and moving metaphor of exile.

In August 2011, the news of Dragan Klaić's untimely death arrived. In the days and weeks to follow, numerous obituaries celebrating his exceptional intellect and personality appeared in various media outlets, from leading papers in the countries of the former-Yugoslavia to the

Guardian. The obituary published by his family included a code which inextricably linked Klaić with his inimitable sense of being at home in exile:

> Many will remember his brilliant mind, his generosity, his deep commitment to friends and work, his sense of humour, and his capacity to love, share and support. His joy of life came shining through his never-ending appetite for good books, opera, theatre, museums, and of course the best food and wine. Above all he enjoyed sharing these experiences around the Ikea table with friends who visited us from all over the world.
>
> (http://www.balkankult.org/bk/files/592/en/DRAGAN.pdf)

The Ikea table – the symbolic object of the exilic non-place – remained a feature in the immigrant's writing, in his everyday life, and even in his death. Hence, the exilic identity becomes redefined not by its decontextualization – placelessness – but by its ties to a multiplicity of places and non-places.

The Toronto home of my cousins Željko and Pejka has its own Ikea items, it is also warm and comfortable, clean and somewhat North American. It is hospitable, yet it does not give away too much about its inhabitants, except for one detail. On the central living room wall, right above an ergonomically designed Ikea chair, is a poster, painted in broad, curvy strokes, of a skier racing at full speed. The poster fits nicely in the environment, matching the colours on the walls and the patterns on the furniture. Only when one spots the title – 1984 SARAJEVO OLYMPIC GAMES – does it become clear what this poster really is – not a mere decoration, but an intervention in a private, exilic non-space. Like Klaić's Ikea table, the poster is a code item through which the exilic non-place becomes domesticated. It is the process in which things that contradict one another and create a sense of ambiguity begin to cohabit. Yet, the poster, this exilic code item that invokes another place in the comfort of its owners' Canadian home, was not a camouflaged trauma, a disguised scar, not even a piece of incurable nostalgia. When asked about the poster, the family refers to its beauty with lightness and glee in their voices because it is about their relationship to Sarajevo that they have managed to negotiate under their own terms. They chose to relate to the memory of the city by literally and metaphorically framing one of its most utopian performative moments – Sarajevo the Olympic city, where their lives were young, safe and prosperous and where the future looked bright, modern and fast. The skier on the poster was indeed Sarajevo, as it appeared in 1984 in vibrant colours and broad energetic brushstrokes. Like many others, Pajka and Željko have lost their city, but they have kept its energy and vitality as captured in the image of the invincible Olympic skier.

Identities

The Balkan bloodbath was to a great extent about claiming and reclaiming national, ethnic and religious identities, and zealously affirming them on the basis of exclusivity and difference. Nothing mocks this better than exile. Identity – especially when considered on the level of the homogenous and the national – becomes porous and negotiable. In the year 2000, Canadian director Ken Finkleman made a series of television films entitled *Foreign Objects*. One of them was based on an actual massacre that happened in Kosovo, when a pair of Serbian extremists killed a family of Kosovo Albanians. Finkleman tried to gather together as authentic a cast as possible from the population of ex-YU Torontonians. Alongside a couple of Kosovo Albanian actors, he hired a Bosnian to play a Serb, a Croatian to play another Albanian, and a Serb to play a Serb. The Serbian character, who could not have been further from the notion of the heroic Serbian male identity – always unjustly wronged and never guilty – was even more complicated by the fact that a Serbian actor was to play the murderer.

Much could be said about using events and stories situated in the Balkan conflicts to make cinematic parables of savagery and evil, as well as about the tendency to cast East European actors as villains in English-speaking movies. What interests me here, though, is how these actors approached their original national identities and their roles. My informant about this project, writer Dragan Todorović, who doubled as the actor playing the murderous Serb, had agreed to take part in the film after much deliberation. Although his role reinforced the trend of casting villainous Serbs as antagonists in films, the massacre had indeed taken place and after researching the actual event, Todorović agreed to do the project. For him, enacting the role and serving as a consultant on Finkleman's script became a critical vehicle – a way to reflect on his personal outrage over Serbia's atrocities in Kosovo. Todorović shared several off-camera moments with me including the laughter that ensued when Bosnian actor Emir Geljo (who also played a Serb in the film) told dark and hilarious jokes about besieged Sarajevo. Notably, Todorović and the Kosovo Albanians involved in the project did not shy away from discussing politics, particularly the Kosovo issue and the conflict with

Serbia. Of course, they did not always agree, but the discussion never turned into a quarrel. Even if they could not be persuaded to change their views, both parties in the conversation had a strong understanding of the different experiences of history, place and identity that had shaped their perspectives. This kind of conversation between a Serb and a Kosovo Albanian is still hard to imagine in Belgrade or Priština (the capital of Kosovo).

The reasons that this conversation was possible in Toronto are several: the place itself – its distance from the disputed Balkan territories and its relative neutrality towards the respective imagined communities – likely loosened the grip on the Serbian and Albanian participants that blood and place would have held elsewhere. In addition, the actors were hired for a project where identity (either the actor's own or the one performed in the film) involved taking on a role. Moreover, the original, 'authentic' identities of most of the actors had already been hyphenated through the experience of exile – negotiating distance and belonging to at least two places. The exilic context has enabled a kind of openness within which identity is neither singular nor exclusively bound to one place. In other words, exilic identities (at least of the most recent diasporas emerging out of the Balkan conflicts) have undergone a process by which they become more fluid and less written in the blood and stone of national imaginaries.

The wars in the Balkans instigated the most recent diasporic wave from this region to Canada, the United States and Western Europe. The first wave left Tito's Yugoslavia in the aftermath of the Second World War. Unlike previous generations of expats who have established tight-knit communities largely based on shared ethnicity, the communities of new immigrants from 'post-Yugoslavia', as Klaić called it, have been more open and porous:

> The post-Yugoslav diaspora is a large, fragmented and dispersed community. [...] Quite a large number of my friends and colleagues, academics, intellectuals and artists in their thirties and forties sooner or later left by choice, seeking in emigration the multicultural context that we all once enjoyed in Yugoslavia and which we were deprived of in 1991.
>
> ('The Post-Yugoslav Exile', p. 39)

The older generation of immigrants who had escaped communism were united by shared imaginaries of alternative ideological projects, mainly of royalist and bourgeois orientation. The homogeneity of these communities is grounded in their consensus on remembering and interpreting the past and the ways it shapes their dreams for a better political future for the country they left so long ago. The new generation has no shared national and ideological projects; rather, it was catapulted into its exilic existence precisely because it had been traumatized by imaginaries and projects of this kind.

When I started this book, I believed that my case studies, memories, fragments and glimpses into the shared exilic life of 'post-Yugoslavian' (Klaić) diasporas would enable me to claim that these emerging immigrant communities had established their own heterotopic spaces in the multicultural fabric of Toronto. I hoped that our private spaces, communal events, ethnic restaurants and shops would produce new spatial identities and relations – heterotopias of Belgrade and Sarajevo in Toronto. Perhaps, even, a kind of a scattered and fragmented Yugoslavian heterotopia. Ethnic restaurants and shops have emerged, so have communal and cultural events related to post-Yugoslavian communities, but they did not give rise to the kinds of heterotopias that invoked and reconstituted a sense of place or community in singular and readily recognizable terms. There are at least two reasons why exilic heterotopias of Sarajevo and Belgrade have never really emerged in Toronto: the first has to do with the relationship to memory, the other to history.

On a tiny street in a small pocket in the north-east end of Toronto, there is a store that sells food products that any post-Yugoslavian would instantly recognize – *ajvar* (a Macedonian vegetable spread), *burek* (a pie mainly associated with Bosnia), *bajadere* and *kiki bombone* (Croatian sweets that were part of many Yugoslavian childhoods), and so on. Next-door is a small, ethnic joint known for its *kebabs* that is owned by a Bosnian. Further down the street, a Serbian hairdresser has set up shop. On sunny, quiet days, the shopkeeper, the cook and the hairdresser sit in front of their establishments to smoke and chat. I used to jokingly refer to this street as *Mali Zvornik*, after a provincial Bosnian town that I have never visited. The sight of this little street in Toronto fed into my imaginaries of another place that I regarded as familiar, but which I never actually knew. I often visited my '*Mali Zvornik*' in Toronto for my supply of comfort food and occasionally, to indulge my nostalgia for *kiki bombone* – a chewy, pink candy that tasted of strawberries and childhood.

I stopped calling the place *Mali Zvornik* the moment I truly related the name to the actual place – one that suffered enormously during the war, but was far from the glare of the media spotlight. The taste of *kiki bombone* still brought happy memories, not only my own, I believed, but memories uncomplicated by the wars that I could share with any post-Yugoslavian. When I read Dubravka Ugrešić's book, *The Ministry of Pain* (*Ministarstvo Boli*), the pink, strawberry-flavoured candy of my childhood suddenly lost its innocence. In her book, Ugrešić describes her life as an exile in Amsterdam where she taught in a university department of Slavic Studies and Languages. Many of Ugrešić's students had ties to the former Yugoslavia and had been traumatized by the country's breakdown. Early in the book, her reflection on memory and manipulation and the banality of evil turns *kiki bombone* into a metaphor revealing that nostalgia is never innocent:

> Evoking memories has been a unique manipulation of the past, as much as their prohibition. Regimes in our former country were pressing the *delete* button, while I kept pressing *restore*. There, the regime was manipulating millions of people, and here, I have been manipulating a few. They were erasing the Yugoslavian past, ascribing to 'yugoslavianism' guilt for all the misfortunes, including the war itself, and I was concerned for the everyday existence that marked our lives and established a voluntary *lost & found* service. Both manipulations were clouding the reality. I wondered, would I not – evoking warm images from our shared past – suppress recent images of the war's bloody reality. Would I not – inviting my students to invoke the taste of *kiki bombone* – erase a case of a Belgrade boy stabbed by his peers only because he was Albanian. [...]
>
> On the other hand, everything was connected and went in pairs. Death alone was chewing *kiki bombone*. People were murdered and they were murderers, they were robbers and they were robbed, they were rapists and they were raped with cheap refrains of the everyday in the background. Soldiers fell hit by bullets, while dragging a TV – their loot – towards the trench. Death was walking hand in hand with the garbage of the trivial. Hence the detail with the *kiki* candy could be perpetuated in numerous variants. In an image of a child hit by a sniper, blood streaming out of its mouth mixed with the sweet saliva of *kiki bombone*.
>
> (*Ministarstvo Boli*, pp. 64–5)

We may all share the tastes, smells, colours and brands of former Yugoslavia, but since the early 1990s, they have acquired different connotations and metaphors filtered through different experience of war and exile. Hence, we have been reluctant to impose interpretations on our shared memories and uncomfortable with claiming a shared exilic cultural space. Nevertheless, a somewhat paradoxical relationship to history has emerged as a possibility – an opening *of* space and an opening *in* space: on the one hand, historical baggage as heavy as lead comes between us; on the other, there was a limit to the amount of history that we could carry with us.

Open space

'City life is the "being together" of strangers', writes Iris Marion Young (quoted in Massey, 'Conceptualization of place', p. 83). Exilic city life (at least as long as post-Yugoslavian exiles are concerned) is the 'being together' of people who share complicated and variously interpreted histories. The last diasporas from the Balkans have neither reconstructed their homogenous national imaginaries nor invoked multicultural heterotopias of former Yugoslavia. This is not to say that communities based around ethnic and regional backgrounds have not emerged. Serbs often hang out with other Serbs, Croats with Croats, Bosnians with Bosnians, but they do not form closed, tightly knit communities. They also mix with various *others* engaging with diverse ad hoc communities that include expats from different regions and ethnicities of former Yugoslavia, immigrants from other parts of the world and long-time Canadians. These communities are spontaneous rather than predetermined by ethnic or other alliances, temporary rather than fixed, dynamic and porous rather than static and closed. The communication is at most times unmediated; politics and war are neither constant topics nor the proverbial elephant in the room. What distinguishes the mode of interacting, belonging and being in the city is *improvisation*.

Improvisation, as a mode of exilic individual and communal being, enables utopian performative moments to take place on stage and in the everyday life of the city. These moments occur on various levels – from private gatherings to public and cultural events. At times they reflect the urban ideal proposed by geographer Kevin Robins, who looks for ways 'to match community and security with the kind of openness that can stimulate a positive sense of challenge and contestation' ('Prisoners of the City', p. 17). Robins calls for rethinking 'the notion of place as settled, enclosed and internally coherent' (p. 58) and calls for 'its replacement or supplementation by a concept of place as a meeting-place, the location of the intersections of particular bundles of activity spaces, of connections and interrelations, of influences and movements.'(quoted in Massey, 'Conceptualization of place', pp. 58–9).

In 2001, my play, *Not My Story*, directed by Serbian-Canadian artist Dragana Varagić was staged at the Toronto Fringe Festival (Illustration 20). Subsequently, it was restaged for a mainstream run in 2004. The play referenced Chekhov's *Three Sisters*, transporting the women to the world of post-Yugoslavian immigrants living in Canada. The cast and production team included a diverse group of expats from various regions of former Yugoslavia as well as Canadian actors, producers and other contributors to the project. This mixed creative team attracted a variety of audiences, including a larger than usual interest of various post-Yugoslavian communities since at the time there were few other cultural events that related to their context. Ticket queues stretched along the pavement in front of the theatre, eliciting the curiosity of passers-by. Immigrants from other places were interested to see how someone else's immigrant experience had been portrayed. Regular Toronto theatergoers and critics came to see the work of local theatre makers involved in the show, but just as often to discover for themselves what all the fuss was about. This created a spontaneous, urban communal moment – an accidental gathering of diverse people that was neither premeditated nor pre-negotiated. The theatre and the space around it became a temporary meeting-place (Robins) for an exchange that was not necessarily confined to one's immediate and familiar communal context. The project created a sense of beyond that Young ascribes to the modern city: 'The modern city means always having a sense of beyond, that there is much human life beyond my experience going on in or near these spaces, and I can never grasp the city as a whole' (*Conceptualization of Place*, p. 83).

This was partly an immigrant project, because of its theme and of the background of some of the team members, but it was not a piece that belonged to any singular Balkan diasporic community. Rather, it was a project that was part of Toronto's theatre offerings for the season, beyond ethnic ghettoization or self-ghettoization. The production was a success not only in a theatrical sense but also in a communal one. The excellent actors, the director, the dramaturge and the entire team were able to capture the Chekhovian mixture of sadness and comedy. The diverse creative team endowed the play with a certain openness and attracted an even more diverse audience which was, perhaps, the most interesting part of the event. All of us who were involved in the project loved to listen to the audience night after night – many laughed, some even cried, but not necessarily in the same places. Two memories of the production further illustrate the key features of these ad hoc exilic communities – porous space and improvisation.

April Productions, in conjunction with **The Toronto Fringe Festival** presents:

HAPPINESS CHANNEL

Written by **Silvija Jestrovic**
Directed by **Dragana Varagic**

With:
Cynthia Ashperger
Jason Jazrawy
Rena Polley
Stephen Sparks
Gregory Thomas
Dragana Varagic

Andjelija Djuric/Costume and Set Design
Milija Gluhovic/ Assistant Director
Joanne Mackay-Bennett/ Production Manager
Yana Meerzon/Dramaturg
Daniela Misetic/Stage Manager
Terri Park/Lighting Design
Dragoslav Tanaskovic/Music Composer and Sound Design

DUŠAN

Where? St. Vladimir Institute, 620 Spadina Ave. (south of Harbord)

July 6 @ 9:00 PM / July 8 @ 4:30 PM
July 10 @ 7:30 PM / July 12 @ 4:30 PM
July 13 @ 1:30 PM / July 14 @ 6:00 PM
July 15 @ 10:30 PM

Tickets: Advance Ticket Sales $10
By Phone: 862-2222 or in person at Box Office, 29 Brunswick Ave.
All others at door $8

Illustration 20 Poster for *Not My Story,* designed by Dušan Petričić

In 2004, when the second run of *Not My Story* closed in Toronto, Croatian actress Cynthia Ashperger threw a party at her home. She was one of my immigrant 'three sisters', alongside Canadian actor Rena Polly and Serbian actor Dragana Varagić, who had also directed the show. The diverse mix of the party reflected the demographic of the project. To the delight of everyone present, musician Dragoslav Tanasković, who composed the score for the show, started to play the piano. At one point someone asked if he could play a particular Croatian song. He did so and then immediately joked that he should play a Serbian one for reasons of parity. The guests played along with the joke. When Croatian party-goers requested another Croatian song, the Serbian group waited until it was finished before asking for another Serbian song, and so the tunes volleyed back and forth with all of us singing all the songs together. Eventually exhausted, the musician came up with an 'ace' finale. 'Enough!' he said, 'Now we're going to sing a song that we can all agree on.' As he started to play *Mamma Mia*, everyone burst into laughter. The improvisation that had taken place along musical and national lines turned into an impromptu satire of our differences and reinforced the utter absurdity of the conflict whose bloody outcome has permanently marked this generation of post-Yugoslavian exiles. Our shared exilic context allowed us to make light of our differences and to indulge in a satirical improvisation that started and ended in laughter.

Several years after he arrived as a refugee in Toronto, Sarajevo poet Goran Simić opened a café which he envisaged as a creative space and a meeting-place. Unlike national imagined communities, upon which the gathering places of older generation diasporas from the region were modelled, this place was not limited either by native language or by any homogenous ethnic demographic. It was a place one could enter easily without negotiation. Bosnians who frequented the place where immediately joined by other post-Yugoslav expats. Simić's Canadian friends and fellow writers came along, but so did random visitors who lived in the neighbourhood as well as a few rougher street characters whom the poet had befriended. In terms of creative output, there was no fixed agenda. Most of the time, the walls of the café were adorned with abstract clay masks – reflections of the exilic experience – by Sarajevo artist Sasha Bukvić. Some evenings, Simić read his poetry, often alongside fellow Canadian poet, Fraser Sutherland. Other times, they brought in actors to read from the new play that the poets were developing with a local prostitute, another frequent visitor at the café. Even though the café was relatively short-lived due to mundane financial issues, its temporality contributed to its syncretic, transient and shifting identity.

The exilic city does not operate as an ideal open space at all times, in fact it rarely does. Immigrant realities, like any other, and in some cases more than others, involve hardship, misunderstandings and disappointment on all levels – systemic/political, collective and personal. Yet sporadic glimpses of the exilic, open city can emerge in brief moments where its openness unfolds through utopian performatives. This openness is more than a fleeting look at an unattainable ideal; it is a genuine experience of openness and encounter that long after the utopian moment has passed, reverberates and cumulatively shapes communal realities. Although, as Young admits', liberatory possibilities of capitalist cities have been fraught with ambiguity' (quoted in Massey, 'Conceptualization of place', p. 83), the city still works as a place for unmediated encounters:

> The social differentiation of the city also provides a positive inexhaustibility of human relations. The possibility always exists of becoming acquainted with new and different people, with different cultural and social experiences; the possibility always exists for new groups to form or emerge around specific interests.
>
> (p. 84)

So far, I have talked about individuals and communities and how they have encountered and shaped their exilic spaces casting the city in a relatively passive role. It is worth remembering that the relationship between the exile and the city is a two-way street.

To look into exilic Toronto in relation to Canadian immigration policy and its multiculturalism on a programmatic level exceeds the scope of this analysis. I have been more invested in the relationships between the exile and the city that are relatively unmediated by representatives, leaders, state institutions and bureaucrats (although some support must be acknowledged, such as, in relation to the given case studies, the Arts Council's funding for *Not My Story*). So how does Toronto interact with its exilic communities? How has it been involved in shaping its spaces into meeting-places for ad hoc communities? There is an undeniable multicultural aspect to a city like Toronto, which is not to be confused with multiculturalism as a governmental policy. Although the official policy might figure as a contextual aspect, the multiculturalism that I have described here is an everyday, lived experience which may or may not conform to governmental policies. The experience of intense, *lived* multiculturalism through the everyday movements and rhythms of the city, as opposed to the *conceptual* multiculturalism of governing bodies, allows space for immigrant identities to be involved in shaping the city and, in return, to being shaped by the city. This is not meant to imply that the mutual reshaping between the exile and the city is an easy process and that immigrant identities have a readily available place.

Yet Toronto's eclectic map, with its mixture of diverse ethnic neighbourhoods, means that the boundaries of ethnicity and class are slightly more porous than in some other places. In comparison to the long and turbulent histories of Belgrade and Sarajevo, Toronto emerges as a relatively young place, less burdened and fixed in the closed communal narratives that are often impenetrable to newcomers. Toronto's distinction from the palimpsests of the Balkan cities allows immigrants more flexible, heterogeneous ways to be part of the city. Consequently, the notion of 'meeting-place' not only unfolds through encounters of people with one another, but is also a point of encounter between an individual and/or a collective with the moving, transient body of the city itself. To meet-in-the-city also means to come face to face with it – to form a relationship to one another – to link one's own history with the everyday life of the city.

Sense of time

> It was not too difficult becoming an émigré because the condition runs in my family. Ever since childhood I have been aware that several generations of my ancestors embarked on an émigré life, and that those who did not manage to leave on time usually lost their lives.
>
> (Klaić, 'The Post-Yugoslav Exile', p. 33)

I have talked so far about sense of place – a contested space of memory (the Balkans), and the possibilities within fragmented exilic spaces – whereby the idea of a shared (if at times charged) space among post-Yugoslav expats emerges. Another dimension that is often shared warrants mention here. It is the sense of time by which I mean both *historical time* and a sense of *timing*.

It is New Year's Eve, 2003, when a group of post-Yugoslavs, most of them from Belgrade and a few from Sarajevo, including my cousin Željko, gather around my dining-room table for the festive evening. At one point, the conversation diverts towards the topic of war and someone asks Željko about his escape from Sarajevo. Željko begins his story, describing the early days of the siege, his neighbours and the shelter where they spent the nights. His story is full of details and miniature anecdotes. We can picture his flat, his kitchen, we see the plate of cabbage rolls as he places it in the microwave, we see his fingers setting the timer to exactly 30 seconds, since this is the exact time needed to warm the cabbage rolls to perfection. He transfers the rolls to a plastic container, washes the plate, walks out of the apartment, and locks the door. We follow Željko, container of cabbage rolls in hand, as he descends the stairs to the shelter. We almost jump from our seats when the grenade hits. The next morning, we follow him upstairs, we try to feel through Željko's eyes the shock of reaching one's home only to find a pail of rubble and smoke. 'Everything was gone', he says, 'except for one single item that remained intact – the microwave plate'. We all laugh. The clock strikes midnight, we have forgotten about the New Year. Champagne is opened hastily and New Year's hugs are quickly exchanged. 'Željko, please continue', pleads one of the guests as we quickly return to our seats.

For most of us, the moment when exile began does not correspond to the date that we left the country. The word 'immigrant' officially appeared in my documents in 1995, although my legal status had changed a few times over the years. The physical and material circumstances of my situation have also changed several times: from my internal, self-imposed exile in Belgrade, to my initial immigrant days in Toronto – selling American jeans in a store run by an Indian expat and washing dishes in an Italian family-run eatery – and beyond. Željko's exile also began before he arrived in Canada with the official status of war refugee. In fact, his exile began the moment that the grenade landed on his flat. His physical exile followed several months later. What we share is the experience of rupture and discontinuity through both external factors and an internal sense of timing that have shaped our histories.

It is that shared sense of time that brought us around my dining-room table on that particular New Year's Eve in 2003 where we sat riveted by Željko's story. We shared a sense of *historical time* through which some of us recognized the political moment when our internal exiles began; and a *sense of timing* of when to board our flights to Canada. Then, of course, there was Željko's impeccable sense of timing. For if the cabbage rolls had taken any longer to be perfectly warmed than precisely 30 seconds, there would have been no story to share.

Notes

Part I Belgrade: The City of Spectacle

1. When the protest was over, Ognjenović, a distinguished theatre director and playwright, was forced by the authorities to resign from the position of Artistic Director of the National Theatre. By the mid-1990s, the National Theatre was tightly controlled by cultural officials of Milošević's regime, prompting a few members of the ensemble to leave the theatre in protest. In post-Milošević years, Ognjenović became Serbia's ambassador to Denmark.
2. For lyrics of the Patti Smith song, go to: http://www.metrolyrics.com/people-have-the-power-lyrics-patti-smith.html
3. After the events of 5 October 2000, when Milošević was overthrown, Lečić became Minister of Culture in the newly formed Serbian Government. He remained Minister of Culture for the next three years.
4. OTPOR was a political organization (of mostly students) active from 1998, whose agenda was the political struggle for democracy against the regime of Slobodan Milošević. Occasionally, members of OTPOR were arrested for their political activities. Nowadays, OTPOR is no loner an active organization and some of its prominent members have become leading figures of the political establishment in Serbia.
5. Zoran Djindjić was one of the most prominent figures of the Serbian political opposition to Milošević. He became Prime Minister of Serbia in 2001. In March of 2003, Djindjić was assassinated by a former paramilitary soldier with links to organized crime.

1 City-as-Action

1. See Dubravka Knežević's 'Marked in Red Ink', an article that deals with the anti-regime protests in Serbia that opens with an analogy to the French Revolution.
2. Although students had assumed control of the buildings, it was not possible to fully prevent the infiltration of regime supporters. On more than one occasion, mature 'students', whom nobody had seen before, tried to take the upper hand in decision-making. The infiltration of groups and institutions considered subversive, under the pretence of like-mindedness and camaraderie, was one of communism's tried and true tactics.
3. See S. Jestrovic, 'Theatricalization of Politics/Politicization of Theatre', *Canadian Theatre Review*, no 103. University of Texas Press, 2000: 42–7.
4. This fear was not entirely unfounded. After all, in the protests in 1991 two people were killed, while a number of others was beaten and arrested. In the course of the Milošević regime, journalist Dušan Reljić was kidnapped and held for questioning at an undisclosed location for several days; Slavko Ćuruvija, editor of the newspaper *Telgraf*, was gunned down; Milošević's

mentor turn political opponent was found dead after missing for a few years; and so on. Numbers of journalists and other prominent public figures that openly expressed their views against Milošević received threats. Nevertheless, disturbing as this account of the regime's violence was, for over ten years internal retributions of this kind had been relatively limited in numbers, serving perhaps more as a warning than as a systematic way of eliminating oppositional voices. Milošević's regime appropriated a tactic practised in the later years of Tito's Yugoslavia, where dissidents were not officially allowed, but they were not persecuted either. Milošević's regime went one small step further in this strategy; it did not so much repress oppositional voices, as simply ignore them. To openly oppress the opposition would only have made it stronger; to ignore it, to deny it, to cut all its outlets and treat it as non-existent was a much more efficient way of disempowerment.

5. The work of this company has been closely related to the city itself , which often emerged as both a performance site and a protagonist. For instance, the first performance of *DAH* was based on Brecht's poetry and it took place in Knez Mihailova Street in 1991. It both coincided with the disintegration of Yugoslavia and was a reaction to the ensuing bloodbath in the Balkans. The company has since devised numerous projectsm often using streets and found spaces as artistic outlets to actively engage and confront Serbian cultural and political reality. Remaining outside the cultural establishment, *DAH* has created performances that in one way or another explore the role of art 'in dark times' as the title of Brecht's poem has it. See also Brecht, *Bad Time for Poetry: Was it? Is It?*.
6. Nikola Džafo, *Led Art: 1993–2003 Dokumenti Vremena*. Novi Sad: Multimedija Centar Led Art, 2004.
7. Independent Radio B92 was the chief voice of Serbian resistance to Milošević's regime.
8. The Venetian gondola, depicted in Nikola Džafo's sculpture, used to be a status symbol representing the rise of the working class to lower middle class in the 1960s, when the borders of Tito's Yugoslavia opened to the West and shopping trips to Trieste became common. The Venetian gondola, usually displayed on the shelf in the living room, was the main souvenir from these trips – testimony of the first encounter between communist ideals and Western consumerism, as well as a memento of everyday life in Tito's Yugoslavia.
9. Author Jovan Čekić.
10. Author Milorad Cvetičanin.
11. Turbo-folk is a type of commercial music played in Serbia and other parts of the Balkans. It mixes traditional folk tunes with electronic instruments, usually set to sentimental lyrics. It became very popular in the early nineties and is associated with bad taste, kitsch, provincialism and lack of political consciousness.
12. In 2000, Sara Vidal put together a monograph dedicated to the *Bivouac* performance.
13. Quoted from the article 'Operacija Puz' ('Operation Snail'), by B. Batic published in the Serbian weekly magazine *NIN*, 10 January 1997, pp. 16–17.

2 At the Confluence of Utopia and Seduction

1. It is important to note that the repertoire of leading Serbian theatres in the 1980s was rather eclectic and, although the obsession with national identity and history was evident, shows with very different thematic and aesthetic concerns were produced alongside one another. For that reason, theatre critic Ksenija Radulović, analysing the repertoire of the 1980s, argues that the outburst of Serbian national sentiment in theatres may not have been a result of a premeditated, strategic cultural policy with the tendency to foreground national identity and assert a univocal national perspective. See Ksenija Radulović, 'Nacionalni resentiman na sceni' ['National sentiment on stage'], *Teatron*, no. 118, [Belgrade] 2002: 1–16.
2. The show was directed by Arsenije Jovanović, an established practitioner, whose work has not normally been related to national themes and traditional staging. Shortly after this performance, he turned to the exploration of the performance of sound.
3. Ironically, this view was not shared by other republics in the Yugoslavian Federation. Quite the contrary, the neighbouring republics felt dominated by Serbia. Yet under its shadow and that of Tito's Yugoslavia, they had also started to rediscover their own suppressed national sentiments.
4. I am grateful to Janelle Reinlet for pointing out to me the analogy between the improvisational scenario of *The Battle of Kolubara* and the 'Dominus vobiscum' ('The Lord be with you') salutation followed by the 'Et cum spiritu tuo' ('And with your spirit').
5. In her article, *'Invitation to the Battle: Reception of the 'patriotic' repertoire from the eighties' ('Poziv na bitku: recepcija 'patriotskog' repertoara osamdesetih' Teatron*), Slavica Vučković gives a detailed account of the mixed critical response to the *Battle of Kolubara*.
6. The title 'the most RESISTANT actor' is a word-play with the name of the organization OTPOR, since the word 'otpor' means 'resistant' in Serbo-Croatian.
7. See: http://www.vekoltours.com/online/index.php?option=com_content&task=view&id=95&Itemid=207&lang=EN
8. See: http://www.globus.com.hr/Clanak.aspx?BrojID=307&ClanakID=8519&Stranica=4

3 Epilogue: Endemic Geopathologies

1. In writing that the regime 'drove us out of Belgrade', I deliberately refer to the city rather than to the country for two reasons. Firstly, because there is no single name for the country that would be fully accurate. I can no longer call the country Yugoslavia, since it has disintegrated, nor can I identify Serbia as my place of origin. For a long time, I was able to refer to my place of origin only through negation, by naming what it no longer was (i.e., 'ex-Yugoslavia' or 'the former-Yugoslavia'). The second reason that I refer to the city rather than to the State is to emphasize my own Belgrade-centredness, which later in this section I acknowledge to be a problematic aspect of Serbian civic resistance.
2. Michael Warner understands publics and counter-publics as processes generated through discursive practices (*Publics and Counter-Publics*. New York: Zone

Books, 2002, p. 67). According to Warner, publics and counter-publics are particular and exclusive processes rather than fixed entities.

3. *Klub svetskih putnika* is still in business and because of its unusual setting and live-music it is often featured on tourist websites.
4. This dynamics between public and private spaces of Belgrade confirms Warner's claim of private space as a myth, because it is effectively conditioned and shaped in relation to public spaces.
5. Čavke was the legendary drummer of the famous Serbian rock band, *Električni orgazam*. When the war broke and Yugoslavia's downfall began, Čavke took part in an anti-war project that gathered a few leading local musicians. The project is best known for its anti-war song, *Rimtu-ti-tuki*. Soon after the filming of *Ghetto*, Čavke emigrated to Australia where he lived until his premature death in 1997.
6. A number of radical political performances in Belgrade could qualify as Invisible Theatre though (as the title of Milena Dragićević-Šešić's NTQ article suggests). The difference was in using and inventing strategies more organically suited to the local culture. Nevertheless, the population these performances addressed was mostly limited to the urban milieu.
7. Joseph Roach defines It-effect as personality-driven mass attraction (*It*. Ann Arbor, MI: University of Michigan Press, 2007, p. 3).
8. These attempts at performing the city had not managed to mobilize a large number of citizens, since the citizen's saw through the regimes appropriation of the counter-spectacle. The owner of the infamous Pink TV was one of the prominent figures on the bridges, where he was singing and playing guitar.
9. The military term 'collateral damage' was widely used in the English-speaking media in news broadcasts about the NATO bombing. The bombing campaign was justified as an intervention that only aimed at legitimate military targets, which included the infrastructure of Serbia (roads, bridges, factories, television stations) and not at the civilians of Serbia. The campaign was also marketed as 'humanitarian bombing' whose aim was to liberate Kosovo Albanians from Serbian oppression and free democratically inclined citizens of Serbia from Milošević. In the news broadcasts (CNN, BBC, etc.), civilian casualties of the bombing were reported as 'collateral damage', which made the actual dead bodies of Serbian civilians less real.

Part II Sarajevo: Imaginaries and Embodiments

5 City-as-Body

1. The usage of this term is inspired by the MA dissertation of my former student Diego dela Vega Wood.
2. See T. Wartenbaker *Credible Witness*; the term is derived from *hysterical paralysis* – a psychiatric condition caused by extreme anxiety that incapacitates the body.
3. For more, see Branislav Jakovljevic, 'Theatre of Atrocities: Towards a Disreality Principle'; and Patar Ramadanovic, 'Simonidas on the Balkans'.
4. When the Dossier on Markale was written, in the 1990s, this claim offered still more proof of the jingoistic attitude and militant nationalism of Serbian politicians. Post 9/11 and post 7/7 terrorist attacks, it is hard not to notice a

similar kind of racist rhetoric towards Islam in tabloid and Western right-wing media.

5. Variations of this sacrifice myth, however, appear in other Balkan regions as well.

6 Theatricality versus Bare Life

1. I have translated 'embalmed' literally ('balzamovani' in the original). In the local jargon the word can also mean *intoxicated, being in an altered state,* which is what it means in the context of the quoted paragraph. I have decided to go with the literal translation because of the duality that the meaning of this word evokes – dead, yet preserved.
2. However, this applies to downtown Sarajevo and certain neighbourhoods where most of the cultural activity was taking place. The city was essentially divided, so there were suburbs that were controlled by Serbian forces and neighbourhoods cut off from the rest of the city.
3. MESS is the acronym for the Sarajevo Festival of Small and Experimental Stages, that Haris Pašović had resurrected during the war. MESS was responsible for a variety of cultural projects in the besieged city and remains active. The FAMA collective was involved in a number of projects during the war including the publication of the *Sarajevo Survival Guide*. More recently, FAMA has launched an interactive museum of the Sarajevo siege. See http://vimeo.com/23039488
4. Suada Kapić is a Bosnian author and activist.
5. Tvrdko Kulenovic is a well-known Bosnian author and academic.
6. John Fine and Robert Donia are American history Professors who published extensively on the history of Bosnia and Herzegovina. See J. Fine, J. Vine and R. Donia, *Bosnia and Herzegovina: A Tradition Betrayed*. New York: Columbia University Press, 1994.
7. Erika Munk's lecture was on theatre in extreme circumstances.

7 Theatre as Ideal City

1. Andreas points out an aspect of common knowledge within the local Serbian context when it comes to the involvement of ex-criminals in the war:

> [...] Belgrade could keep up the appearance of non-involvement on the front stage, while engaging in covert facilitation backstage. Many of these irregular fighters from Serbia were wooed to Bosnia by the prospect of looting and selling stolen goods on the black market. Indeed many of the irregulars were common criminals. In the 1980s and early 1990s, many Yugoslav criminals operating in Western Europe had returned home in the face of intensifying police pressure and tighter immigration restrictions. Conveniently, 'the Bosnian war had just started', wrote a journalist for the Belgrade independent weekly *Vreme*, 'creating the opportunity for low risk robbery in patriotic costume'.
>
> (*Blue Helmets and Black Markets*, p. 24)

See also Uroš Komlenović, 'State and Mafia in Yugoslavia', *East European Constitutional Review* 6.4, 1997: 70–3.

2. According to the former Bosnian Chief of Police Intelligence, who commented on the death of one of the criminals/fighters, Caco, who was killed by the Bosnian army in an arrest attempt that allegedly went wrong, and was later rehabilitated: 'He [Caco] was the executor and witness of atrocities and killings. He was in the chain of command. And he needed to disappear. Without his death the ones who killed him would also never been held responsible' (*The Fixer,* p. 90).
3. On the issues regarding allegations of UNPROFOR crime, corruption and profiteering see Andreas's, *Blue Helmets and Black Markets*; Joe Sacco, *The Fixer*; David Rieff, *Slaughterhouse*; Carol Off, *The Lion, The Fox, and the Eagle.*
4. The 2002 census was the first count of the population in post-Dayton Bosnia and Herzegovina. Repulika Srpska, the part governed by Bosnian Serbs, refused to take part in the census exercise.
5. Former Yugoslavia was the only country that had Muslim as a nationality, not just a religious denomination. Hence the constituent nationalities of Yugoslavia included Serbs, Croats, Muslims, Slovenians and Macedonians. During and after the war, Bosnian Muslims transformed themselves into the Bosniac nation and the word 'Muslim' as a national identification was replaced with the word 'Bošnjak' (Bosniac), a descriptive that was associated with the medieval Bosnian state.
6. See Roger Friedland, 'Religious Nationalism and the Problem of Collective Representation', Annual Review of Sociology 27, 2001: 125–52.

Works Cited

Agamben, Georgio. *Means Without Ends*. Trans. V. Binetti and C. Casarino. Minneapolis, MN, and London: University of Minnesota Press, 2000.

Anderson, Benedict. *Imagined Communities: Reflections on the Origin and Spread of Nationalism*. Rev. edn., London: Verso, 1991.

Andreas, Peter. *Blue Helmets and Black Markets*. Ithaca, NY, and London: Cornell University Press, 2008.

Andrić, Ivo. '*Aska i Vuk* [Aska and the Wolf]', *Pripovjetke*. Sarajevo: Svjetlost, 1984.

——. *Na Drini Ćuprija* [*Bridge Over the River Drina*]. Sarajevo: Svjetlost, 1984.

Arendt, Hannah. 'Appendix/judging: Excerpts from lectures on Kant's political philosophy', in *The Life of the Mind*. Ed. Mary McCarthy. New York: Harcourt, 1978, pp. 255–72.

——. *Essays in Understanding 1930–1954*. New York: Schocken Books, 1994.

Augé, Marc. *Non-Place: Introduction to an Anthropology of Supermodernity*. Trans. J. Howe. London and New York: Verso, 1995.

Bachelard, Gaston. *The Poetics of Space*. Trans. Maria Jolas. Boston, MA: Beacon Press, 1969.

Bakhtin, M. M. *The Dialogic Imagination: Four Essays*. Ed. Michael Holquist. Trans. Caryl Emerson and Michael Holquist. Austin, TX, and London: University of Texas Press, 1981.

——. *Rabelais and his World*. Trans. Helene Iswolsky. Bloomington, IN: Indiana University Press, 1984.

Batić, B. 'Operacija Puž [Operation Snail]', *NIN* [Belgrade], 10 January 1997: 16–17.

Baudrillard, Jean. 'No Reprieve For Sarajevo', *Liberation*, 8 January 1994. Available: www.uta.edu/english/apt/collab/texts/reprieve.html

Beckett, Samuel. *Waiting for Godot*. New York: Grove Press, 1954.

Bogdanović, Bogdan. 'The Ritual Murder of the City', in *Balkan Blues: Writing Out of Yugoslavia*. Ed. J. Labon. Evanston, IL: Northwestern University Press, 1998, pp. 37–75.

Brecht, Bertolt. *Bad Time for Poetry: Was It? Is It?* Ed. John Willett. London: Methuen, 1995.

Brook, Peter. *The Empty Space*. London: Penguin, 1990.

Butler, Judith. *Bodies that Matter*. New York: Routledge, 1993.

——. *Frames of War*. London and New York: Verso, 2009.

Carlson, Marvin. *The Haunted Stage: The Theatre as Memory Machine*. Ann Arbor, MI: University of Michigan Press, 2001.

Chaudhuri, Una. *Staging Place: The Geography of Modern Drama*. Ann Arbor, MI: University of Michigan Press, 1995.

Ćirić, Sonja, 'Majca i Pesnica [T-Shirt and a Fist']', *Vreme* 468, 25 December 1999: http://www.vreme.com/arhiva_html/468/14.html

Debord, Guy. *Society of Spectacle*. Detroit, IL: Black and Red, 1983.

——. *Comments to the Society of Spectacle*. Trans. Malcolm Imrie. London: Verso, 1998.

De Certeau, Michel. *The Practice of Everyday Life*. Trans. Steven Rendall. Berkeley, CA: University of California Press, 1988.

Diamond, Elin. 'Blau, Butler, Beckett and the Politics of Seeming', *TDR* 44.4, 2000: 31–43.

Diklić, Darko. *Teatar u ratnom Sarajevu 1992/1995*. Sarajevo: Biblioteka Manhattan, 2004.

Dolan, Jill. *Utopia in Performance: Finding Hope at the Theater*. Ann Arbor, MI: University of Michigan Press, 2005.

Donia, Robert. *Sarajevo: A Biography*. London: Hurst, 2006.

Dragićević-Šešić, Milena. 'The Street as Political Space', *NTQ* 17.65, 2001: 74–86.

——. 'Nevidljivo pozoriste na ulicama Beograda [Invisible Theatre on the Streets of Belgrade]', Centre for Cultural Decontamination Archive.

Drakulić, Slavenka. *How we Survived Communism and even Laughed*. London: Hutchinson, 1991.

Dukovski, Dejan. *Powder Keg*. Skopje: Macedonian National Theatre, 1994.

Džafo, Nikola. *Led Art: 1993–2003 Dokumenti Vremena*. Novi Sad: Multimedija Centar Led Art, 2004.

Erickson, Jon. 'Defining Political Performance with Foucault and Habermas', in *Theatricality*. Ed. Thomas Postlewait and Tracy C. Davis. Cambridge: Cambridge University Press, 2003).

FAMA Collective. *Sarajevo Survival Guide*. Sarajevo: FAMA, 1993.

Foucault, Michel. 'Of Other Space: Utopias and Heterotopias', *Rethinking Architecture: A Reader in Cultural Theory*. Ed. Neil Leach. London: Routledge, 1997, pp. 350–6.

Friedland, Roger. 'Religious Nationalism and the Problem of Collective Representation', *Annual Review of Sociology* 27, 2001: 125–52.

Galloway, Steven. *The Cellist of Sarajevo*. Canada: Knopf, 2008.

Glenny, Misha. *The Fall of Yugoslavia*. London: Penguin Books, 1996.

Goldsworthy, Vesna. 'Invention and In(ter)vention: The Rethoric of Balkanizationn', in *Balkan as Metaphor*. Ed. D. Bjelić and O. Savić. London and Cambridge, MA: MIT Press, 2005.

Golub, Spencer. *Evreinov: The Theatre of Paradox and Transformation*. Ann Arbor, MI: UMI Research Press, 1984.

Habermas, Jurgen. *Moral Consciousness and Communicative Action*. Trans. Christian Lenhardt and Sherry Weber Nicholsen. Cambridge, MA: MIT Press, 1996.

Hadžimuhamedović, Amra. 'Grad Razdrag: O spolizaciji kao alternative rekonstrukcije', *Sarajevske Sveske* 20–1, 2008.

Jakovljević, Branislav. 'Theatre of Atrocities: Towards a Disreality Principle', *PMLA* 124.5, 2009: 1813–19.

Jess, Pat and Doreen Massey. 'The Contestation of Place', in *A Place in the World?* Ed. Doreen Massey and Pat Jess. Oxford: Oxford University Press, 1995, pp. 134–74.

Jestrović, Silvija. 'Theatricalizing Politics/ Politicizing Theatre', *Canadian Theatre Review* 103, University of Toronto Press, 2000: 42–7.

Judah, Tim. *The Serbs*. New Haven, CT: Yale University Press, 1998.

Kalyvas, Stathis. *The Logic of Violence in Civil War*. Cambridge: Cambridge University Press, 2006.

Kaminer, Wladimir. *Ich bin kein Berliner*. Munchen: Goldmann, 2007.

Karahasan, Dževad. *Sarajevo, Exodus of a City*. Trans. Slobodan Drakulić. New York: Kodansha Press, 1994.

Kershaw, Baz. *The Radical in Performance*. London and New York: Routledge, 1999.

Keyserling, Count Hermann. *Europe*. Trans. Maurice Samuel, New York: Harcourt Brace, 1928.

King, Russell. 'Migration, globalization and place', in *A Place in the World?* Ed. Doreen Massey and Pat Jess. Oxford: Oxford University Press, 1995, pp. 5–45.

Klaić, Dragan. *Exercises in Exile: The Reshaping of an Expat at the Ikea-Table*. Amsterdam: Cossee, 2004.

——. 'The Post-Yugoslav Exile: An Interim Account', in *Gulliver: The Time is Out of Joint*. Amsterdam: Felix Meritis Papers 8, 1997, pp. 33–42.

Knežević, Dubravka. 'Marked in Red Ink', *Theatre Journal* 48.4, 1996: 407–18.

Komlenović, Uroš. 'State and Mafia in Yugoslavia', *East European Constitutional Review* 6.4, 1997: 70–3.

Labon, Joanna et al. *Balkan Blues: Writing Out of Yugoslavia*. Evanston, IL: Northwestern University press.

Lefebvre, Henri. *The Production of Space*. Trans. Donald Nicholson-Smith. Oxford: Blackwell, 1992.

Markowitz, Fran. *Sarajevo: A Bosnian Kaleidoscope*. Chicago, IL: University of Illinois Press, 2010.

Marin, Louis. *Utopics: Spatial Play*. New Jersey: Humanities Press, 1984.

Massey, Doreen. 'The conceptualization of place, in *A Place in the World?* Ed. Doreen Massey and Pat Jess. Oxford: Oxford University Press, 1995, pp. 45–87.

Medenica, Ivan and Ksenija Radulović. '"Nemam tu šta da tražim"' ['"There is Nothing I Seek Here"'], Interview with Mirjana Miočinović], *Teatron* 118, 2002: 39–41.

Milosavljević, Aleksandar. 'BITEF je gotov – sezona je pocela' ['BITEF Is Over – Theatre Season Begins'], *Teatron* 89, Belgrade: Museum of Theatre Art, 1994: 185–91.

Milošević, Diana. Dah Theatre website: http://www.dahteatarcentar.com/index_eng.html

Mujkić, Asim. 'We, the Citizens of Ethnopolis', *Constallation* 14.1, 2007: 5–17.

Off, Carol. *The Lion, The Fox, and the Eagle: A Story of Generals and Justice in Yugoslavia and Rwanda*. Toronto: Random House, Canada, 2000.

Owens, Patricia. '"Reclaiming 'Bare Life"?: Against Agamben on Refugees', *Journal of International Relations* 23/24 , 2009: 567–82.

Panovski, Naum. 'Goran Stefanovski's Sarajevo or Sara in the Horror Land', *PAJ* 16.2, May 1994: 47–52.

Petrović, Gorana. 'Beograd Festival u funkciji oblikovanja imidža Beograda' ['The Function of Belgrade Festival in Shaping the Image of Belgrade'], *Kultura*. Belgrade: Centre for the Study of Cultural Development, 2009.

Prodanović, Mileta. *Stariji i lepši Beograd* [*Prettier and Older Belgrade*]. Belgrade: Stubovi Kulture, 2004.

Radulović, Ksenija. 'Nacionalni resentiman na sceni' ['National sentiment on stage'], *Teatron* 118, [Belgrade] 2002: 1–16.

Ramadanović, Petar. 'Simonides on the Balkans', *Balkan as Metaphore.* Ed. D. Bjelić and O. Savić. Cambridge, MA: MIT Press, 2005, pp. 351–65.

Rieff, David. *Slaughterhouse: Bosnia and the Failure of the West.* New York: Simon & Schuster, 1995.

——. 'Murder in the Neighbourhood', *Dissent* 49.1, 2002 (available: http://www.dissentmagazine.org/article).

Roach, Joseph. *It.* Ann Arbor, MI: University of Michigan Press, 2007.

Robins, Kevin. 'Prisoners of the city: Whatever could a postmodern city be?', *New Formations* 15, Winter 1991: 1–22.

Rose, Gillian. 'Place and identity: A sense of place', *A Place in the World?* Ed. Doreen Massey and Pat Jess. Oxford: Oxford University Press, 1995, pp. 87–133.

Sacco, Joe. *The Fixer: A Story from Sarajevo.* London: Jonathan Cape, 2004.

——. *Safe Area Giražde.* London: Jonathan Cape, 2007.

Sadler, Simon. *The Situationist City.* Cambridge, MA: MIT Press, 1998.

Schechner, Richard. *Environmental Theatre.* New York: Applause, 1994.

Šehić, Faruk. *Apokalipsa iz recicle bina [Apocalypse from the Recycling Bin].* Sarajevo: Buybook, 2008.

Sennett, Richard. *Flesh and Stone.* London and New York: Faber & Faber 1994.

Sherwood, Seth. 'Belgrade Rocks', *New York Times,* 16 October 2005 (available: www.nytimes.com/2005/10/16/travel/16belgrade.html).

Soja, Edward. 'Thirdspace: Expending the Scope of the Geographical Imagination', in *Architecturally Speaking: Practices of Art, Architecture and the Everyday.* Ed. Alan Read. London: Routledge, 2000.

Sontag, Susan. 'Waiting for Godot in Sarajevo', *PAJ* 16.2, 1994: 87–106.

——. *Regarding the Pain of Others.* London: Penguin, 2003.

Stefanovski, Gorna. ' Tales from the Wild East' (available: http://www.eurozine.com/articles/2009-03-24-stefanovski-en.html).

Stojaković, Dušan. 'Three Shrines for One Wish' ['Tri hrama za jednu zelju'], *Vecernje novosti* 20.01, 2008 (available: http://www.naslovi.net/2008-01-20/vecernje-novosti/tri-hrama-za-jednu-zelju/549603).

Taylor, Diana. *The Archive and the Repertoire.* Durham, NC, and London: Duke University Press, 2003.

Todorović, Dragan. *The Book Of Revenge: Blues for Yugoslavia.* Toronto: Vintage, 2006.

Toole, David. *Waiting for Godot in Sarajevo: Theological Reflections on Nihilism, Tragedy, and Apocalypse.* London: SCM Press, 1998.

Turner, Victor. *From Ritual to Theatre: The Human Seriousness of Play.* New York: Performing Arts Journal Publications, 1982.

Ugrešić, Dubravka. *Ministarstvo Boli.* Beograd: Fabrika knjiga, 2004.

Veltruský, Jirí. 'Man and Object in the Theatre', *A Prague School Reader on Esthetics, Literary Structure and Style.* Ed. Paul Garvin. Washington: Georgetown University Press, 1964, pp. 83–91.

Vidal, Sara. *Bivouac: Générik Vapeur.* Paris: Seus et Tonka, 2000.

Vučetić, Slavica. 'Invitation to the Battle: Reception of the "patriotic" repertoire from the eighties', *Teatron* 118, 2002: 12–16; original in the newspaper *Danas,* 7 February 1984).

Vučković, Slavica. 'Poziv na bitku (Recepcija "patriotskog" repertoara iz osamdesetih)' ['Call for Battle (Reception of the "patriotic" repertoire from the eighties')], *Teatron* 118, [Belgrade], 2002: 12–17.
Warner, Michael. *Publics and Counter-Publics*. New York: Zone Books, 2002.
Wartenbaker, Timberlake. *Credible Witness*. London: Faber Plays, 2001.
Wilde, Oscar. 'The Decay of Lying', *Collected Works of Oscar Wilde*. Hertfordshire: Wordsworth Editions, 1997.
Whybrow, Nicolas. *Art and the City*. London, New York. I. B. Tauris, 2011.
Žižek, Slavoj. *The Metastases of Enjoyment*. London: Verso, 1994.

Index

GPSR Compliance
The European Union's (EU) General Product Safety Regulation (GPSR) is a set of rules that requires consumer products to be safe and our obligations to ensure this.

If you have any concerns about our products, you can contact us on

ProductSafety@springernature.com

In case Publisher is established outside the EU, the EU authorized representative is:

Springer Nature Customer Service Center GmbH
Europaplatz 3
69115 Heidelberg, Germany

www.ingramcontent.com/pod-product-compliance
Ingram Content Group UK Ltd.
Pitfield, Milton Keynes, MK11 3LW, UK
UKHW020419250726
13967UKWH00007B/2724